Praise for *The Debt Bomb*

"The five loveliest words in the English language are those that begin the First Amendment: 'Congress shall make no law . . .' Notice the most underused word in contemporary Washington: 'No.' Fortunately, Tom Coburn uses it with gusto in attacking the crisis so well described in this book. He is a man with a plan, and the steely determination to implement it."

— **George F. Will**, nationally
syndicated columnist

"Dr. Tom Coburn is the real deal. He's not a politician; he's a citizen in office. Day in and day out, he's been fighting to shrink the federal government, and has been attacked by his own party and the political opposition for doing so. Now he's written a book outlining in stark terms the problems the nation is facing. Dr. Coburn is a real American hero, and he's standing against the tide in the United States Senate. If you want the truth, from the inside, you need to read this book."

— **Mark Meckler**, cofounder and
National Chairman of the Tea
Party Patriots

"*The Debt Bomb* is superb. It's a smart, gutsy, and captivating take on how Washington got us into this mess—it then gives the taxpayers some real answers and solutions as to how to get out of it! If you're sick and tired of Washington politicians making excuses and pandering mush, this book will be a sheer delight. Tom Coburn tells the truth, and tips over everyone's sacred cows."

— **Al Simpson**, former
U.S. Senator

"Nobody understands our nation's fiscal nightmare better than Dr. Coburn, and no one else has proposed more concrete ways to attack our fiscal problems. Tom Coburn gets it. He readily admits there is no easy way out of the fiscal mess our politicians have gotten us into. And he is bold enough and smart enough to propose real solutions that will put our fiscal house in order. Tom Coburn is my hero."

— **Erskine Bowles**, White House
Chief of Staff under President
Bill Clinton

"Tom Coburn is a rare breed in a town filled with big spending Democrats and big government Republicans. As a fellow member of the Class of 1994, I've seen Tom stay true to the values of our cause while others sold out to Washington's highest bidders. With America's future hanging in the balance, Tom has written a book that warns of a coming debt bomb that threatens to destroy our economy and our future. If you want to know how Washington can avert the coming crisis, read this important book."

— **Joe Scarborough**, host of
MSNBC's *Morning Joe*

"*The Debt Bomb* has the bold answers and insights the American people have been clamoring for. Dr. Coburn's willingness to go big exposes the appalling lack of leadership in the White House and Congress. *The Debt Bomb* should be required reading for any American who wants to force our elected leaders to step up and join Dr. Coburn in addressing this urgent threat."

— **Larry Kudlow**, Reagan
administration economist and
host of CNBC's *The Kudlow
Report*

"In *The Debt Bomb*, Tom outlines how all Americans can work together to strengthen our critical health and retirement security programs, reform our tax code, and lift our crushing burden of debt. Dr. Coburn has accurately diagnosed the problem and offers a sensible prescription to solve it. More than anything, he makes a compelling case for urgency and action before the crisis becomes incurable."

— **Representative Paul Ryan**, Chairman of the House Budget Committee

"No one in Congress has done more to shift the debate from growing government to cutting spending than Tom Coburn. When others were silent, he courageously stood up to big spenders in both parties, exposed the wasteful earmarks like the Bridge to Nowhere, and called for an end to corporate welfare that undermines our free market economy. In *The Debt Bomb*, Tom outlines bold, decisive action to save our nation from fiscal collapse. It's a privilege to fight alongside him to defend freedom."

— **Senator Jim DeMint**

"It's high time we had a ruthless and compassionate conversation about the American tax policy, Senator Coburn takes a big step in this book."

— **Dylan Ratigan**, host of MSNBC's *The Dylan Ratigan Show*

"Senator Coburn gives the reader a fascinating inside look at his courageous efforts to end congressional boondoggles, root out waste in government, and defuse the debt bomb. He is a strong voice for common sense and fiscal sanity, unafraid to dig into details and stand up to the leadership, even in his own party."

— **Alice M. Rivlin**, Brookings Institution, former Director of the Office of Management and Budget under President Clinton

"As someone who courageously supported the recommendations of the Bowles-Simpson Commission and as a member of the Senate's bipartisan Gang of Six, Tom Coburn has demonstrated a commitment to improving America's unsustainable long-term fiscal outlook through bipartisan solutions. In *The Debt Bomb*, he shows us why he has devoted so much time and energy to addressing America's fiscal challenges, which pose a primary threat to the future prosperity of all Americans, including the most vulnerable in our society."

— **Peter G. Peterson**, former Secretary of Commerce under President Nixon and author of *Running on Empty*

"Throughout his distinguished career, Senator Tom Coburn has been one of the most consistent advocates for fiscal sanity and responsibility in Washington. Based on unambiguous evidence and moral principle, *The Debt Bomb* not only articulates the dangerous consequences of our runaway spending, but also offers courageous, responsible, no-nonsense solutions for restoring America to prosperity. This is an important book at a critical time in our nation's history."

— **Bill Bennett**, former Secretary of Education under President Reagan and host of *Morning in America*

THE DEBT BOMB

A Bold Plan to Stop Washington from Bankrupting America

U.S. Senator
Tom A. Coburn, M.D.

with John Hart

THOMAS NELSON
Since 1798

NASHVILLE   DALLAS   MEXICO CITY   RIO DE JANEIRO

Published in Nashville, Tennessee, by Thomas Nelson. Thomas Nelson is a registered trademark of Thomas Nelson, Inc.

Thomas Nelson, Inc., titles may be purchased in bulk for educational, business, fund-raising, or sales promotional use. For information, please e-mail SpecialMarkets@ThomasNelson.com.

Library of Congress Cataloging-in-Publication Data

Coburn, Tom A.
   The debt bomb : a bold plan to stop Washington from bankrupting America / Tom Coburn; with John Hart.
      p. cm.
   Includes bibliographical references and index.
   ISBN 978-1-59555-467-3
   1. Government spending policy—United States. 2. Debts, Public—United States. 3. Bureaucracy—United States. 4. United States—Politics and government—2009– 5. United States—Economic policy—2009– I. Hart, John. II. Title.
HJ7537.C63 2012
336.3'40973—dc23   2011053178

Printed in the United States of America

12 13 14 15 QGF 6 5 4 3

This book is dedicated to every American from every persuasion who wants a realistic explanation of where we stand and who wants to renew confidence both in ourselves and our republic.

Contents

Introduction

AMERICA TODAY FACES ONE OF THE GREATEST THREATS TO ITS existence since our founding. The threat does not come from any foreign army or terrorist network, but from our own government and its unsustainable spending. If we don't change course in the near future—most likely the next two years—America as we've known it could soon be a shell of its former self.

We could face a sudden economic collapse worse than the Great Depression, or we could enter an era of managed decline and waning influence.

What is certain is that maintaining our present course is a mathematical impossibility. If we ignore this problem, we will condemn future generations to a lower standard of living with less freedom and less opportunity. Sooner or later, our "debt bomb" will go off.[1]

Our quandary is not unexpected. History has shown time and time again that debt can bring nations to their knees. Great powers such as

Britain, Spain, France, the Ottomans, the Soviet Union, and the Roman Empire declined economically before they contracted, collapsed, or were conquered. In many cases, only a few years separated the height of their power from their irreversible decline and demise. Our founders understood this history very well: John Adams warned, "Democracy never lasts long. It soon wastes, exhausts, and murders itself. There was never a democracy yet that did not commit suicide."[2]

HOW WE LOST CONTROL

In order to avoid this fate and defuse our debt bomb, we need to retrace our steps, go back to the beginning, and look at how we got off course. America was founded not only on a shared belief in individual liberty and freedom but also on a healthy skepticism of political power. Our founders had lived under the tyranny of monarchs—the ultimate career politicians of their time—and were determined to establish a different system in America. As Thomas Jefferson said, "The natural progress of things is for liberty to yield, and government to gain ground."[3]

Jefferson, in particular, warned the real threat to democracy would be the cost and scope of government itself, especially expansions of government that were not paid for. "I consider the fortunes of our republic as depending, in an eminent degree, on the extinguishment of public debt," Jefferson said. Ignoring debt, he warned, would lead America toward "the English career of debt, corruption and rottenness, closing with revolution."[4]

Not all of our framers shared Jefferson's concern, yet they put aside their differences and drafted a Constitution—the grand bargain of their time—that sought not only to balance the powers of government between branches but also to severely *limit* those powers so that citizens, not politicians, would be in charge. The purpose of limiting government was not to deprive those less fortunate. In fact, the goal was the opposite. Our founders believed a free society required limited government *in order for* individual liberty to flourish. As government was limited, freedom and opportunity would expand. Our system was designed so free men and women would create healthy, prosperous families and communities that would look after one another, free of government harassment, intrusion, and interference.

We are where we are today because career politicians have prostituted the founders' clear intention to limit government in the name of "doing good." For decades both parties have grown government well beyond the boundaries of the Constitution and created the very problem our founders sought to avoid—a deeply indebted government that is threatening the very survival of our republic.

Today Jefferson's fears are coming true. The growth of government has created a debt that now exceeds the size of our economy.[5] In the past decade alone, the size of government has doubled under both Republicans and Democrats. In 2001, spending under President Clinton was $1.86 trillion[6]; spending in 2011 was a staggering $3.8 trillion.[7] And we are now borrowing from future generations nearly $4 billion *every day* or $41,222 *every second* just to keep government running.[8] The federal government borrows more money in a couple of days than my home state of Oklahoma spends in an entire year.[9]

Our annual deficit in 2011—$1.3 trillion—was the size of our entire federal budget just fifteen years ago.[10] This number also exceeds the gross national products of all but twelve nations on earth, including Australia, Mexico, and South Korea.[11] Meanwhile, our cities and states are on the verge of bankruptcy in part because of the burdens Washington politicians have placed on states in the name of providing benefits.

Most troubling of all is that our national debt may have already passed the tipping point. In their groundbreaking book about debt and deficits, *This Time Is Different: Eight Centuries of Financial Folly*, economists Carmen Reinhart and Kenneth Rogoff show that nations whose debt equals 90 percent of their economy see at best much slower growth and at worst a total economic collapse.[12] At $15 trillion our national debt is now past that point.

So how did we get where we are? What took the most successful republic in history and put it on its backside? There is only one answer. *We have allowed the elite political class to buy our loyalty at the cost of our freedoms.*

How to Regain Control

Our nation's best hope is to reclaim our heritage that combined a strong belief in individual liberty with a healthy skepticism of government. President Reagan put it well in his farewell address: "Ours was the first revolution in the history of mankind that truly reversed the course of government, and with three little words: 'We the People.' 'We the People' tell the government what to do; it doesn't tell us. 'We the People' are the driver; the government is the car. And we decide where it should go, and by what route, and how fast. Almost all the world's constitutions are documents in which governments tell the people what their privileges are. Our Constitution is a document in which 'We the People' tell the government what it is allowed to do. 'We the People' are free."[13]

I believe we can be free of a legacy of debt and decline if you—"We the People"—rethink what government can, and should, do in the twenty-first century. To do that, it is the responsibility of every citizen to ask politicians hard questions and then hold them accountable:

- Just how many government programs reflect our founders' intent? Are those programs constitutional? Do they fit within

the domain the founders so carefully laid out before us?
Do they lead to independence, self-reliance, and personal
responsibility, or do they lead to dependency?

- If these programs already exist, are they being run efficiently?
  Are they achieving their stated goals, and can we even
  measure their progress? And most important, can we *afford*
  them?

If we have this debate and make the hard choices that need to be
made, an era of renewed prosperity and freedom is within reach.

I'm confident we can make these changes because everywhere I go
in Oklahoma and across the country, I find honest, hardworking people
who want to be treated like adults and be presented with the facts. I find
people who would support massive changes once they learn about the
vast amount of waste, duplication, and sheer stupidity throughout the
federal government.

I'm especially encouraged because I spend a lot of time talking to
grandparents. Washington elites often suggest our nation's seniors—of
whom many are grandparents—are a roadblock to reform because they
don't want to change safety net programs such as Medicare and Social
Security. This is fundamentally false. I've asked thousands of seniors
in town hall meetings, "Raise your hand if you're willing to sacrifice to
make sure your kids and grandkids have a higher standard of living." Not
once in my thirteen years of holding town hall meetings have seniors not
raised their hands en masse. When presented with the facts, no grand-
parent would sacrifice a grandchild's future so the elderly can maintain
the same level of benefits. In the end, it will be the grandparents who give
Washington politicians the courage to change. Seniors get it. The only
way to save these programs—and preserve a level of benefits similar to
what we have today—is to change them.

Finally, I'm hopeful because although we may be past a tipping point in terms of the size of our debt, we may also be past the tipping point in terms of what Americans will tolerate from Washington. Congress's approval rating slipped to an all-time low of 9 percent near the end of 2011, which makes me wonder where those 9 percent have been.[14] The public's frustration is the major reason we who are fighting for solutions have seen progress over the past few years. The success we've had, such as our improbable victories against pork-barrel spending, is because "We the People" have said enough is enough.

SOLUTIONS ARE WITHIN REACH

Even though the challenges before us are great, there are solutions. Some solutions may require sacrifice, but most Americans *are* willing to make sacrifices in the short term to secure freedom and prosperity in the long term. The people I know, by and large, are not afraid of doing hard things, particularly when it will give the next generation a better life. Previous generations of Americans have risen to great challenges before and built the greatest society with the most liberty and most dynamic economy ever known to humanity. And the truth is, right now the "hard" things are not that hard, but they will become very hard if we ignore the problem.

Most of all, though, the solutions will require politicians to sacrifice what they value above all else—their images, reputations, and political careers.

The solutions, I am convinced, begin with retracing our steps and taking the path of limited government and less debt. Again, limiting government does not mean we create a society that does not care for those who cannot care for themselves. Instead, it means we redirect our charity and enable those who depend on us to succeed. A solution means we require all who receive such a bounty to meet the expectations of personal responsibility up to their ability. It means we quit creating programs that are gamed by those who take advantage of the people who play by the rules. And most of all, a solution means we stop passing on to future generations of Americans responsibilities that are truly ours today.

Change of the magnitude that is necessary (I've detailed at least $9 trillion in savings in my deficit reduction plan *Back in Black*[15]) will require a top-down and bottom-up renewal to happen simultaneously. Perhaps the best news for America is, many problems in Washington can be solved by changing *who* is in Washington. The typical member of Congress is a wonderful and engaging individual with noble intentions but little real-world experience. If we are to solve the problems in front of us, we must elect individuals with backgrounds similar to those of our founders—people full of life experiences paid for with hardship, hard work, and disappointment; people who are willing to give up the comfort of today for a better tomorrow for America.

Still, real solutions will never be enacted without popular consent. If politicians in Washington refuse to back real solutions, "We the People" have a moral obligation to replace those politicians.

From my vantage point in the Senate, I can assure you that taking the time to be informed and hold Washington accountable makes not just a minor difference, but the decisive difference. I understand that for Americans who are busy raising families and working, politics—especially during an election season—is an interruption rather than a hobby. Yet, politics has never been a more necessary interruption. As C. S. Lewis once said, "A sick society must think much about politics, as a sick man must think much about digestion . . . We think of such things only in order to be able to think of something else."[16]

That "something else" is what we all long for—a more stable and prosperous future for those we love.

We have two paths we can travel. One will lead us to the same outcome as those republics before us—decline and disintegration. The other path is much more difficult. It is a path built on service, hard work, and delayed gratification. It is a path born of hardship, but one that leads to very great rewards. The path that will cheat history is marked by courage, standing firm, and saying no to the continued abandonment of the very core principles that made America great.

On a personal note, I would add that at sixty-four I am in my last term in the Senate and am very unlikely to ever hold another public position. I voluntarily limited my terms in the Senate to two. When I served in the House, I also limited my terms. Yet, I have tried to approach every term, and each decision, as if it were my last.

Most of all, I want to finish the race strong, secure a future for my grandkids, and give back to a country that has given me so much. I was blessed to have had a very full life before running for Congress. I was fortunate enough to have built a business, and as a physician I delivered more than three thousand babies before I was first elected to serve in the House of Representatives in 1994. I'm also a three-time cancer survivor, which I hope has given me a little extra perspective on the things that matter versus the things that are fleeting.

If you yearn for an America where freedom is everyone's ally, join me in holding the entire establishment accountable to do what is in the best long-term interest for our country, our families, and our future.

PART I

The Problem

Where We Are and How We Got Here

1

Red Ink Rising

Our national debt is our biggest national security threat.

—Admiral Mike Mullen, Chairman of the Joint Chiefs
of Staff under President Obama, June 24, 2010[1]

Imagine that it started like this on August 4, 2014, in Tokyo.

A dozen of the top investors in Japan filed into a serene conference room overlooking Tokyo Bay. It was an early morning meeting in the Japanese branch of Entrust mutual funds, one of the largest managers of mutual funds in the world. Entrust, like dozens of other private funds, along with foreign governments, buys the U.S. Treasury bills that allow the U.S. government to function. When we borrowed money to pay for our government programs, these were the people from whom we got the money. Even this far into the Great Recession, which was now also known as our Lost Decade, few Americans realized it was the willingness of foreign governments and funds like Entrust that enabled the U.S. government to borrow the money it needed to pay our troops, write Social Security checks, and pay benefits for programs such as Medicare and Medicaid. Everything we took for granted was possible as long as people like those gathered in Tokyo this Monday morning agreed that U.S. debt was a safe bet.

The meeting began with an overview of economic indicators. The news in Japan, and Europe, was encouraging. In both regions a recovery was finally taking root after several years of turmoil and defaults. The United States was a different story.

Hiroshi Suzuki, the head of Entrust, spelled out his growing concerns. Nearly two years into the new Republican president's term, he said, the administration—along with a narrow Republican majority in the Senate and a majority in the House—had failed to pass a long-term deficit reduction plan and was not likely to pass any significant legislation this close to the midterm elections.[2] If action was put off until 2015, he argued, the 2016 presidential elections would take over and nothing would happen until 2017 at the earliest. By that point, Treasury bills would be worth far less than they are today.

"The Americans have waited too long. I recommend selling our holdings of U.S. Treasury bills before the Americans have a chance to devalue their currency any further. We have an obligation to make wise investments for our own aging population," he said.

One dissenting voice, Akira Yamamoto, a former finance minister, argued that it was too soon to sell U.S. debt. The fundamentals of the U.S. economy were very, very strong. The United States still had a diversified economy, with abundant natural resources, untapped energy reserves, and a world-class university system.

"A few key reforms to the tax code and entitlement programs and a new energy policy would allow the American economy to grow at an impressive rate. This could very well be another American century, not a Chinese century," Yamamoto said.

Plus, he reminded the group, three years earlier Bill Gross, the head of

PIMCO—which managed the world's largest mutual fund—had made a decision similar to the one Mr. Suzuki was proposing. Gross sold his holdings of Treasury bills in 2011 with the expectation that they would be worth less in the future. Later that year, Gross admitted he'd acted prematurely.[3]

While the group understood the logic behind Mr. Yamamoto's argument, it seemed the political leadership in the United States was committed to the status quo, a path of self-destruction.

While Europe and Japan were resolving their debt crisis, the United States Congress was standing still. Congress had spent months trying to repeal Obamacare—a vital goal and a campaign pledge of the new president and every Republican. While the law had been effectively crippled by the courts and legislative action, the new Congress and president could not rally around a credible replacement plan. One such plan, the Patients' Choice Act—backed by Paul Ryan (R-WI) and myself—was defeated by Republicans frightened by special interests who falsely whispered it was a tax increase, while moderate Republicans and Democrats complained it was a backdoor attempt to end Medicare and Medicaid.

The new president said things would be different, but one of his first acts was to create another deficit reduction commission instead of offering a specific reform package. Outlining explicit tax and entitlement reforms would be too risky with such a narrow majority in Congress, White House aides argued. This new commission would be modeled after the Base Closure and Realignment Commission that successfully downsized military bases after the end of the Cold War. The new commission, called TRAC—the Tax Reform and Entitlement Action Commission—was lampooned. The president was so afraid of mentioning entitlement reform that the *E* was dropped from the acronym. The *Wall Street Journal* editorialized: "We need a solution, not another lap around the same TRAC. Plus, we already have a commission with ample authority. It's called Congress."

The rest of the world wasn't laughing. Without addressing its growing health care costs, everyone understood America's debt would rise far beyond sustainable levels. The world also understood that in the past three years, other commissions had been formed and had failed. President Obama had rejected the findings of his own debt commission—the Simpson-Bowles Commission—in 2010. The supercommittee that was formed in 2011 to avert a debt crisis had also disintegrated.

While Congress slept, the Federal Reserve continued to print money and keep interest rates artificially low to prevent housing prices—which had been stagnant for four years—from falling. It was obvious to those meeting in Tokyo the morning of August 4, 2014, that the Americans were going to inflate and devalue their way out of a crisis. That meant their holdings would be worth less.

Mr. Suzuki offered his closing argument: "Some of the smartest investors in America have declined to buy their own government's debt. It's time to look for other opportunities."[4]

As the Tokyo meeting wrapped up, eleven of the twelve board members voted to sell Entrust's holdings of U.S. Treasury bills. Over the next hour, markets were calm. Then at 10:25 a.m. Tokyo time, the *Wall Street Journal* Asian edition, Bloomberg, and Reuters posted small news items about Entrust's sell-off.

Nothing happened immediately. Then, thirty minutes later another large fund in Asia sold its holding of U.S. Treasury bills. At noon, three more firms released their holdings. By 2:00 p.m., dozens of private firms across Asia as well as some of the top global firms had dumped their holdings of U.S. debt. At 2:31 p.m., the sell-off went into overdrive when the government of Singapore released its holdings of Treasury bills. The news of the Singapore sell-off spread like wildfire.

At 3:00 p.m. Tokyo time, the markets in Europe opened. Almost immediately every major private firm was dumping its holdings of U.S. Treasury bills. The value of the dollar had already dropped 10 percent compared to the euro and yen. With a European sell-off under way, the governments of Asia faced a difficult decision. Asian markets were about to close. Dumping U.S. debt would damage the U.S. and world economies, while holding U.S. debt would result in billions in losses. Most finance ministers realized the sell-off had already passed the point of no return—the U.S. economy would already be severely damaged. Japan, the second-largest holder of U.S. debt in the world, sold its holdings of Treasury bills. China, the world's largest holder of U.S. debt, would wait it out. The Chinese had other plans.

Less than an hour after the European markets opened, the dollar was in a free fall. Every other European and Asian government was dumping U.S. debt. At about 3:00 a.m. Washington time, the chairman of the Federal Reserve, who was vacationing—along with the president and most of Congress—received a call from a frantic aide who said a crash was under way. At 4:00 a.m., the chairman, the Treasury secretary, and the president's Council of Economic Advisers held an emergency conference call. They asked the White House chief of staff to wake the president, who was with his family at Camp David.

The president said it was important not to panic and raise the specter of bailouts. "There will be no bailouts on my watch," he said.

Americans woke to the horrifying news that the value of the dollar was dropping precipitously. Everything they owned—their life savings, retirement plans, and homes—had now lost a third of its buying power compared to other currencies. And there was no way to predict if we had hit bottom. At the same time, the price of oil jumped 50 percent because of the declining value of the dollar.

The president took the unusual step of holding a press conference at 8:00 a.m. Eastern Time, an hour before trading on Wall Street would begin. Global markets had overreacted and made decisions out of fear, he told reporters. The fundamentals of the U.S. economy were as strong today as they were yesterday. Everything would be all right.

Yet, when markets on Wall Street opened, the Dow lost 10 percent of its value in fifteen minutes. Trading was automatically halted. An hour later trading resumed, and the Dow lost 20 percent of its value. Trading was halted for the remainder of the day and would remain closed indefinitely by presidential executive order. Still, the value of the dollar continued to fall. Afraid that their life savings were disappearing, Americans began to trickle into banks and line up at ATM machines. At first it was orderly. With news of the sell-off deteriorating, a bank run was in progress. Americans were withdrawing funds at record paces. Bank websites crashed. When one bank in Berkeley, California, tried to close early, a mob shattered the windows and demanded access to their funds.

A week into the crash, the dollar had lost 50 percent of its value compared to other currencies, and the price of oil had doubled to $240 a barrel. Inflation also was beginning to pick up. Rumors of mass layoffs swirled. That's when the protests got out of control. In scenes not witnessed in America since the assassination of Martin Luther King Jr., entire city blocks were set on fire. Banks, other financial institutions, and government buildings were targeted primarily, but in many places the looting was indiscriminate. Anything that would hold its value—gold, silver, precious stones—was a target.

Ironically, Wall Street itself saw the least amount of violence. Perhaps it was the memory of 9/11. New Yorkers had seen the thin veneer of civilization peeled back not long ago and didn't want to return to that place. This was a financial catastrophe, but we would pull together. Our way of life, not our very lives, was slipping away.

The president deployed the National Guard to dozens of cities. Congressional leaders wanted to return to Washington but were encouraged to stay out of the city for security reasons. The president didn't want to create the appearance of imposing martial law in the nation's capital. Many members of Congress were more than happy to stay home. The nation was only six weeks away from a debt-limit increase. Neither side wanted to contemplate the tax increases and benefit cuts that would be necessary to fix this problem.

The president decided to reopen Wall Street the last week of August after the value of the dollar seemed to bottom out. The Federal Reserve also increased interest rates by a full basis point (a 20 percent increase) to stop the hemorrhaging and begged foreign governments not to dump our debt. When the markets opened at the end of August, the Dow lost 8 percent of its value, then crept up and stabilized at 7,000 points. In less than a month, the Dow had lost 40 percent of its value; the dollar was worth half of what it had been before August 4, and inflation was sure to markedly increase.

Congress would not have six weeks to sort out what to do. With the economy paralyzed, tax receipts to the Treasury plummeted. Because our government was operating on borrowed money—we were borrowing $6 billion a day—we didn't have the reserves to pay Social Security, Medicare, and Medicaid benefits as well as veterans' benefits and student loans. The entitlement trust funds had been robbed long ago.

With the rest of the world not wanting to see the United States face a complete default and bankruptcy, the leaders and finance members of the G-20 convened in Rio to make the United States an offer—and an ultimatum.

In exchange for the privilege of borrowing money from the international community, the United States would accept several fundamental reforms. First, the retirement age for entitlement programs would be immediately raised to 72. Benefits would be severely means tested. And tax rates would double for most Americans.

The finance minister from India summarized the meeting: "The United States has seen this coming for decades, especially the last five years. Future Congresses and presidents can modify these policies as they please. But if the United States wants to borrow money, they would be wise to operate within these parameters. These are merely the reforms they could have enacted themselves long ago."

Members of Congress expressed outrage but saw few alternatives. Borrowing a play from Greece's playbook, some called for a referendum on the deal. Congress passed a resolution disapproving of the G-20 plan, but they could not bring themselves to vote on the substance of the actual agreement because doing so would highlight their failure to anticipate the crisis. The president, by executive order, accepted the agreement.

Three years later, in 2017, the United States would begin to recover from the crash of 2014. Tax rates were lowered significantly, and a few deductions would be added back into the code. The draconian cuts to entitlement programs were scaled back slightly. The unemployment rate had peaked at 24 percent (true unemployment was probably closer to 30 percent) and started to come down.

Two years later, in 2019, the recovery would run into difficulty.

That summer, the People's Republic of China was conducting annual military exercises in the Taiwan Strait, when thousands of vessels suddenly headed straight for Taiwan. When satellite images of the maneuver reached Washington, the president threatened military action. The Chinese responded swiftly and curtly that they would dump our debt if we interfered. They also reminded the president that they had reached military parity with the United States. Our military leaders realized an intervention not only would cripple our economy but would likely lead to the loss of two or more aircraft carriers and would subject U.S. cities and military installations to cruise missile attacks, if not a nuclear exchange.

That afternoon China annexed Taiwan. The Chinese made one face-saving gesture. Because we had declined to access our own energy reserves, China extended the privilege of allowing us to purchase oil from their South American allies.

Although this scenario—the Entrust firm and its partners—is fictitious, we will face a calamity if we continue to ignore the unmistakable lessons of history and the economic and military threats posed by excessive debt, especially debt to foreign nations. Debt puts great powers in a weakened and vulnerable condition.

A crisis could be triggered by other events. In a weakened and unstable global economy, military conflict could break out with devastating human and economic consequences. We could face a crash in our stock market and see widespread civil unrest. Many in our government and law enforcement agencies believe we are already on the cusp of widespread unrest even without an acute debt crisis.

Admiral Mullen, therefore, is not exaggerating when he calls our debt our greatest national security threat. What makes his statement so remarkable is that for most of America's history, threats to our national security have been described in military terms: the size of opposing armies, the number of ICBMs, and—in a post-9/11 world—the determination of terrorists to kill civilians. Our military leaders, of all people, have no reason to downplay such threats, so Admiral Mullen's decision to identify America's greatest vulnerability in *economic* rather than military terms should be a wake-up call for every American.

History also shows that for great nations, the end can come quickly. Those who think we have years to debate these issues are courting disaster. Harvard historian Niall Ferguson asks, "What if collapse does not arrive over a number of centuries but comes suddenly, like a thief in the night? Great powers and empires are complex systems, which means their construction more resembles a termite hill than an Egyptian pyramid . . . including the tendency to move from stability to instability quite suddenly."[5]

If Tom Clancy could capture our moment, he might call it "Red Ink

Rising." In a very real sense, the threat from borrowing from countries like China is greater than the threat of war with China. A sudden, catastrophic collapse is more likely to be triggered by an act of enlightened self-interest rather than by coordinated hostility. Sooner rather than later, a major fund or government will just decide one day that buying U.S. debt is a bad bet. And with one gust of wind, the house of cards will come crashing down.

FACING THE FACTS

America is already bankrupt. We may not believe it. We may not yet feel its full effects. But we are effectively bankrupt. Our debt now exceeds the size of our entire economy. Our payments on our obligations—our unfunded liabilities—exceed our income as far as the eye can see. No amount of obtainable growth or tax revenue will be enough. There simply is no possible way we can finance our long-term liabilities without fundamentally reimagining what government can do in the twenty-first century.

The 90 Percent Tipping Point

Advanced economics like ours that pass a 90 percent debt-to-GDP ratio are less common because they do not survive.

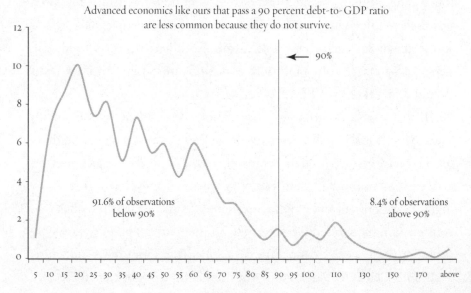

Our economy is already slowing by 25 to 33 percent right now because of our debt burden. As Reinhart and Rogoff argue, our economy slows by 1 point of Gross Domestic Product (GDP) when we hit a debt-to-GDP ratio of 90 percent, which we hit in 2010 (see chart below).[6] And each point of GDP growth missed equals one million jobs not created.[7] Our lackluster economy has proven them correct.

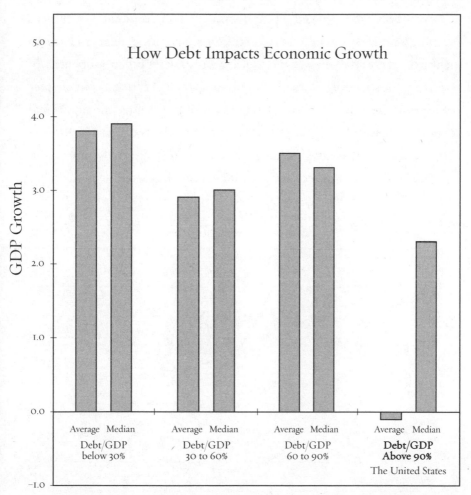

How Debt Impacts Economic Growth

Advanced economies like ours with excessive debt (above 90 percent of GDP) experience much slower, or negative, economic growth.

Meanwhile, our real unemployment rate is closer to 20 percent than 9 percent when you factor in people who have given up or are working only part-time. The decline in housing prices since 2007 is worse than during the Great Depression.[8] Finally, our recession is also the deepest of any we've experienced since the Great Depression. As the graph below shows, our recessions have been getting longer and more severe because our debt is creating a drag on our economy.

We are so overleveraged—heavily indebted—additional government spending and borrowing, such as "stimulus" spending, tends to have no effect or make matters worse. In other words, any potential benefit of government spending (which is highly suspect as I'll discuss in chapter 6) is negated by the harmful consequences of borrowing and additional debt. Think of it this way: we've ordered a seventh credit card just to pay off interest on the other six credit cards we've maxed out.

The bad news is, the economy could get much worse.

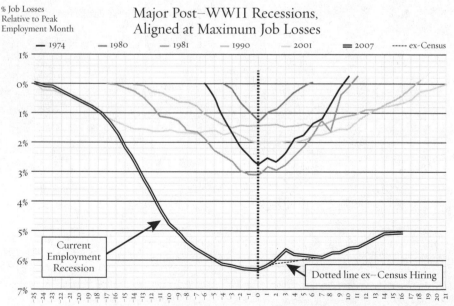

% Job Losses Relative to Peak Employment Month

Major Post–WWII Recessions, Aligned at Maximum Job Losses

Months, Aligned at the Bottom of Recession

WHY THE DEBT IS A THREAT

As the opening scenario suggests, the debt bomb could be triggered by a sudden loss of confidence in our economy. We could see the collapse of the stock market, a further collapse in housing prices, runaway inflation, and social unrest on an almost unimaginable scale. This outcome is much likelier than a slow or gradual decline. The rest of the world simply won't give us the option of managing our decline. Before we reach that final triggering event, however, the existence of a debt bomb in the center of our national life will be a source of fear that erodes consumer confidence and dissuades businesses from investing and hiring. Erskine Bowles, former president Clinton's chief of staff, with whom I've served on President Obama's National Commission on Fiscal Responsibility and Reform, aptly says our debt is a "cancer that will destroy the country from within."[9]

Following are the stages describing how that crisis could unfold.

Debt Bomb, Stage 1: Congress tries to maintain the status quo on spending and entitlements

America's debt crisis is essentially a spending-and-entitlement crisis. The vast majority of our long-term debt comes from entitlement spending, particularly in health care entitlements—as well as the interest costs associated with serving the debt that comes from entitlement borrowing and spending. As the chart on the following page shows, we are on a completely unsustainable course. Spending, especially on entitlement programs like Medicare and Social Security, will rise substantially in coming years. Meanwhile, the interest costs associated with this spending—and borrowing—will rise exponentially.

Using official government estimates, our total unfunded liabilities are $61.6 trillion.[10] Medicare and Social Security alone make up 75 percent of those liabilities. However, using real-world accounting practices employed by businesses and corporations, called *generally accepted*

Sources of Long-Term Debt

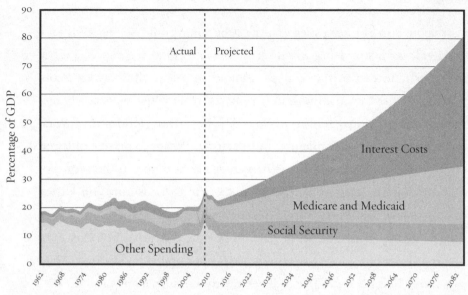

Source: Veronique de Rugy, Mercatus Center at George Mason University/CBO

accounting principles, or GAAP, Michael Tanner with the CATO Institute estimates our unfunded liabilities may be closer to $119.5 trillion.[11]

Fortunately, chairman of the Federal Reserve Ben Bernanke is honest about the math. As he explained in early 2011, "By definition, the unsustainable trajectories of deficits and debt that the [Congressional Budget Office] outlines *cannot actually happen*, because creditors would never be willing to lend to a government whose debt, relative to national income, is rising without limit."[12] Bernanke added, quoting a famous line from economist Herbert Stein, "If something can't go on forever, it will stop."[13]

If current patterns hold, Washington will continue to behave as if there is no entitlement crisis. We'll hear increasingly dire warnings and more earnest promises to do something, but no one will act decisively until we experience more economic pain. Then, as in the scenario described earlier, it will stop.

It is also important to note that every year we delay, the problem gets harder to solve. The hole we've dug for ourselves gets deeper and the sides steeper each year we don't act.[14] Yet Congress and key committee chairs have spent years kicking the can down the road. However, by 2014, and probably much sooner, there will be nowhere to kick the can. We'll hit a wall, and the can will bounce back at our shins. In 2022, tax revenues will only cover the cost of Medicare, Social Security, and interest payments on the national debt. We'll simply have nothing left to fund every other function of government. That means we'll have to do one of three things: (1) shut down every federal agency and scuttle our aircraft carriers; (2) borrow a couple trillion dollars every year to fund the other

Our Unsustainable Course: In the near future, Medicare, Medicaid, Social Security, and Interest Payments will consume all available revenue.

Percentage of GDP

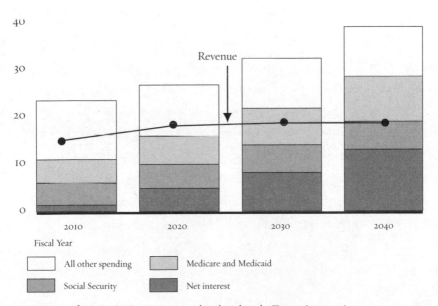

Note: Data are from GAO's January 2010 analysis based on the Trustees' assumptions for Social Security and Medicare

government functions, if we can even borrow the money; or (3) enact massive tax increases, which will further slow economic growth.

Debt Bomb, Stage 2: The United States faces additional credit downgrades

Government has been able to live on borrowed money for so long because, unlike families and individuals, it has the power to print money, borrow, and refinance its own debt essentially when it pleases. Government does this by, for instance, raising the debt limit—its de facto credit card limit—and then borrowing from creditors at home and abroad. Today, we are more vulnerable to debt crisis than in our past because almost one-third of our debt is held by foreigners, which makes us dependent on remaining in the good graces of creditors outside our country.[15]

This approach has worked because the international financial community has, up to this point, had confidence in the ability of the United

Proportion of U.S. Public Debt Holidngs (%)—March 2011

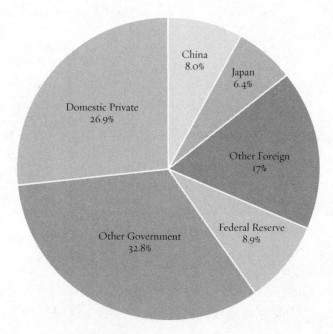

States to repay its debts. Our debt has been perceived as a safer bet than other countries with, for instance, less diverse economies or more serious demographic problems. Yet sooner or later, our debt won't seem like such a safe bet.

In April 2011, Standard & Poor's (S&P), a financial service company that is one of the Big Three credit rating agencies, fired a shot across Washington's bow when they downgraded our long-term credit outlook from "stable" to "negative." S&P said, "We believe there is a material risk that U.S. policymakers might not reach an agreement on how to address medium- and long-term budgetary challenges by 2013."[16]

In August, after months of failing to agree to a long-term deficit reduction plan, S&P made good on their threat and downgraded our rating from AAA to AA+. Congress had been warned and had done nothing. So we were downgraded, and rightly so. If we continue to kick the can down the road, we can expect further downgrades and increased interest costs.

Debt Bomb, Stage 3: Interest rates markedly increase, harming consumers and sending interest payments on the national debt soaring

If our rating continues to deteriorate, and if international creditors lose confidence in our ability—and our will—to pay off our debts, we could see a crash in bond prices along with skyrocketing interest rates. This will cause a decrease in the relative value in the dollar with a reciprocal increase in the price of oil, which is a major reason why we must have an energy policy that immediately causes us to explore and consume our own energy resources.

The crisis in Europe in 2011 shows how volatile bond prices can become when nations become deeply indebted. In the first week of November 2011, for instance, rates on Italian bonds (which measure their cost of borrowing) jumped more than 100 basis points or 1 percent.[17] Meanwhile, interest rates jumped more than 300 basis points in Greece.[18]

Again, rates will go up for the same reason consumers are forced to pay higher interest rates for mortgages. Interest rates reflect risk. International markets will decide lending money to the United States is riskier than it was in the past: the greater the perceived risk, the higher the interest rates. This stage could be delayed in the short term because of the debt crisis in Europe. As the euro weakens, the dollar will strengthen. Yet this reprieve may give us a false sense of security and delay reform even longer.

Still, the Federal Reserve will not be able to keep rates low forever. We have maintained near-historic-low interest rates in recent years in part because the Federal Reserve has tried to stimulate the housing market and stabilize home prices. When interest rates go up—and they have nowhere to go but up—we will all suffer enormously. Loans for homes, cars, and education will cost more and the government will spend—and borrow—more to cover interest payments on the national debt.[19]

If interest rates return to their historic average of about 6 percent, interest payments on the national debt will be the largest line item in the budget by 2020. Interest payments alone on our debt will rise by at least $150 billion per year per point of increase in rates.[20] As the *Wall Street Journal*'s Allysia Finley notes, "A return to normal interest rates will ultimately raise the country's interest costs by $350 billion a year, or $3.5 trillion over a decade. If the super committee couldn't even agree on $1.2 trillion cuts, how will Congress ever cut three times that?"[21]

External forces will also push interest rates higher. Top economists have warned me that the world will hit a debt wall and liquidity crisis around 2013, when the world's available liquid assets ($9 trillion) won't be able to meet sovereign debt requirements (about $13 trillion).

Debt Bomb, Stage 4: Inflation soars, and the value of the dollar declines

In this fourth and final stage we experience a debt crisis. Borrowing enough money to fund our military and other programs will become much more expensive. Because we will be spending more on interest payments, it will be virtually impossible to balance our budget with spending cuts and revenue increases. The hole will be too deep and the sides too steep to climb out.

Meanwhile, the so-called solutions government would turn to at this point would make the problem much worse. Politicians would essentially try to save themselves by destroying the middle class with a tactic Reinhart and Rogoff call "financial repression."[22] Financial repression happens when, to solve a debt crisis, the government uses tools that rob working families. One of the time-honored tools of financial repression is the debasement of currency and inflation. Reinhart and Rogoff call debasement an "Old World favorite"[23] and point to the example of King Henry VIII of England nearly five hundred years ago: "For economists, Henry VIII of England should be almost as famous for clipping his kingdom's coins as he was for chopping off the heads of its queens."[24]

In Henry VIII's time, debasement was accomplished by reducing the gold and silver content of coins. In today's world of paper money, we simply print more, which the Federal Reserve has already done, and may continue to do.

Inflation will then accompany currency debasement. Inflation will make government debt seem smaller by shrinking the value of the dollar. Yet, for individual Americans, inflation will be an insidious hidden tax increase that will make everything you buy more expensive, and everything you own worth less. If our government tries to inflate its way out of a debt crisis, much of your life savings will be wiped out. Milton Friedman put it well: "Inflation has been irresistibly attractive to sovereigns because it is a hidden tax that at first appears painless or even pleasant . . . It is truly taxation without representation."[25]

Other nations will see this as their chance to make what could be a decisive move against the dollar. For years, our global competitors have been trying to find ways to move away from a financial system called Bretton Woods that puts the U.S. dollar at the center of the global economy. In 1944, as World War II was still raging, delegates from the forty-four allied nations met in Bretton Woods, New Hampshire, to set monetary policy for the postwar era. The delegates decided each country would establish the U.S. dollar as the world's reserve currency, thereby tying its currency to the U.S. dollar. This policy continues to this day. If we experience a debt crisis, Bretton Woods would likely be undone and the value of the dollar would fall even further.

Finally, the bottom would fall out of the middle class. Unemployment would soar, while the cost of living would increase. Real wage growth has already been stagnant in recent years, and it will be the middle-class and lower-income families that pay the price for Washington's refusal to act.[26]

A Decade of Wage Stagnation

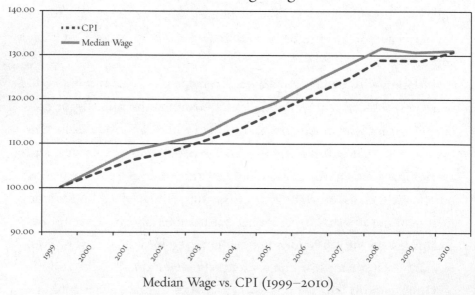

Median Wage vs. CPI (1999–2010)

OTHER VIEWS—WHAT ABOUT WALL STREET, THE BIG BANKS, AND THE BUSH TAX CUTS?

Americans understand that we are in a financial mess, but there is naturally disagreement and confusion about the causes. Let me touch on two other explanations.

First, many Americans want to blame Wall Street and bad decisions among big banks for our recent economic crisis. They are right to be critical of Wall Street. Without question, Wall Street played a major role in triggering the subprime mortgage crisis. In fact, Senator Carl Levin (D-MI), chairman of the Senate Permanent Subcommittee on Investigations, and I released a detailed report excoriating some of these bad actors.[27]

Out of greed and carelessness banks did make loans people could not afford and then the financial system used exotic and questionable trading tools to pass around and sometimes hide these toxic assets. Yet, Congress itself set up a system of perverse incentives that allowed and even encouraged these loans. Politicians wanted the strokes that come along with providing "affordable" housing, so they pushed banks to make bad loans and then refused to do oversight over entities such as Fannie Mae and Freddie Mac, the Office of Thrift Supervision, and the Securities and Exchange Commission until it was too late.

Not surprisingly, the "Blame Wall Street" argument is extremely popular with career politicians who refuse to cut spending and want to defend the status quo. Politicians love to blame everyone but themselves. Fortunately, the American people get it and won't be easily duped. A USA Today poll revealed that when asked whom they blame more for the poor economy, 64 percent of Americans name the federal government and 30 percent say big financial institutions.[28]

Blaming Wall Street alone is simplistic and dangerous because it takes the focus off the greater threat, which is our debt and Washington's refusal to act to reduce it. Plus, the subprime mortgage crisis merely exposed the underlying weaknesses in our economy that were created by a government that is too big to succeed. *From 2001 to 2007 the underlying growth rate of the economy minus the housing bubble was a meager 1 percent.*[29]

Second, I have heard probably hundreds of speeches on the Senate floor blaming our economic turmoil on the Bush tax cuts and the wars in Iraq and Afghanistan. President Bush does deserve his share of blame. In many respects, his administration was a fiscal disaster. President Bush squandered a historic opportunity to exercise fiscal restraint at a time when Republicans controlled all three branches of government. He refused to rein in excessive spending and failed to veto Republican appropriations bills loaded with earmarks. He also made no serious effort to pay for the wars in Iraq and Afghanistan by cutting spending. President Roosevelt, on other hand, proposed cutting spending by 10 percent during World War II.[30] In fact, I voted against all but one war spending bill because Congress and the Bush administration were not serious about paying for the wars by cutting spending rather than borrowing.

The Bush administration also brought us the tragedy of compassionate conservatism—the well-intended but flawed belief that big, activist government could be tamed by Republicans and directed to serve the poor. Finally, instead of reforming Medicare, President Bush and a Republican Congress expanded Medicare through the creation of the prescription drug benefit.

Still, these are critiques conservatives have made of Bush for years. The arguments heard most often on the floor come from members looking to blame someone else for their own inaction.

For instance, blaming our debt on the wars simply does not add up. The average annual cost of our missions in Iraq and Afghanistan is about

$123 billion,[31] which is not much more than the $100 billion we may waste every year in Medicare fraud alone.[32] Clearly, Medicare is a bigger problem—and one politicians don't want to solve.[33]

The Bush tax cuts, on the other hand, are costlier but are still dwarfed by the cost of entitlements. Over the next ten years, the Bush tax cuts will "cost" $3.5 trillion in terms of what they add to the debt while entitlements will cost about $23 trillion.[34] Plus, even if we got rid of the Bush tax cuts and therefore raised taxes, that $3.5 trillion in so-called savings would not necessarily go to more revenue to reduce the debt. Raising taxes would likely hurt the economy, prolong our pain, and lead to less revenue than if we did the responsible thing and threw out the current code and replaced it with one that was simpler and fairer. Plus, Congress would spend the money that came from new revenue rather than decrease the debt.

Still, this does not mean we should not try to offset the deficit consequences of tax cuts with spending cuts. Tax cuts generally create revenue by generating economic growth, but not always enough to cancel out the harmful effects of borrowing, which is a form of deferred taxation that depresses growth. In other words, if tax cuts are likely to increase the deficit it is wise to offset or cancel out this negative effect with spending cuts. I voted against extending the Bush tax cuts in 2010 precisely because Congress was not willing to offset the tax cuts with spending cuts. Had Congress cut spending as they enacted the Bush tax cuts, our economic and employment outlook would be significantly stronger than it is today.

Nonetheless, blaming the Bush tax cuts for our debt problem ignores the root causes of our debt and the long-term sweep of history. The problems we face today are the consequences of policies enacted in the 1930s that put Congress in the business of doing things outside of its enumerated powers.

As the graph below shows, government spending started to consume an ever-increasing share of our economy in 1930, until it reached today's unsustainable and dangerous levels. George W. Bush only served for a fraction of that time.

The Spending Explosion—It Started Long Before Bush and Obama

U.S. Government Spending as Percent of U.S. GDP from Fiscal Year 1890 to Fiscal Year 2010

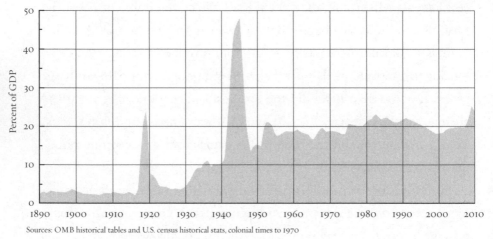

Sources: OMB historical tables and U.S. census historical stats, colonial times to 1970

WILL WE IGNORE THE WARNINGS?

Understanding the nature of this threat and how to deal with it is the defining challenge of our time. We are not alone in our predicament. What is unfolding is essentially the collapse of the International Welfare State. At the time of this writing, countries such as Greece, Italy, Spain, Portugal, Ireland, and Japan are at serious risk of default. The European Union is hanging by a thread.

Ironically, Jin Liqun, the supervising chairman of China Investment Corporation, China's sovereign wealth fund, has offered one of the most insightful—though self-serving—critiques about what is happening in Europe. He said, "If you look at the troubles which happened in European countries, this is purely because of the accumulated troubles of the worn out welfare society. I think the labour laws are outdated. The labour laws induce sloth, indolence, rather than hard [work]. The incentive system is totally out of whack."[35]

It isn't the banks or the free-market system that is to blame. It is the disruption of the free-market system by career politicians who promised things European economies could not afford. Europe brought on its crisis by creating disincentives to work. If we don't reduce our debt burden, we will be in the same position in the very near future.

The risks for us are not just material. Our basic freedoms are at stake. A depression, which would be global, is a real possibility. This outcome would be cataclysmic. Historians generally agree that the last major depression and its instability was a factor that led to the rise of Nazi Germany and World War II. A weakened America would be far less capable of defending not only itself but its allies. Even if we wanted to intervene against a rogue state or competing power, we may not have the means to do so. And the world will suffer the consequences along with us.

Other nations have been down this path before. Spain, France, and Britain all had overextended economies and debt crises like ours in the years preceding their declines. Rome, of course, is the best example. Rome used emergency economic fixes for years and collapsed when it ran out of people to tax. It could no longer afford to pay its army and defend its borders. It was only a matter of time before it was besieged by barbarians and burned. Economist Bruce Bartlett has written, "The fall of Rome was fundamentally due to economic deterioration resulting from excessive taxation, inflation, and over-regulation. Higher and higher taxes failed to raise additional revenues because wealthier taxpayers could evade such taxes while the middle class—and its taxpaying capacity—were exterminated."[36]

I've spent countless hours over the past two years laying out the threat of a debt crisis to our national leaders. The vast majority agree the threat is real enough to warrant dramatic action at the earliest opportunity. Senator Dick Durbin (D-IL) calls the ideas I've presented in this chapter my "doomsday speech," but he says it persuaded him to think about our challenges in a new light. Most national leaders understand that if we don't solve this problem on our terms, the international financial community will dictate the terms of a solution to us. As much as Dick Durbin and I might disagree, we would rather negotiate a solution with each other than with another government or other international holders of our debt.

Unfortunately, Washington has a notoriously short memory. The economic crisis of 2007 and 2008 took most policymakers by surprise. Imagine if, in 2008, a politician had predicted that housing prices would fall 25 percent over the next three years, a rate of decline worse than the Great Depression. No one would have believed him. Yet that is precisely what happened.

The difference now is, the next stages of our debt crisis are entirely predictable. But if Washington continues to govern as if a crisis is not around the corner, we will invite a crisis sooner than anyone expects.

Fortunately, at least a few policymakers in Washington understand the urgency and severity of the threat before us. Today, a band of U.S. senators is meeting away from the cameras to discuss ways to cheat history and defuse our debt bomb.

IN THE BUNKER

"Well, I hope everyone can sleep tonight," said a senator as he left a closed-door briefing on the state of our nation's fiscal health. It was a biting February morning in our nation's capital. Nearly forty senators representing both parties had gathered belowground in the Capitol

Visitor Center at the invitation of Senator Mike Crapo (R-ID), Senator Kent Conrad (D-ND), and me. The message the presenters—budget experts Kyle Bass, who predicted the mortgage meltdown of 2007/2008; and Frank Brosens—delivered was stark: our looming debt crisis is much more severe, and more urgent, than most had realized.

A few weeks later we hosted another early-morning session that was also closed to the press, again with about forty senators from both sides of the aisle. This meeting happened only days before a possible government shutdown on April 5, 2011. Yet, we were concerned about a more serious shutdown—a shutdown of our economy. The senators sat in rows, as if students again, while staff stood in the back, close to the coffee, scones, and briefing materials they passed out to senators as they filed in. The presenters were renowned economists Carmen Reinhart of the University of Maryland and Kenneth Rogoff of Harvard, coauthors of the best-selling book titled *This Time Is Different: Eight Centuries of Financial Folly.*

Reinhart and Rogoff speak with a degree of clarity and authority unusual for academics. They were ideal visitors to help us pause and think. Both economists had hundreds of years of data at their fingertips and were unquestionably nonpartisan. Neither had any ax to grind.

Reinhart and Rogoff had spent much of the past year dismantling the mistaken belief that "this time is different"—the notion that this particular group of policymakers in this moment in history was somehow smarter than all the others and could run up debt forever without catastrophic consequences. A key conclusion of their work is that economies like ours slow down considerably when our debt-to-GDP ratio reaches about 90 percent.

They wrote, "We have been here before. No matter how different the latest financial frenzy or crisis always appears, there are usually remarkable similarities with past experience from other countries and from history.

Recognizing these analogies and precedents is an essential step toward improving our global financial system, both to reduce the risk of future crisis and to better handle catastrophes when they happen."[37]

After Reinhart and Rogoff made brief opening comments focused on the urgency and scope of the problem, the student senators began asking questions with a sincere curiosity cynics would find disarming.

Johnny Isakson, a Republican from Georgia and always a gentleman, stood up to ask his question: "Do we need to act this year? Is it better to act quickly?"

"Absolutely," Rogoff said. "Not acting moves the risk closer," he explained, because every year of not acting adds another year of debt accumulation. "You have very few levers at this point," he warned us.

More hands went in the air.

Senator Mary Landrieu, a Democrat from Louisiana, asked how concerned we should be about revenues and tax rates. Neither Reinhart nor Rogoff said we could fix our debt problem with just tax increases. Both emphasized the need for comprehensive tax reform and tax code simplification. Reinhart said the mortgage interest deduction discourages savings, while Rogoff told me later, "The current code is a jalopy."

Senator Bob Corker (R-TN) asked how relevant it was where our debt is bought—at home or abroad.

"Very relevant," Rogoff responded. "You have less leverage when it's external."

Senator Kent Conrad, the chairman of the Senate Budget Committee, said our current deficits were severe because we had very low revenues due to a slow economy combined with very high spending. He then offered his own stern warning to the assembled senators. Turning around in his chair in the middle of the room, he explained to his colleagues that when our high debt burden causes our economy to slow by 1 point of GDP, as Reinhart and Rogoff estimate, that doesn't slow our economy by 1 percent but *25 to 33 percent* when we are growing at only 3 or 4 GDP points per year.

Reinhart echoed Conrad's point and explained that countries rarely pass the 90 percent debt-to-GDP tipping point precisely because it is dangerous to let that much debt accumulate. She said, "If it was not risky to hit the 90 percent threshold, we would expect a higher incidence."

Senator and former governor Mike Johanns, a Republican from Nebraska, asked, "Is there a point at which the debt market rebels?"

"I don't want to be fire and brimstone," Rogoff said. "No one knows when this will happen." Yet, he added, "It takes more than two years to turn the ship around . . . Once you've waited too long, it's too hard to take radical steps."

Waiting, of course, always seems to be the course of action in Washington. For this discussion, at least, senators were looking for a course of action.

Senator Durbin asked about the dangers of not investing in areas like education.

Reinhart acknowledged the importance of what she called "human capital formation," but said those sorts of investments are hardest hit in a crisis. "Doing an adjustment in response to a crisis doesn't work very well," she explained. Earlier Rogoff said the effects of controversial measures such as tax cuts and stimulus spending tend to be exaggerated in the popular media. "Debt is the problem," Rogoff clarified. "You have a debt crisis because of debt."

"Thank you for your depressing presentation," Durbin said in closing, to self-conscious laughter around the room.

These private exchanges, in which senators had the humility and curiosity to be students again, were a welcome departure from business-as-usual posturing. This was a view of the Senate the American people almost never see but would be encouraged to witness. These meetings were happening because you—We the People—were putting enormous pressure on Congress to get serious about spending and deficit reduction. And there was remarkable agreement about the severity of the problem, even though some in the room, such as Mary Landrieu, Scott Brown, Dick Durbin, and Rand Paul, were very far apart on solutions.

After the meeting in the Capitol Visitor Center, I walked back through the Capitol tunnel and subway to the Russell Senate Office Building with Reinhart and Rogoff. As we walked, Reinhart remarked, "I've seen this movie a thousand times. I know how it ends."

We then sat in my office for an informal debriefing. They put an even sharper point on their warnings.

Reinhart said bluntly that if we don't act quickly to reduce our debt burden, "financial repression is coming." She also said a "massive hidden tax on the middle class" will be imposed on the country through government policies that will try to manage a debt crisis. This could include negative rates of return on pensions and inflation. "Don't underestimate the power of necessity," she concluded.

Rogoff agreed and said our government would try to manage a debt crisis "at every margin and from every angle."

I asked Rogoff where he saw short-term inflation headed.

"I see inflation at 2.5 to 3 percent, but it's hard to predict," he answered. "When you get killed is when people don't buy your debt."

Reinhart and Rogoff had identified our real problem, and the danger ahead. Our entire government and system depend on people buying our debt. When that stops, the party is over.

To avoid that fate, let's look at how we got here, and how we can get back on track.

THE PROBLEM

We have already passed the tipping point. Our debt is already preventing the creation of one million jobs a year.

If we refuse to reduce our debt, the government will try to shrink the size of our debt through financial repression. Inflation will be increased by decreasing the value of our currency, which is known as debasement. This option will destroy the middle class.

If we try to go down this path the rest of the world may not let us get very far because the value of the Treasury bills they own will decrease.

We will then become Greece. Because we failed to reduce our debt on our own terms, the rest of the world will dictate the terms to us.

2

The Triumph of Politicians

You ask, how it has happened that all Europe has acted on
the principle, "that Power was Right." Power always sincerely,
conscientiously, believes itself right. Power always thinks it
has a great soul, and vast views, beyond the comprehension of
the weak; and that it is doing God service, when it is violating
all His laws. Power must never be trusted without a check.

—JOHN ADAMS TO THOMAS JEFFERSON, FEBRUARY 2, 1816[1]

TO MANY AMERICANS, THE SOLUTIONS TO OUR FISCAL PROBLEMS
are blindingly obvious: spend less, borrow less, keep taxes low, and
reform entitlement programs in a way that protects the poor. One reason
I released *Back in Black*, which includes $9 trillion in deficit reduction
recommendations, was to show that it is possible to make these changes.[2]

For years, voters have been sending the same message to Washington:
make the hard choices now that will secure liberty for future generations.
However, numerous elections over the past forty years, including those
described by pundits as "change elections" in which power shifts between
parties, have failed to fundamentally fix the problem. Different parties and

presidents have pursued competing goals, of course, and those distinctions are by no means trivial. Yet, at the end of the day, we're still going bankrupt. Spending has skyrocketed, and our debt has now hit a critical level.

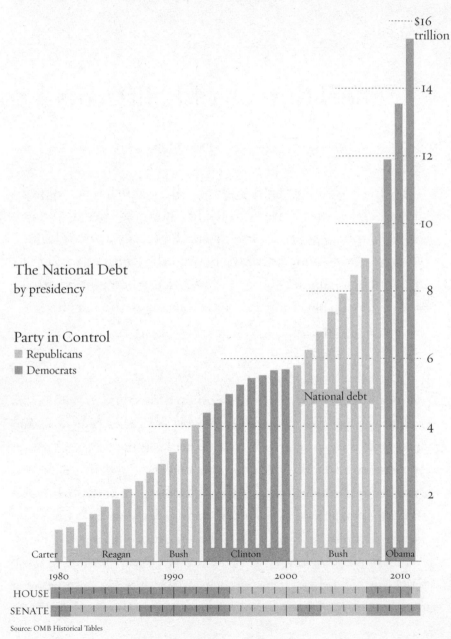

The National Debt
by presidency

Party in Control
■ Republicans
■ Democrats

National debt

Carter   Reagan   Bush   Clinton   Bush   Obama

1980   1990   2000   2010

HOUSE
SENATE

Source: OMB Historical Tables

This begs the questions: Why is real change so elusive? How did we let things get so bad? Why is it so hard to cut spending? And why does Washington defend the status quo so intensely? As the chart shows on the previous page, spending has exploded under both Republicans and Democrats.

WHAT'S WRONG WITH WASHINGTON?

Washington abounds with explanations of why the system is broken. Many say money in politics is the problem. Industries and special interests spend millions protecting their subsidies by co-opting politicians who need huge sums of campaign cash to win. Yet, this explanation does not go far enough. We know from experience that no amount of campaign finance reform or ethics reform will be enough. As long as government touches so many aspects of our lives, we will have money in politics. The way to reduce the influence of money, therefore, is to reduce the size of government. Even then, there are other forces at work.

Others point to structural problems such as *gerrymandering*, the art of drawing congressional district boundaries in ways that protect incumbents. Gerrymandering lets politicians choose their voters rather than letting voters choose their representatives. Finally, many argue that Washington is so sharply divided along partisan and ideological lines that commonsense solutions are next to impossible to enact.

All these problems are real symptoms of a deeper problem. *Careerism*—the philosophy of governing to win the next election above all else—is the root of almost all that ails Washington. Careerism is the dark matter of the political universe. It is the unseen force that bends decisions, and character, in ways that defy common sense and obvious explanations.

CAREERISM TRUMPS IDEOLOGY

I'll never forget being pulled aside on the Senate floor by a well-known Republican senator who wanted to know why I was taking so many controversial stands against earmarks and popular spending programs. He was genuinely curious about what made me tick.

"*Why* do you do what you do?" he asked.

"I don't care if I get reelected," I responded. "I really don't."

His face looked ashen. He knew that I knew we were acknowledging the fundamental problem in Washington. Virtually all members of Congress come to Washington with noble and pure intentions. Over time, however, a subtle shift occurs. The desire to do the right thing is supplanted by the desire to hang on to power so the politicians can do the right thing at some point in the future, when it is safer or when success seems more likely. Yet, the moment to do what is right is never today. It is always a mirage just beyond the horizon of the next election. Consequently, the perfect political moment to fix the nation's problems never arrives.

This particular senator was like many Republicans. He was seen as generally conservative but played the Washington game, spent money we don't have on things we don't need, and avoided rocking the boat so he could get reelected and do good things down the road. He knew it and I knew it. And he was embarrassed by his double-mindedness.

REAL VALUES VERSUS ASPIRATIONAL VALUES

One way to understand the power of careerism is to look at the difference between real values and aspirational or nominal values. Think of this as the "actions speak louder than words" principle. Real values reflect behavior. They are who we really are. Nominal values, on the other hand, reflect aspirations. They are what we would like to be.

Everyone in Washington wants to do the right thing—govern in a fiscally responsible manner that helps Americans fulfill their aspirations—but their behavior, sadly, tells a different story. Republicans almost uniformly say the problem is spending, but only very few members participate in the actual work of identifying and eliminating wasteful and low-priority spending. Most Republicans prefer to spend money and try to get reelected. Cutting spending, therefore, is a nominal value, not a real value.

Democrats have the same problem. Democrats aspire to values like economic justice, equality, and protecting entitlement programs; but their behavior says something else. Instead of fixing the programs upon which the poor depend, many Democrats support policies that will bankrupt those very programs. Many Democrats also engage in class warfare rhetoric and complain about tax cuts for the rich, yet they refuse to end tax breaks for the rich and other direct payments to millionaires.[3] With Democrats, economic justice is often a nominal value, not a real value.

At the end of the day, our $15 trillion national debt is a monument to Washington's real values—self-preservation and careerism. (See appendix B for a list of votes that illustrate the Senate's real values.)

WASHINGTON'S "INNER RING"

Perhaps the best description of *careerism* comes from C. S. Lewis's book *The Weight of Glory*. Lewis describes human nature as pursuing the "Inner Ring." Lewis, incidentally, was a close friend and colleague of J. R. R. Tolkien, who wrote about another ring that is better known—the Ring of Power—in his *Lord of the Rings* trilogy. Both rings warn of the seduction of power and position.

Lewis's Inner Ring is a place where people can feel important and secure knowing they are "in the know." Every form of government has had Inner Rings, from the Roman Senate to the King's Counsel in Britain to today's Congress.

Lewis said that the pursuit of the Inner Ring makes good men do bad things. He wrote, "As long as you are governed by that desire you will never get what you want. You are trying to peel an onion; if you succeed there will be nothing left. Until you conquer the fear of being an outsider, an outsider you will remain."[4]

Inner Rings are not isolated to politics—they exist in all fields and all areas of life. Most of us have felt the fear of losing power, position, and prestige and have known people who cling to positions for the wrong reasons and then justify unethical behavior to maintain their positions. Careerism in Washington is different in the sense that Washington amplifies, and then aggressively exploits, basic human insecurities and the desire to feel significant, accepted, and loved.

For instance, the culture of Washington specializes in providing politicians with various rationalizations to convince them they are on the right track when they are really becoming part of the problem. It helps members "go native" and make the transition from principled outsiders to political insiders in several ways.

Washington is populated with what is essentially a permanent feudal class of media elites, politicians, lobbyists, experts, and staffers who are inclined to be self-referential and self-reinforcing insiders. Washington has its own circuit of events, balls, and dinners that tend to draw the same insular crowd to every event. Most of these people really are delightful, but they are frequently disconnected from the real world, and a surprising number have never had a real job outside of politics.

Washington is still quintessentially American in the sense that almost anyone can break in, but once you are in, you are considered part of the ruling class, and the ruling class protects its own. When a member of

Congress is elected, he or she is quickly surrounded by people from this ruling class—party leaders, lobbyists, interest groups, and staff—who have a vested interest in keeping the member in power. Unless the member has a very clear sense of purpose and mission and is not afraid to lose an election, this group tends to take over and implement its unspoken and subtle indoctrination process.

Members of Congress, who have gained access to one of the most coveted Inner Rings—leadership offices—desperately want members from their party to stay in power so they themselves can stay in power. For congressional leaders, their positions depend not on their ability to solve problems but on their ability *to win and maintain seats for their party*. If new members want to do good things, party leaders tell them they first have to stay in power. Then they can do good things. Solving problems is fine, but it is something to be done down the road, once everyone's position is more secure. Again, that moment never seems to arrive.

Lobbyists, special-interest groups, and even think tanks also have a vested interest in keeping members in power, particularly when a member has given special access to these groups. Outside groups give members not only campaign cash for acting on behalf of their clients, but also prestige, honor, and even badges of purity for voting the way they want. Heads of these groups often hold themselves up as judges in a purity pageant that rewards politicians for adhering to arbitrary goals and narrow pledges that are designed to elevate parties and interest groups at the expense of the country.

For instance, if you want to mindlessly defend the status quo on Social Security and Medicare, AARP will laud your virtue even if your rejection of reform jeopardizes the very programs you want to protect. Similarly, if you want to present yourself as a conservative for low taxes, you can sign Americans for Tax Reform's Taxpayer Protection Pledge and then go about your business borrowing, spending, and earmarking as usual. Even though those actions keep tax rates high and government big, ATR will be happy to give you a badge of purity.

Whatever path a member of Congress chooses politically or ideologically will be affirmed by groups who have a vested interest in protecting the status quo. Washington lets you choose your ideology, and interest groups will provide the justification. You tell these groups what feels good to you, and they'll make sure you feel right about your positions, however contradictory and counterproductive they may be.

Finally, staff members—the eyes and ears of Congress—know their jobs depend on their bosses staying in power. And as members of Congress climb the congressional ladder, so do staff. If members themselves don't have a clear vision, the default advice from staff will be to play it safe and avoid offending the powers that be in Washington. This is an enormous problem among committee staff, in particular. Staff routinely leave the Hill to double or triple their salaries working for groups they were previously responsible for regulating or overseeing. If a member of Congress is not highly committed to oversight, all too often committee staff undermine oversight and avoid confronting industry groups or agencies for whom they may someday work.

When disgraced lobbyist Jack Abramoff was released from prison, he confirmed this fact. As one report showed, "Abramoff boasted that in his heyday he had 100 lawmakers under his thumb—usually because he'd promised their staffers high-paying future jobs. 'The moment I said that to them . . . that was it. We owned them,' he said. 'Everything we want, they're going to do.'"[5]

Together, these players in the ruling class—party leaders, media personalities, heads of special-interest groups, and staff—reinforce Washington's incumbent protection system that is rigged to keep politicians in office for as long as possible.

Our founders wrote the Constitution to guard against the problem of careerism. They knew they couldn't outlaw ambition and insecurity. Instead, they designed the Constitution to be a containment chamber for the human drive for power. Just as in a nuclear reactor, political energy, when contained, can do good things and solve problems. The problem today is, the reactor has been breached. Politicians are asked to manage powers and responsibilities our founders never intended to delegate to Congress. As a result, only the most resolute members survive the system, and the country is now endangered by a system that is in meltdown.

Again, it is the scope of government itself—not money—that leads legislators to become dependent on Washington's permanent feudal class. Our government today is so massive that it is impossible for any one member to know everything. As a result, members have become highly dependent on staff, lobbyists, and interests who are all too eager to label their obedience and ignorance as purity to whatever cause the interest group champions.

The media exacerbates this problem. Reporters treat every member of Congress like an expert because the media itself has a voracious appetite for content and conflict. Some members feel enormous pressure to comment on everything. They themselves know that the power to cast a vote on a topic does not convey expertise, and most work very hard to be informed. Yet, a legion of outside voices is always ready to step in and gloss over a member's lack of knowledge with talking points and other tips on how to fake it.

THE THREE ROOTS OF CAREERISM: PAROCHIALISM, TRADITION, AND PARTY

Careerism expresses itself in several ways. Some are obvious. Certain members become camera moths once elected. If a camera light comes on, they run to it. Yet most expressions are more subtle. For instance,

I have repeatedly tried to force Congress to fix decaying roads and bridges before funding lower-priority earmarks, such as the infamous Bridge to Nowhere in Alaska—a proposed $223 billion bridge to an island with fifty inhabitants—and beautification projects, such as squirrel sanctuaries. I've had some success, but the battles over such simple choices have been epic at times. This obvious inability to set rational priorities in all areas of government, big and small—from defense to transportation to health care to entitlement reform—is the most common expression of careerism. Politicians refuse to set priorities for a simple reason. Saying no might make someone mad, and then he or she might not give you money or vote for you. As a result, nothing changes.

On the surface, our government is made of three branches—the executive, judicial, and legislative. But the real story of how Washington works is under the surface. Below the three branches of government are the three roots of careerism—parochialism, tradition, and party. These roots run deep and are cracking the foundations of our republic.

The Triumph of Parochialism

Career politicians in Washington tend to govern on the basis of parochialism over principle. *Parochialism*—making decisions based on what will benefit a politician's state or district—seems innocuous and even laudable. Certainly, there is nothing wrong with wanting to help your state or district. But when that instinct also aligns with a politician's careerist impulses, it becomes very convenient for politicians to justify all sorts of mischief and assume powers that do not exist in the Constitution.

Interestingly, the oath of office makes no mention of a representative or senator's district or state, but instead affirms the Constitution. The oath reads:

I do solemnly swear (or affirm) that I will support and defend the Constitution of the United States against all enemies, foreign and domestic; that I will bear true faith and allegiance to the same; that I take this obligation freely, without any mental reservation or purpose of evasion; and that I will well and faithfully discharge the duties of the office on which I am about to enter: So help me God.[6]

Nowhere has parochialism been more evident than with Congress's gluttonous appetite for earmarks—special-interest pork projects targeted to individual districts and states by individual members—in the 1990s and the last decade. For twenty years earmarks were the gateway drug to Washington's spending addiction, mostly under Republican rule. As earmarks increased, so did overall spending levels.

Earmarks: The Gateway Drug to Congress's Spending Addiction

(Number of earmarks, total federal government spending, in trillions of dollars, by fiscal year)

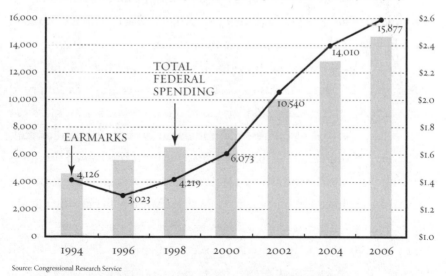

Source: Congressional Research Service

All this was justified as a public service and an expression of Congress's constitutional authority to exercise its so-called power of the purse. In practice, the earmark process was a celebration of careerism, and a form of legalized bribery.

Case in point: on July 13, 2005, the Senate Committee on Environment and Public Works sent me this memo:

> The high priority project allocation amount contained in this letter *is a target*. Please remember that these amounts may change. The conference is currently negotiating state highway formula distribution and pending the outcome of those negotiations, *these allocation amounts may need to be reduced* to ensure the formula structure works.
>
> Target Allocation Amount for Senator Coburn: $45,000,000

As the memo makes plain, each senator received an allowance—what Representative Jeff Flake (R-AZ) calls "walking-around money"—to spend on earmarks as they saw fit. I had no idea why my allowance was $45 million and not $10 million or $100 million, and neither did anyone else. The phrase "high priority project allocation" was a farce. These figures had nothing to do with our state's infrastructure needs, and everything to do with our political needs. As politicians, the "high priority project" was extending our careers. Each senator was supposed to just take his or her money, dole it out and keep his or her mouth shut.

The staffer who sent me this memo obviously was not familiar with my history of opposing earmarks and exposing thinly veiled attempts at bribery. In 1998, for instance, a staffer for then House Transportation Committee chairman Bud Shuster (R-PA) left a voice mail offering me $15 million for pork in my district, which I played for *ABC World News Tonight*. It is memos like this that inspired disgraced lobbyist Jack Abramoff to call the House Appropriations Committee an earmark "favor factory."[7]

Earmarks were used to stage bring-home-the-bacon ribbon-cutting ceremonies and, in many cases, to solicit campaign contributions in exchange for special projects. One of the more famous examples involved the sordid tale of how a powerful congressman from Alaska, Don Young, took an unusual interest in an earmark in Florida along Coconut Road.

In 2005, Young, one of the cocreators of the "Bridge to Nowhere" earmark and then chairman of the Transportation and Infrastructure Committee, flew to Lee County, Florida, for a fund-raiser. Lee County had successfully secured $10 million to expand a highway along a hurricane evacuation route. Young pulled in $40,000 at the event. One of the top contributors was developer Daniel Aronoff, who happened to own four thousand acres along a stretch called Coconut Road.

When Young returned to Washington, language in a bill the House and Senate had already passed was mysteriously edited. Instead of directing $10 million for "widening and improvements for I-75," the language was changed to "Coconut Rd. interchange I-75 Lee County." In other words, instead of directing the funds to the hurricane evacuation route as promised and, more important, as the House and Senate agreed to, someone changed the language to benefit Daniel Aronoff, a top contributor whose land value would increase because of the project.[8]

Keith Ashdown, then with Taxpayers for Common Sense and now a member of my staff, stated, "This goes beyond the intent of the technical corrections process. It's supposed to be about getting your punctuation right, not about making sure that your major benefactor is getting their pork . . . I've seen little gimmicks and little tricks used to make sure somebody's friend or contributor is taken care of but this is by far one of the more underhanded, surreptitious examples I've seen—ever."[9]

Young initially denied responsibility for the change and wrongly claimed local residents and the local congressman, Connie Mack, requested the edit. After I pushed for a House-Senate task force to investigate the origin of the earmark, Young's office admitted they made the change but claimed they were only correcting an error.

Columnist George Will said of the affair, "Unlike another fragrant slab of recent pork, the $233 million Alaskan Bridge to Nowhere, Coconut Road goes somewhere. It runs straight into the dark heart of Washington's earmark culture of waste, corruption and anticonstitutional deviousness."[10]

Proposed earmarks like the Bridge to Nowhere, Coconut Road, and the Woodstock Museum—a museum celebrating the famous free love gathering in 1969 that now received free money—finally forced Congress to accept an earmark moratorium in 2011, yet the culture of parochialism and careerism in Congress is alive and well. For instance, members continue to push for parochial projects through phone-marking—a tactic members use to avoid a paper trail and transparency rules by calling agency heads to cajole them to fund certain grants or risk budget cuts to their agency. President Obama, in fact, threatened to make public requests that continued to come this way. It's a shame he didn't make good on that threat.[11]

Parochialism also continues to thrive in defense contracting and transportation funding. Defense contracts are often distributed across the country not according to need or cost, but on how to continue the life cycle of the weapon system. Defense systems made from parts built in twenty or thirty states are harder to kill than systems built in one state, regardless of their relevance to our strategic needs. Transportation earmarks also continue through programs that require states to spend money on things like bike paths and other lower-priority beautification projects instead of essential roads and bridges.

Another egregious form of parochialism are tax earmarks—special-interest spending programs placed in the tax code designed as credits or deductions that benefit particular groups or industries. One example of tax earmarks has been subsidies for biofuels like ethanol that are fiercely defended, not surprisingly, by members from corn-growing states, or whatever state creates your favorite "green" biofuel. Ethanol has also been protected by the tradition of holding presidential caucuses in Iowa early in the nominating process. Thankfully, support for the credit is on the wane and it may permanently expire.

Other tax earmarks have gone to Hollywood movie producers, racetracks, the tackle-box industry, and more.[12] Tax earmarks are also a favorite among the leaders of special-interest groups who sometimes act like career politicians who have never been elected. To borrow a phrase from conservative blogger and earmark foe Erick Erickson, for these "coin-operated . . . conservatives"[13] tax earmarks are a two-for-one special. Protecting tax earmarks generates large contributions from the industries that benefit from them, while protecting these provisions also gives politicians cover to say they are supporting a tax cut.

The argument that tax earmarks are tax cuts, of course, is ludicrous. Tax earmarks have nothing to do with taxes. They are pure spending programs that are hidden in the code so they can receive extra special-interest protection. Tax earmarks are especially insidious because they are de facto tax increases on everyone who can't hire a lobbyist or donate to an interest group. Keeping tax earmarks in place does not "cut taxes" but rather keeps tax rates higher for everyone else.

The Triumph of Tradition

Another root of careerism along with parochialism is tradition for tradition's sake. When I was first elected to the Senate, the phrase I heard most often was "Let me explain how things work around here." Every new class of members of Congress, especially senators, endures these lectures.

Early in my term in the Senate, a young legislative director from the office of a well-known and established conservative senator wanted to meet with me urgently to explain how the Senate worked, particularly with regard to earmarks. Even though I had served three terms in the House and challenged the process repeatedly and publicly, I apparently needed a refresher course now that I was in the Upper Chamber.

I sat down with this earnest and well-intentioned aide, even though it seemed he was acting independently of his boss. Our meeting was cordial, though not particularly informative, and we each went on our ways. It was the first of many times my office would be instructed about "the way things are done around here."

The most striking lecture about the preeminence of tradition came in the spring of 2008 when Republican appropriator Senator Pete Domenici (R-NM) wanted to pass a bill authorizing new federal land designations. The bill had passed Domenici's committee unanimously, so he assumed it was noncontroversial and should sail through the Senate. However, the bill had several problems.

First, it would borrow and spend new money—about $50 million—instead of reducing money from other accounts. Second, it was irresponsible for Congress to approve new land designations when the National Park Services was already facing a $9 billion maintenance backlog. This was a classic Washington response: Why solve an old problem when you can create a new program?

Domenici thought my objections were hardly reasonable. In fact, he was livid that a junior senator who was not on the committee dared to oppose his bill. *That just wasn't how things were done around here.* If you aren't on the committee, you aren't supposed to meddle with committee business.

I thought this line of reasoning was more than a little imperial. I respected Senator Domenici, but I had been elected to represent taxpayers in Oklahoma, who would have to pay for this bill, along with taxpayers in the other forty-nine states. As their elected representative, I had not only the right but the responsibility to stop and amend bad legislation.

In my mind, the concerns of 300 million Americans far outweighed the convenience and conventions of ninety-nine senators.

Domenici said on the floor:

> So, basically, there have been no reasons for holding up these bills . . . I do not believe the judgment regarding park boundaries in Wyoming, a land exchange in Arizona, a water project in Colorado, should supplant that of the 23 members of the committee—that one Senator should supplant that.
>
> Those 23 members of this committee make their judgments on information compiled by a professional staff with a combined service of relevant departments in Congress of over 70 years on the Republican staff side alone. They spend a great deal of time on these bills. They know more than anyone else. They give that knowledge to us, the 23 members, and we vote. It is not as if these bills are put together, brought here, much time, effort and money and resources are put into them before they are put together and before we ask the Senate to pass them. I hope we will not find ourselves in this bind again.[14]

In other words, it was wrong for me to question not only the wisdom of the senators on the committee but their staff. I didn't care if the committee had a thousand years of staff experience. None of those staff members were elected. They had zero constitutional authority.

It was unusual for Domenici to publicly acknowledge the open secret about the extent to which committee staff run the show in Congress. Domenici and most appropriators delegate their decision-making authority to staff members who often cultivate cozy relationships with special-interest groups they hope to one day work for, earning salaries of $300,000 to $500,000 or more.

Domenici also claimed that the bill, which he said was merely an authorization bill—a bill that creates programs but doesn't directly fund them—did not spend any money and that therefore my objection was baseless. Appropriators often make this argument but contradict themselves in their own press releases, in which they brag about how mere authorization bills are going to create jobs in their state. In the Senate, authorization bills always signal Congress's intent to spend real money, and lots of it.

As I explained to Senator Domenici:

We are not passing these bills under the assumption they are not going to be appropriated. We are passing these bills under the assumption they will be appropriated.

As a matter of fact, the promise is made as we pass this. And either it is a hollow promise you are sending back home so you can say, yes, I did this, and lie to your constituents, or we are going to appropriate the money. It is one or the other. So either we are dishonest with whom we are telling we are doing something for or we absolutely intend to appropriate it. There isn't any other option.

I will finish up by saying this . . . We are in tremendous economic straits in the long term. This debate is not about the lands bill. It is about will we change the philosophy, will we honor our oath, and will we start doing what is right in the long term for those who come after us . . .

Am I frustrating the Senators from New Mexico? You bet. Are our children worth it? You bet. I am not going to stop. I am going to stand and say we are going to think long term, we are going to start protecting property rights, we are going to start thinking about our children, and we are not going to give up because we get lectured because we are not doing it the way we have always done it. The way we have always done it has us bankrupt. It is time for a change. Republicans and Democrats alike, our children are worth it.[15]

The Triumph of Partisans

The final root of careerism in Washington is partisanship. In many respects partisanship *is* careerism. Partisanship, more than anything else in Washington, prevents long-term solutions. Short-term political goals almost always trump the best interests of the country. The moment to take risks necessary to defuse the debt bomb never arrives. Nothing ever changes, until it's too late to change.

Like many dysfunctions in Washington, partisanship is presented as a rationalization for doing good. Partisans argue the chief goal of politicians should be to give their respective party as much power as possible so they can do good things for the country. In the real world, this rarely happens. Rigid partisans tend to advocate positions that betray the principles upon which their parties were founded. Instead of advancing principled solutions, partisanship reinforces the status quo.

This is precisely what derailed the Republican revolution in the 1990s. When I was elected in the historic 1994 election, leaders like Newt Gingrich (R-GA), Dick Armey (R-TX), and Tom DeLay (R-TX) were widely viewed as solid ideological conservatives. Yet, their principled conservatism disappeared when they were in power. In office, they were partisans first and principled conservatives second.

Our revolution started with a burst of principled reforms in the first one hundred days, but most members soon went native. Armey betrayed the term limits movement by sabotaging the vote and ensuring the measure would fail. He said term limits weren't necessary because the good guys had won. Partisanship trumped principle. Fortunately, Armey today is like the Armey before he had power—principled and articulate—which highlights the problem with careerism.

Newt Gingrich reversed the gains we made toward reducing spending by violating a Republican budget deal and agreeing to budget-busting omnibus bills beginning in 1997. Gingrich also became distracted by what people in Washington call "shiny objects"—secondary issues and distractions that don't necessarily advance primary goals. Gingrich lost himself in personal struggles and saw the Monica Lewinsky scandal as a shortcut to Republican gains. In 1998, I confronted him about our failure to articulate a positive, detailed conservative agenda and how our failure to lead was demoralizing our base. His response: "Clinton has already motivated our base." Gingrich the partisan won the argument against Gingrich the principled conservative. Republicans, by the way, were shellacked in the 1998 elections.

As this process unfolded, the other members of the Class of 1994 felt as though we were insurgents who had been abandoned and betrayed by our own generals. I helped mount a coup to replace Gingrich as Speaker in 1997. That effort failed, but when Republicans lost seats in 1998, I helped gather six other Republicans who vowed that we would not vote for Gingrich for Speaker under any circumstance. Because Gingrich knew that he would lose the speakership if he lost six votes in our narrow majority, he resigned from Congress.

I left the House in 2001 because I was following my pledge to limit my terms. By then, parochialism and partisanship had undermined the foundations of the Republican Party. The divide between conservatives and party insiders was getting wider. Conservatives were aghast that Republican appropriators were embarking on an orgy of pork-barrel spending unparalleled in human history. Yet, at that time, President Bush's chief political adviser, Karl Rove, was talking about the possibility of a permanent governing majority for Republicans. Meanwhile, lobbyists and party insiders Jack Abramoff and Grover Norquist were helping Tom DeLay (R-TX), the Republican whip at the time, on the K Street Project[16]—a project that was designed to populate K Street lobbying shops with loyal Republicans instead of reducing the size of K Street by reducing the ways in which government interferes with our lives and necessitates lobbying.

It was only a matter of time before our majority collapsed. On May 24, 2001, Republican senator Jim Jeffords defected and gave control of the Senate to Democrats. Republicans regained control of the Senate in 2002. In 2005 and 2006, years of overspending and earmarking caught up with the party. Republicans were decimated in the 2006 elections.

Republican fantasies of a permanent governing majority weren't jettisoned, however, just put off for another day. Democrats, of course, have the same dreams, which bring us to today's impasse.

CAREERISM AT THE IMPASSE

I have spent much of the past two years in meetings with members from both parties trying to solve the debt problem. It has felt like pushing twenty boulders up a mountain of ice. My colleagues are well intended, and I love them dearly as individuals, but there is no real leadership in either party. Both sides do the same calculation: "If I tell the voters the truth, they won't like me and they won't vote for me." They then convince themselves that they can't do the right thing now because they won't have the power to stay in office. The force bringing these boulders—and solutions—back to earth is careerism.

If members of Congress knew their current term would be their last, I have no doubt we could defuse the debt bomb within a matter of days. The fact that we haven't passed such a bill has much more to do with careerism than ideology. Bridging the gap between conservatives and liberals is easy compared to bridging the gap between courage and cowardice.

Both parties today are putting their short-term political interests ahead of the country. Both present their positions as tough and principled to their respective partisans, but what we often see is posturing and false purity.

For example, politicians in both parties try to score points by promoting their refusal to compromise with the other side. In most cases, this posturing has nothing to do with principle and everything to do with careerism—pandering to one side's respective political base in order to gain popularity and win reelection.

Democrats claim their line in the sand is protecting entitlement benefits for the poor and seniors. Convinced of the virtue of their goal, partisan Democrats rationalize their decision to dismiss, demagogue, and demonize anyone who proposes entitlement reform.

This position, however, is entirely about protecting Democrats, not the poor or seniors. If entitlement programs are not reformed, they will collapse and bring our economy down with them.

Republicans, meanwhile, say their line in the sand is "no tax increases." I'm glad so many Republicans are talking tough about the problem being overspending, not under-taxation. I've been making that case since 1995. If these same Republicans, who continue to vote for more spending, had been as resolute since 1995, the problem would be much easier to solve. Every dollar of deficit spending Republicans backed—along with Democrats—was a deferred tax increase. Our present challenges prove that deficits do matter.

Republicans know it is possible to increase revenue without raising tax rates on anyone. In fact, you can cut tax rates, cut spending, and see an increase in tax revenue. Senator Marco Rubio (R-FL) nailed this point when he said, "We don't need new taxes. We need new taxpayers."[17] Ultimately, smart tax policy stimulates real growth, which, in turn, creates jobs and revenue. If revenue is considered undesirable, then so is job creation and growth, which is ludicrous.

In the real world, putting one dollar on the table in order to get ten dollars back, or even three or four dollars back, would be a great deal. In Washington, however, this kind of agreement is seen as heresy to careerists on both sides. In a 10 to 1 deal ($10 in cuts for every $1 in tax revenue), Democrats would see only "cuts" while Republicans would see only "tax increases," even though such a deal would prevent the very cuts and tax increases they each say they want to avoid.

I realize this logic only works when cuts can be made today, not in some distant time. Politicians will always embrace the politics of instant gratification that favors revenue increases over cuts. I've seen this tendency firsthand on many occasions. Still, a deal that can truly guarantee a significant net reduction in the size and scope of government, through entitlement reform, for instance, in exchange for limited revenue increases is a deal worth taking.

Again, if Admiral Mullen is correct that our debt is our greatest national security threat, doing nothing is a recipe for mutually assured destruction. The reality is, doing nothing to solve the problem is both a tax increase and a benefit cut for seniors and the poor. Doing nothing violates the core principles of both parties, while solving the problem is consistent with those values. Doing nothing is the real betrayal and the heresy.

Career politicians in Washington can draw lines in the sand all day, but those lines have already been washed away by a rising tide of debt. There are no lines left to hold. We are under siege and surrounded by an enemy of our own making. We'll either fix the problem together, or suffer enormously together. As much as I would enjoy serving in a conservative supermajority, it will never happen before the debt bomb explodes. A liberal supermajority is equally impossible. And if we refuse to make the effort and talk to one another, what is the alternative? Will the Chinese and other foreign governments give us a better deal than another party within our own country?

The late Tony Blankley, who had a front-row seat to the Gingrich revolution as his top communications adviser, offered a remarkably candid and stinging indictment of the problem of what he calls "governing while drunk on partisanship"—what I call being drunk on careerism. Blankley wrote:

> If future historians look back on the ruins of the American economy after a U.S. bond crisis struck in the second decade of the 21st century, many causes will be noted . . . But the central indictment for the catastrophe that ended American prosperity and world dominance will be justly laid at the feet of those Washington politicians who continued to play for short-term partisan advantage, even as the economic earth was beginning to move under their feet.
>
> Even if there is only a one-in-three or a one-in-six chance of the bond crisis hitting before 2013, the down side risk of such a calamity is so immense that no responsible Washington political leader would take it. It is like playing Russian roulette with our future. Would anyone put a six-shooter with even one bullet in the chamber to his or her head? Of course not. Yet that is where, so far, the Democratic Party leadership (and some elements of the GOP Senate) have placed themselves.[18]

Does this mean Republicans should just accept whatever deal Democrats propose? Of course not. The process has to be one of verify, then trust, and verify again. The only deal worth accepting is one that solves the problem, saves America, and in so doing, dramatically reduces the size and scope of government. Such a solution is possible, but careerists on both sides are standing in the way.

When it seemed a breakthrough might be possible in the summer of 2011, columnist David Brooks said the Republican Party "is being offered the deal of the century: trillions of dollars in spending cuts in exchange for a few hundred billion dollars of revenue increases."[19]

He continued:

A normal Republican Party would seize the opportunity to put a long-term limit on the growth of government. It would seize the opportunity to put the country on a sound fiscal footing. It would seize the opportunity to do these things without putting any real crimp in economic growth.

The party is not being asked to raise marginal tax rates in a way that might pervert incentives. On the contrary, Republicans are merely being asked to close loopholes and eliminate tax expenditures that are themselves distortionary.

This, as I say, is the mother of all no-brainers.[20]

WASHINGTON CAN BE CHANGED

The only group that has the authority to settle this debate and avert a debt crisis is informed citizens. Free people armed with the facts can demand that both parties put aside careerism and save the country. Free people do have the power to replace career politicians who have long since passed their expiration date.

The tragedy of career politicians is the tighter they hold on to power, the likelier they are to lose their positions. The opposite is also true. I made very clear during my campaign that I would not try to bring home the bacon for Oklahoma. That position upset some people but it also built trust. While I'm a staunch constitutional conservative, the typical Oklahoman knows I care about the long term more than about short-term politics. If Congress had the courage to simply be honest and propose real solutions instead of trying to protect the status quo, the body as a whole would regain the American people's trust, even if the solutions seemed unpopular at first.

Amid all the talk about Washington being broken, there is ample evidence members can be rotated—or fired—when people simply get engaged. The public did this in 2010 when they fired dozens of career politicians who were no longer effective. In Pennsylvania, for instance, Democrat primary voters defeated Arlen Specter, who switched parties for the sole purpose of winning reelection. Specter didn't want to face now senator Pat Toomey in the Republican primary, so he became a Democrat. Voters saw through his self-serving rationalization and threw him out of office. Similarly, in Utah, Senator Robert Bennett stayed in office too long, supported earmarks, and grew hesitant about cutting spending. As a result, the people of Utah threw him out of office and elected Mike Lee. In Florida, conservative Marco Rubio beat Charlie Crist, who gave every indication he would be another go-along-to-get-along career politician. In Wisconsin, voters elected Ron Johnson, a former CEO who had real-world experience in the private sector. "We the People" made the difference.

It's true that reelection rates are disturbingly high historically, but it is also true that nothing is stopping politicians from being fired en masse. In 1980, for instance, the reelection rate was only 55 percent.[21] If 50 percent of senators up for reelection (thirty-three senators) are defeated each cycle, that's sixteen new senators each cycle, which is enough to change the direction of the country.

To Washington elites, the careerism explanation may seem simplistic, but I am convinced it is true. Anyone trained in science knows the principle of Occam's razor—sometimes the simplest explanation is the best. That's true in politics as well. So much hinges on whether a politician is disposed to hang on to power or let it go in service to the country.

Any visitor to the U.S. Capitol will make a stop in the majestic rotunda in the middle of the Capitol. The painting they will see of one of our most important presidents displays George Washington resigning his military commission in 1783.[22] The painting represents the virtue of politicians giving up power when they could keep it for themselves. Washington's decision to give up power was the final battle of the American Revolution, which established our nation as a republic rather than a monarchy.

Washington's second great resignation came when he left the presidency voluntarily after two terms, when he could have become a de facto king. One of his principal warnings in his farewell address was against accumulating debt:

> As a very important source of strength and security, cherish public credit. One method of preserving it is, to use it as sparingly as possible; avoiding occasions of expense by cultivating peace, but remembering also that timely disbursements to prepare for danger frequently prevent much greater disbursements to repel it; avoiding likewise the accumulation of debt, not only by shunning occasions of expense, but by vigorous exertions in time of peace to discharge the debts, which unavoidable wars may have occasioned, not ungenerously throwing upon posterity the burden which we ourselves ought to bear.[23]

Our founders feared—and expected—we would face a moment like this. That's why they wrote the Constitution. They knew the greatest threat to our republic would not be a foreign army—or a shadowy terrorist cell in a cave—but career politicians and their enablers, who will always seek more and more power. Behind our greatest national security threat is an axis of excuses—careerist Republicans, Democrats, staff, and special-interest groups who reward one another for doing nothing.

If we want to cheat history in 2012 and beyond, we need to go back and look at how those wise Americans cheated history in their day. Their wisdom can guide us to a solution, help us defuse the debt bomb, and preserve freedom for future generations of Americans.

THE PROBLEM

The real disease in Washington is careerism, the fear of losing reelection. All the other dysfunctions of Washington are symptoms of this disease.

The bad habits, such as earmarking, that led to an explosion of spending in the past two decades are expressions of careerism—the desire to win reelection above all else.

Careerism, not ideological commitments, is the cause of our impasse today. Both sides are preoccupied with the acquisition and maintenance of power more than reducing our debt and averting an economic catastrophe.

If Washington politicians valued fiscal responsibility more than getting reelected, we would see fiscally responsible behavior. Our crushing debt burden—$15 trillion and rising as of 2012—is proof that Washington politicians value reelection above all else.

3

The Dying Constitution

In questions of power let no more be heard of
confidence in man, but bind him down from
mischief by the chains of the Constitution.

—THOMAS JEFFERSON[1]

THE REAL GENIUS OF THE FRAMERS OF OUR CONSTITUTION WAS
their determination to check not just the institutions of government but,
more important, *the people* who made up the institutions. As students of
history our founders understood human nature and how people behaved
in a political environment. In a sense, our Constitution is as much a
psychological document as a political document. Our founders knew
politicians would seek to become careerists who would then undo the
republic with excessive spending and debt.

In fact, our founding fathers found the thought of career politicians
so offensive that few among the first members of Congress dared serve
more than two or three terms before going home. They believed passionately in the idea of rotation—a voluntary check and balance in which
members serve for a short time and go home.

The founders' views of human nature are important to consider because some want to dismiss the Constitution as antiquated, outdated, and not terribly relevant to the complexities of modern American life. While our technology is certainly more advanced, people's motivations have not changed much since Adam, much less since the American Revolution. Politicians have always chased the Inner Ring and always will.

The power of politicians, in Jefferson's view, needed to be chained and bound. Government unbound by the Constitution would essentially be a criminal enterprise protected by an unfair application of the law.

Today, our government is a tyranny of good intentions. Politicians believe they are doing good things but have put our very future at risk by making promises they have neither the means nor will to keep. Government has committed generational theft on a massive scale. For the last thirty years we have lived off the next thirty years.

None of this would be surprising to many of our early leaders. They wisely anticipated man's failings because they had a frame of reference and depth of historical knowledge far greater than among politicians today. The process of building the debt bomb started when Washington politicians thought they could outsmart the framers of our Constitution and operate far outside its bounds. If we want to undo the damage government has done to our country, we have to look at how our founders planned to limit the scope of government, and then imagine how a more limited government might look today.

WHY OUR FOUNDERS WANTED TO LIMIT GOVERNMENT

One of the great contributions of the Tea Party movement is it has sparked a national conversation about the Constitution and our founding principles. Not everyone is excited to have this debate, however.

Critics have created various pejorative terms to criticize the Tea Party, such as accusing them of "constitutionalism." Complaining about constitutionalism in a constitutional republic is like complaining about "refereeism" at a football game. It is nonsensical. It is fine to root for one team, or one set of ideas and solutions, but it is foolish to make up the rules as you go along. That's really what the debate is about. Are the rules essentially fixed and reliable, or should one team be allowed to change them on a whim?

All sides agree our founders wanted to balance power between the branches of government, and between the House of Representatives and the Senate. The legislative branch makes laws, while the president executes and vetoes bills. The courts interpret the constitutionality of laws, while the Senate confirms Supreme Court justices, and so on.

However, this is only part of what our founders intended. What mattered as much as *balancing* power between the branches was *limiting* the scope and power of government overall. The most important balance of power in our republic was not going to be between the branches of government but between individuals and the government itself. The whole point of the Constitution was not to protect any particular branch of government per se, but the rights and liberties of individual Americans. If government grew beyond the scope of the Constitution, freedom would be limited by the burden of debt and regulation, which is exactly what we see today.

Again, Jefferson argued plainly that good government was first and foremost government that had a limited role and respected the rights of free people. He said, "A wise and frugal government which shall restrain men from injuring one another, which shall leave them otherwise free to regulate their own pursuits of industry and improvement, and shall not take from the mouth of labor the bread it has earned. This is the sum of good government."[2]

Madison was likewise most concerned about maintaining the right balance of power between the people and the government. He predicted the future when he said, "There are more instances of the abridgement of freedom of the people by gradual and silent encroachments by those in power than by violent and sudden usurpations."[3]

Because Madison and our other framers were concerned about the "gradual and silent encroachments" of future politicians, they placed very clear limitations on the role of government. Their goal was clear: *Whatever is not expressly permitted is prohibited.*

Article I, section 8, of the U.S. Constitution spells out Congress's enumerated powers:

The Congress shall have Power To lay and collect Taxes, Duties, Imports and Excises, to pay the Debts and provide for the common Defence and general Welfare of the United States; but all Duties, Imposts and Excises shall be uniform throughout the United States; [Altered by Amendment XVI, "Income tax."]

- To borrow money on the credit of the United States;
- To regulate Commerce with foreign Nations, and among the several States, and with the Indian Tribes;
- To establish an uniform Rule of Naturalization, and uniform Laws on the subject of Bankruptcies throughout the United States;
- To coin Money, regulate the Value thereof, and of foreign Coin, and fix the Standard of Weights and Measures;
- To provide for the Punishment of counterfeiting the Securities and current Coin of the United States;
- To establish Post Offices and Post Roads;
- To promote the Progress of Science and useful Arts, by

securing for limited Times to Authors and Inventors the exclusive Right to their respective Writings and Discoveries;

- To constitute Tribunals inferior to the supreme Court;
- To define and punish Piracies and Felonies committed on the high Seas, and Offenses against the Law of Nations;
- To declare War, grant Letters of Marque and Reprisal, and make Rules concerning Captures on Land and Water;
- To raise and support Armies, but no Appropriation of Money to that Use shall be for a longer Term than two Years;
- To provide and maintain a Navy;
- To make Rules for the Government and Regulation of the land and naval Forces;
- To provide for calling forth the Militia to execute the Laws of the Union, suppress Insurrections and repel Invasions;
- To provide for organizing, arming, and disciplining, the Militia, and for governing such Part of them as may be employed in the Service of the United States, reserving to the States respectively, the Appointment of the Officers, and the Authority of training the Militia according to the discipline prescribed by Congress;
- To exercise exclusive Legislation in all Cases whatsoever, over such District (not exceeding ten Miles square) as may, by Cession of particular States, and the acceptance of Congress, become the Seat of the Government of the United States, and to exercise like Authority over all Places purchased by the Consent of the Legislature of the State in which the Same shall be, for the Erection of Forts, Magazines, Arsenals, dock-Yards, and other needful Buildings; And

> - To make all Laws which shall be necessary and proper for carrying into Execution the foregoing Powers, and all other Powers vested by this Constitution in the Government of the United States, or in any Department or Officer thereof.

CAN GOVERNMENT MAKE YOU EAT YOUR FRUITS AND VEGETABLES? YOU BET!

Among the enumerated powers listed above, perhaps none has been expanded further beyond our founders' design than the Commerce Clause. Congress's expansion of the Commerce Clause, and the Supreme Court's refusal to rein in Congress, have been particularly instrumental in building the debt bomb.

Again, Article I, section 8, of the Constitution gives Congress the specific, and limited, enumerated power to regulate Commerce with foreign Nations, and among the several States, and with the Indian Tribes.

For most of our history, this enumerated power meant what it says: Congress has the power to regulate the flow of goods across state and international lines. Legitimate applications of this power included the building of railroads and the interstate highway system.

By 1941, however, politicians and judges decided our founders had it all wrong and decided to throw away 150 years of law. As American troops prepared to land on Guadalcanal and North Africa in our epic struggle for freedom, anti-constitutional forces at home decided individual freedom was overrated. The target of their campaign that changed the world was a troublesome Ohio farmer named Roscoe Filburn, whose great offense was growing too much wheat.

During the Great Depression the government had imposed limits on wheat production to drive up prices. Filburn was growing more than he was allowed per acre, and even though he used the excess for himself instead of selling it, he was ordered to cease and desist, pay a fine, and destroy the contraband wheat. Filburn stood his ground and took on the forces of domestic fascism, taking his case all the way to the United States Supreme Court.[4]

In a fateful decision, however, the Court ruled that Filburn was a threat to domestic tranquility. The Court decided that because Filburn used his excess wheat to feed his chickens, he was reducing the amount he would spend on the government-regulated market. Because that market crossed state lines, the Court reasoned, Filburn's contraband wheat affected interstate commerce and could therefore be regulated. This decision set the stage for Obamacare and its individual mandate that says free people must buy health insurance.

Nearly seventy years later, in 2010, the plight of Roscoe Filburn and the divisive debate about Obamacare were fresh on my mind when it came my turn to question Elena Kagan, who had been nominated to replace Justice John Paul Stevens.

When my turn came to question Kagan, I decided to cut to the chase.

I started by asking, "If I wanted to sponsor a bill and it said, 'Americans, you have to eat three vegetables and three fruits every day,' and I got it through Congress, and that's now the law of the land, got to do it, does that violate the Commerce Clause?"

Kagan responded in good humor. "Sounds like a dumb law," she said.

"Yeah," I responded, "but I got one that's real similar to it that I think is equally dumb. I'm not going to mention which it is."

I was referring, of course, to Obamacare.

Kagan continued, "But I think that the question of whether it's a dumb law is different from the question of whether it's constitutional, and I think that courts would be wrong to strike down laws that they think are senseless just because they're senseless."

> COBURN: I guess the question I'm asking you is, do we have the power to tell people what they have to eat every day? . . . I mean, what is the extent of the Commerce Clause? We have this wide embrace of the Commerce Clause, which these guys who wrote this [holding up a bound copy of Federalist Papers] never, ever fathomed that we would be so stupid to take our liberties away by expanding the Commerce Clause this way . . .
>
> I go back to my original question to you: is it within the Constitution for me to write a bill, having been duly elected by the people of Oklahoma, to say—and get it signed by the president—that you have to eat three fruits and three vegetables every day?[5]

Kagan referred back to an answer she had given Senator Cornyn. She explained the Commerce Clause has been interpreted broadly to apply to regulation of any channel of commerce and anything that would substantially affect interstate commerce.

She attempted to answer my real question this way: "But I do want to sort of say again . . . we can come up with sort of, you know, just ridiculous sounding laws, and the . . . principal protector against bad laws is the political branches themselves. And . . . I would go back, I think, to Oliver Wendell Holmes on this. He was this judge who lived . . . in the early 20th century—hated a lot of the legislation that was being enacted during those . . . years but insisted that, if the . . . people wanted it, it was their right to go hang themselves. Now, that's not always the case, but—but there is substantial deference due to political branches—"

COBURN: I'm running out of time. I want to give you another condition: what if I said that if eating three fruits and three vegetables would cut health care costs 20 percent, now—now, we're into commerce. And since the government pays 65 percent of all the health care costs, why—why isn't that constitutional?

KAGAN: Well, Senator Coburn, I . . . feel as though . . . the principles that I've given you are the principles that the court should apply with—

COBURN: Well, I have a little problem with that because if—if we're going to hang ourselves, and as our founders, three of the critical authors of our Constitution thought the judiciary had—had a reason to smack us down, and as Oliver Wendell Holmes, if we want to be doing stupid stuff, we can do stupid stuff, I disagree. I think—you know, and that's not activism. That's looking at the Constitution and saying, well, we're going to ignore it even if it does expand the Commerce Clause, because the Commerce Clause is what has gotten us into a place where we have a $1.6 trillion deficit, that our kids' future has been mortgaged, we may never recover from.

   That's not an understatement at all. In 25 years, they're going to—each of our kids are [sic] going to owe $1,130,000 before they pay—pay interest on that before they do anything for themselves or their kids.

   So the fact is, is that we have this expansive clause, and we have to have some limit on it. And if the—if the courts aren't going to limit it within the original intent, instead of continuing to rely on precedent of this vast expansion of it, the only hope is, is that we have to throw out most of the Congress . . .

And what we find ourselves today on the Commerce Clause is that with—through a period of precedent-setting decisions, we have allowed the federal government to become something that it was never entitled to become, and—and with that, a diminishment of the liberties of the people of this country, both financially and in terms of their own liberty.

KAGAN: Well, Senator Coburn . . . a few points. The first . . . I think that there are limits on the Commerce Clause . . . which are primarily about non-economic activity and Congress not being able to regulate non-economic activity.

[T]he second point I would make is—is I do think that very early in our history—and—and especially I would—I would look to *Gibbons v. Ogden*, where Chief Justice Marshall did, in the first case about these issues, essentially read that clause broadly and—and provide real deference to legislatures and provide real deference to Congress about the scope of that clause, not that the clause doesn't have any limits, but that deference should be provided to Congress with respect to matters affecting interstate commerce.

[A]nd I guess the third point is . . . that $1.6 trillion deficit may be an enormous problem. It may be an enormous problem. But I don't think it's a problem for courts to solve; I think it's a problem for the political process to solve.

COBURN: You missed my whole point. We're here because the courts didn't do their job in limiting our ability to go outside of original intent on what the Commerce Clause was supposed to be.

Sure, you can't solve the problem now, but you helped create it as a court because you allowed something other than what our original founders thought was a legitimate role for the federal government.[6]

At the time I asked this question, many in the media dismissed it as not terribly serious and academic. My point was not to be academic and pretend to be a lawyer. My goal was to bring the real-world experience I did have to bear on one of the most important questions of our time. And it was ironic that some pundits were offended by the *question* more than the *answer* that Congress did in fact have the power to tell us to eat our fruits and vegetables.

I had no intention of embarrassing Kagan or trying to trip her up—if that were my goal, I would not have succeeded. She is a brilliant woman. The *LA Times* ran a story, though, declaring she had "slipped on fruits and veggies."[7]

The exchange highlighted for the country the reason we are in such a deep hole. Congress had deliberately expanded the scope of its power, and not even the Supreme Court felt it had the authority to rein in Congress. No one was watching the store. There was no longer any balance of power between the branches of government. The Supreme Court was designed to check Congress when it got out of bounds. The Supreme Court, however, did not want this role. It would simply make new laws if it didn't like the ones Congress passed.

THE RULE OF RULERS

The evolution and expansion of the Commerce Clause is just one example of how bedrock constitutional principles have been liquefied and reshaped by whimsical majorities. Today we no longer have the rule of law, but the rule of rulers. Being subject to the whim of rulers rather than laws is the very form of tyranny our founders wanted to escape.

Sad to say, the Obama administration has taken the rule of rulers to lengths never before seen in our country. The government has arbitrarily disregarded legal contracts between Chrysler and its creditors. The executive branch has used funds from the Troubled Asset Relief Program (TARP) as a slush fund without any legal authority. The National Labor Relations Board used thuggish logic to tell Boeing they had to build a new $2 billion factory in a non-right-to-work state (Washington) instead of a right-to-work state (South Carolina). We've seen a case against the Black Panthers dismissed for questionable reasons. We've seen countless waivers given to companies who don't want to operate under the health care law for reasons that are indecipherable from a legal perspective— but not a political perspective.

Regarding waivers for Obamacare, columnist Michael Barone makes an important point:

> If Obamacare is so great, why do so many people want to get out from under it?
>
> More specifically, why are more than half of those 3,095,593 [exempted from Obamacare] in plans run by labor unions, which were among Obamacare's biggest political supporters? Union members are only 12 percent of all employees but have gotten 50.3 percent of Obamacare waivers.[8]

There are other examples of the administration ignoring the rule of the law. When the state of Arizona passed a law in 2010 attempting to curtail illegal immigration, the Obama administration's Department of Justice filed an injunction to stop the state from enforcing a law against an activity that was already a federal offense. In its perverse rule of ruler logic, the Justice Department believed it was appropriate to punish a state for attempting to address a problem that was created by the federal government's refusal to enforce existing law and control our borders.

We've also seen the president violate the Constitution and ignore the Senate's advise and consent role by claiming that he can decide when the Senate is in or out of session in order to make four appointments, three of which had never been vetted by the Senate.[9]

Finally, the administration, under the new health care law, is requiring religious and faith-based groups to violate their conscience and pay for contraception, sterilization, and abortion-inducing drugs in employer-provided health plans. This ruling is an assault on the bedrock constitutional principle of religious liberty.

RECLAIMING THE CONSTITUTION— ALL THINGS ARE NOT IN FLUX

Reestablising the rule of law and the limits on the ability of career politicans to spend money is not an impossible task. The American people can undo the legacy of Court-packing with Congress-packing. Sending legislators to Washington who take the Constitution seriously, and will apply it faithfully, will go a long way toward reclaiming our country.

The rule of rulers camp says the Constitution is statist, backward, and antiquated. Yet, it is the progressives who have taken the country backward and turned back the clock on freedom.

Supreme Court Justice Antonin Scalia sums it up well: "Perhaps the most glaring defect of Living Constitutionalism, next to its incompatibility with the whole antievolutionary purpose of a constitution, is that there is no agreement, and no chance of agreement, upon what is to be the guiding principle of the evolution. *Panta rei* ["All things are in flux"] is not a sufficiently informative principle of constitutional interpretation."[10]

Regarding the antievolutionary purpose of the Constitution, Scalia says, its "whole purpose is to prevent change—to embed certain rights in such a manner that future generations cannot readily take them away. A society that adopts a bill of rights is skeptical that 'evolving standards of decency' always 'mark progress,' and that societies always 'mature,' as opposed to rot."[11]

Majorities were never intended to have the power to take away our basic freedoms and the Constitution's limits on government. In the 1943 case *West Virginia State Board of Education v. Barnette*, Justice Jackson eloquently stated, "The very purpose of a Bill of Rights was to withdraw certain subjects from the vicissitudes of political controversy, to place them beyond the reach of majorities and officials and to establish them as legal principles to be applied by the courts. One's right to life, liberty, and property, to free speech, a free press, freedom of worship and assembly, and other fundamental rights may not be submitted to vote; they depend on the outcome of no elections."[12]

And here the critics ask: What about slavery and the rights of women? If the Constitution is antievolutionary and fixed, then should we tolerate these injustices? Of course not.

We should not hesitate to point out the failings of our founders. Clearly, our founders' failure to ban slavery, in particular, left a scar on the Constitution that continues to divide the country. Yet, in spite of their error, they did have the foresight to create an amendment process by which grievous errors could be corrected.

These points are important because as we confront our debt problem we don't need to create a mythical picture of our founding fathers. They were mostly people of faith, yes, and believed deeply in a power beyond government, but they were also full of contradictions. It is helpful to remember that our founders, such as Alexander Hamilton and Jefferson, had different views about the proper role and scope of government. The Constitution, again, was a grand bargain that represented a hard-fought consensus and compromise among wise and learned leaders. Our case for limited government does not depend on creating a perfect picture of our founders. The imperfections of politicians today make the best case for a Constitution that binds their ambitions and chains their egos and good intentions.

CASE STUDIES: IGNORING THE CONSTITUTION IS NOT SMART GOVERNMENT

Today, politicians do not want to debate the views of our founders because very few policies and spending decisions can be justified in light of the Constitution. President Obama, for instance, prefers to frame our key debates as a question of how to achieve "smart government," not as a struggle between big government and small government.[13] I prefer to take the president at his word and trust that he wants to create smart government. So let's look at whether ignoring the Constitution has created smart government.

America's Disability and Dependency Scandal

Few areas of the law better illustrate the danger of Congress stretching the boundaries of the Constitution in the name of "good intentions" than our federal disability programs. The problems with disability programs are twofold. First, they are adding to our debt. In 2011, our largest disability program, the Social Security Disability Insurance program (SSDI) was expected to pay out $129.7 billion in benefits while its so-called trust fund took in only $110.9 billion.[14]

Second, our disability programs undermine freedom because they create dependency and are easily gamed by bad actors who want to cheat the system. Today, a staggering 1 in 18 Americans is considered disabled, which is an impossibly high figure.[15] Between 2000 and 2010, the number of Americans claiming disability benefits[16] increased more than five times the rate of population growth.[17]

The rationale for disability programs is well intended. When people become disabled and cannot work, a compassionate society helps those individuals and prevents them from slipping into poverty and destitution. It is when the federal government gets involved that those intentions become corrupted.

To qualify for disability benefits, claimants must prove that they are essentially unable to perform any kind of work in our national economy, taking into account age, education, and work experience. This requirement, however, is often little more than a speed bump for determined applicants and lawyers who stand to benefit financially from claims. It isn't just disability payments that have skyrocketed. As the *Wall Street Journal* has reported, fees to lawyers who represent disability-benefit applicants have risen 300 percent in the last decade.[18]

I've seen this system up close in my many years in medicine. I have had patients assume I would sign forms declaring them to be disabled when they clearly were not disabled, which suggested other doctors and attorneys had created that expectation. Administrative law judges within the agency can be in on the fix as well. I'll never forget an incident in the 1990s when I testified as a medical expert witness in a case in which I knew the person applying for benefits was not disabled. The judge disregarded my testimony and awarded the claimant benefits in spite of the evidence.

I've also seen this system at work in other areas. After a bad storm in Oklahoma not long ago, I hired a man to help clear trees in my yard. When he completed his work he made an unusual request. He wanted me to write a check to his mother, not to him. Having seen this pattern before, I asked him point blank if he was on disability. He admitted he was, which was odd given his aptitude for manual labor. He wanted me to write his mother a check to protect his eligibility. I ignored his request and wrote him a check instead.

Uncovering and exposing this system has been one of my top priorities in the Senate.

One case that has already come to the nation's attention is the unusual story of Stanley Thornton, a thirty-year-old man who engages in role-play as an adult baby while receiving disability checks from the government. Thornton rose to prominence when National Geographic television ran a segment about his unusual lifestyle.[19] Thornton builds his own custom-made furniture, including a crib and high chair. He even wears adult-sized diapers and drinks from a bottle.

Thornton seemed like an unusual but capable man, so I wrote to the head Social Security inspector general, Patrick P. O'Carroll Jr., looking for an explanation for why he was receiving a disability check. I wrote, "Given that Mr. Thornton is able to determine what is appropriate attire and actions in public, drive himself to complete errands, design and custom-make baby furniture to support a 350-pound adult and run an Internet support group, it is possible that he has been improperly collecting disability benefits for a period of time."

The Social Security Inspector General could not answer my question, but several months later Thornton posted a letter from the Social Security Administration (SSA) on his website, stating that his case had been reviewed by the agency and that he was still eligible to receive disability checks. Thornton then went to the media and demanded that I apologize (after he had threatened to commit suicide if his checks were cut off). I refused to apologize and instead called on Congress to apologize to the American people for creating a system that was so easily exploited by swindlers who wanted to avoid taking personal responsibility. The real problem, though, was not with the adult baby, per se, but with the politicians and bureaucrats who coddled him.

The SSA seemed intent on blocking my investigation and controlling access to information any way they could. In one instance, one of my investigators traveled to Oklahoma City at the request of an administrative law judge to hear a disability case deliberated. When the chief judge learned of his presence he was kicked out because "SSA congressional relations in Washington had not approved" of his presence.

In another instance I sent my staff to a field office only to discover the office had shredded, or was about to shred, the documents we were about to retrieve. Livid, I decided to call the head of the Social Security Administration, Michael Astrue, who likes to describe himself as a poet and critic, to inform him of how our investigation was apparently being obstructed.

"I know you're a poet, so you'll understand what I'm going to say," I opened before explaining how Social Security staff members may be destroying evidence. Astrue responded by trying to shift blame to what he called the "troubled office." I reminded him it was his responsibility, as the head of SSA, to control his own agency. I promised him I would "look under every rock, every folder, and every paper clip" until taxpayers received a full account of how their money was being spent.

Bureaucrats like Astrue had little incentive to manage their agencies well because career politicians in Washington found the task of disability oversight too messy politically. Sending out checks was much more satisfying than conducting oversight even if doing so was bankrupting the country and the very system that provided help to those who were truly disabled. One SSA staffer confided that no other congressional office had asked for the level of detail I requested in twenty-five to thirty-five years. That was the problem. No one was asking.

The redeeming part of the investigation, and the Thornton case especially, has been the public's reaction. Comments from posts ranging from *Huffington Post* to *Fox News* showed that readers were almost universally aghast that public funds were going to an adult baby who seemed capable of working. The American people are willing to help those who truly cannot help themselves, but this was one example where it seemed everyone could agree government had gone too far. The adults were ready to tell the adult babies that enough was enough.

The challenge with such cases is to look past the abuse of the system and see people with dignity who are struggling. Giving people a government check and washing our hands is often the least compassionate response possible. It makes us feel good but makes their lives worse.

The next time someone in Washington or in the media says the Constitution is outdated and those who follow it are quaint, look at what has happened to our disability system. We have the system we have today precisely because career politicians thought they could outsmart our founders and manage responsibilities that were not theirs to manage.

The Constitution and Education

Another area in which we can test the wisdom of expanding the Constitution is education. Those who want to make up the rules as we go along tend to staunchly defend the federal government's role in education, while those who respect the founders' original intent tend to be more skeptical.

Let's look at who is right.

One indisputable fact about our education system is that the status quo isn't working. Since 1965, the federal government has invested more than $2 trillion in American education without improving outcomes. Per-pupil spending at the kindergarten-through-twelfth-grade level has more than doubled since 1970 in real dollars,[20] yet outcomes have not improved. Since 1970, long-term scores in reading, math, and science have remained flat. The pupil-to-teacher ratio has moved from 22.4 pupils per teacher in 1970 to 14.7 in 2011,[21] yet scores haven't improved. Finally, increased federal "investments" in higher education have caused college to become less affordable without improving graduation rates. The list goes on and on and on.

Well-intentioned people on both sides disagree about how to improve education, but we will never move forward if we can't achieve consensus about what the Constitution and the rule of law permit the federal government to do in the area of education. Unfortunately, many voices in this debate are not well-intentioned or reasonable.

Shortly after the 2010 elections, I told radio host Laura Ingraham, "I don't even think education is a role for the federal government. As a matter of fact, Thomas Jefferson said, 'I believe in the federal government having a role for education but the only way to do that is change the Constitution.'"[22]

The liberal blog *ThinkProgress*, the self-appointed guardians of progressivism on the Internet, responded with predictable vitriol and condescension in a post under the headline "Radical Right-Wing Agenda." The author began by asserting that I had never read the document I swore an oath to defend: "Sen. Coburn might want to try to actually read the Constitution before he pretends to know what it allows."[23]

In the very next sentence, the author expressed total certainty about his decidedly expansive interpretation of the "general welfare" clause of the Constitution that has been a matter of great controversy for 220 years. *ThinkProgress* wrote, "Article I provides that '[t]he Congress shall have power to lay and collect taxes, duties, imposts and excises, to pay the debts that provide for the common defense and general welfare of the

United States,' a grant of power that *unambiguously* empowers Congress to raise funds and spend them on programs that are broadly beneficial to American welfare—such as education."[24]

The problem, of course, is that the founders had no such design.[25] As James Madison made crystal clear in Federalist No. 41: "For what purpose could the enumeration of particular powers be inserted, if these and all others were meant to be included in the preceding general power?"

In a private letter to James Robertson, Madison wrote: "With respect to the words 'general welfare,' I have always regarded them as qualified by the detail of powers [enumerated in the Constitution] connected with them. To take them in a literal and unlimited sense would be a metamorphosis of the Constitution into a character which there is a host of proofs was not contemplated by its creators."[26]

An early Supreme Court case, *Marbury v. Madison* (1803), underscored Madison's point: "The powers of the legislature are defined and limited; and that those limits may not be mistaken, or forgotten, the Constitution is written."

If the founders meant to give the federal government a role in education—and many other areas—they would have written it into the enumerated powers. They obviously did not. Jefferson wished the Constitution had given the federal government more of a role in education, but he recognized that no such role existed. This view prevailed for 150 years. Even FDR's administration recognized the federal government had no role in education even as President Roosevelt himself was packing the Supreme Court with progressives.[27]

In 1943, the United States Constitution Sesquicentennial Commission, under FDR's direction, published *The History of the Formation of the Union Under the Constitution*. In a section titled "Questions and Answers Pertaining to the Constitution," it noted:

Q. Where, in the Constitution, is there mention of education?
A. There is none; education is a matter reserved for the states.[28]

If Roosevelt's own commission concluded the federal government had no role in education, there can be little doubt about the plain meaning of the Constitution. Yet, big government fundamentalists insist anyone who deviates from the modern view of the question is an enemy of the state and our children. Of course, their certitude and condescension are designed to compensate for the weakness of the argument.

Americans should ask, what is the "radical" position: questioning the wisdom of an interpretation of the Constitution that has cost billions while providing no benefit to our society, or defending the status quo and the flawed constitutional theory that supports it?

I'd contend that the radical view is defending the status quo.

Let's not forget that the same American progressive movement that gave us a failing education system also gave us a welfare state that is going bankrupt. Their belief in a "living constitution" has sapped the Constitution of its strength and its ability to constrain the ambitions of politicians.

Dismantling the Constitution by growing government and undermining freedom gave us the debt we have today. Republics die when we assume we can have things that were not won with our own blood, sweat, and toil. Career politicians have been less than honest about what history says about republics that lose sight of the character traits of hard work, self-reliance, independence, and charity. They have told us we can depend on them to make the key decisions about our future. Yet, they fail to realize real freedom comes when individuals make the best decisions for their individual lives, unfettered by the wise hands of the elites. Restoring the limits on government will restore liberty and the promise of freedom and prosperity for generations to come.

THE PROBLEM

The Constitution was written to limit the power of politicians, not just our institutions.

In recent decades, politicians have systematically undermined the Constitution to make it easier to spend other people's money and help themselves win reelection.

As the power of politicians to spend has increased, individual liberty has decreased to the point that Congress can pass a law telling you to eat your fruits and vegetables.

Careerism unbound by the Constitution breeds excessive spending and a culture of dependency that has given us an unsustainable debt.

4

Burning Bridges to Nowhere

I will put the Senate on notice—and I don't kid people—if
the Senate decides to discriminate against our State and take
money only from our State, I will resign from this body.

—U.S. SENATOR TED STEVENS

WHEN I RAN FOR THE SENATE IN 2004, A KEY PART OF MY PLATFORM
was a pledge not to seek earmarks for Oklahoma. Earmarks, as I have
said, were a gateway drug to Washington's spending addiction and were
a terrible distraction. We would never tackle our mounting debt and
reform our unusustainable entitlement programs if Congress was preoccupied with pork. As I explained to voters in my state, I would have
no credibility to cut spending and limit the size of government if I asked
for pork. If they wanted pork, I wasn't their guy. As I said when I
announced my intentions to run:

I'm running for the United States Senate to restore our Founders' vision
of limited government.

. . . This generation is on the verge of leaving a disastrous legacy never before seen in our great republic. At the rate our federal government is expanding, with out-of-control deficit spending and with Social Security and Medicare heading for bankruptcy, the threat is very real that we will leave our children and grandchildren an America that will have a lower standard of living than the America we inherited from the previous generation.

Simply put, it would be immoral to allow that to happen.

. . . We can no longer allow career-minded politicians to mortgage the future in exchange for their own personal political gain today.

. . . [Challenging the status quo in government] requires both courage and conviction to take the political risks necessary to produce real change. I am convinced that if those of us on the outside don't attempt to change the way government works, then it will never change.

My opponent, former congressman Brad Carson, thought I was nuts. He argued, "This is a race unprecedented in modern American politics. The question is: Do you think it's the role of a United States senator to fight for your state? Tom Coburn is the only person in either political party who has made doing nothing for our state the basic tenet of his platform."[1]

Oklahoma voters, however, understood my argument and realized that even if I secured "good" earmarks for Oklahoma, they would have to fund wasteful projects in forty-nine other states. I was glad much of the campaign hinged on this question because, when I won, I had a mandate to challenge the culture of Washington and try to end the practice of pork-barrel spending.

The night of my victory in 2004, I received a call from President Bush.

After he congratulated me, I said, "Mr. President, I'm looking forward to helping you cut spending."

There was nothing but silence on the other end.

By the end of 2004, Republicans were becoming increasingly agitated about President Bush's excessive spending. I was determined to follow through on my campaign promise to go after earmarks and wasteful spending even if it meant clashing with my own party.

My campaign was based on a gut feeling and bet that the people of Oklahoma were adults, not children, and would be smart enough to realize earmarking was the gateway drug to Washington's spending addiction. If earmarking could be curtailed, I argued, it would be much easier to address other areas of the budget that were becoming a threat to our national security.

As a member of the House, I had long warned, as had many budget experts, that our unsustainable fiscal course was the greatest long-term threat to our nation. In 2003, as the War on Terror was putting enormous pressure on the Republican Congress to spend, I wrote in my book *Breach of Trust*: "We have no choice but to fight the war that has been thrust upon us, but we can no longer ignore the other battlefront where our freedom is being eroded day by day by an out-of-control federal government that is threatening to bankrupt our nation."[2]

Getting to the point where we could avert our debt crisis would be extraordinarily difficult. In fact, it would be one of the great challenges in our nation's history. The forces in favor of spending were heavily fortified and defended by special-interest groups on both sides. To achieve our goal, I believed we needed to achieve a series of incremental, strategic victories not unlike the island-hopping campaign mounted by General Douglas MacArthur in the Pacific Theater of World War II. MacArthur knew a direct assault on Japan would fail, so he devised an island-hopping, or leapfrogging, strategy that would eventually make victory possible. The same was true from a budgetary perspective. Ending earmarks would give policymakers the credibility, moral authority, and opportunity to confront discretionary spending, duplication, defense spending, and finally, entitlements.

As 2005 started, I was ready to start this campaign. I knew I had to pick my targets carefully, however, and not rush into battle unprepared.

One of the few redeeming aspects of the culture of Washington is the expectation that newly elected senators maintain a low profile for a few months, which promotes humility and restraint, two qualities often lacking in politicians. During this time of holding back and maintaining a low profile, my office was anything but idle. We were actively studying, preparing, and planning. From the beginning, we had an esprit de corps that had carried through from the campaign. We were commandos ready to infiltrate and sabotage the dark heart of Washington's spending culture.

I knew my greatest asset in the Senate was going to be the Senate rules themselves. If politics is war by peaceful means, the Senate rules are an arsenal for change. The stakes for our nation were too high to go into battle half-cocked and unprepared.

In the House, my ability to go after individual projects was very limited. The House is a very hierarchical body, with most power concentrated in the hands of the Speaker, committee chairs, and the Rules Committee. The Rules Committee, in particular, curtails the power of individual members by deciding—usually in consultation with the Speaker—who gets to offer amendments and determine how long they are debated. Our founders designed the Senate, on the other hand, to force consensus and to be a cooling saucer. If you could not come to consensus in the Senate, nothing would happen and laws would not be passed. At our founding, the practice of cloture (cutting off debate with a vote) did not exist. Senators had to get all one hundred members to agree on a path forward. In essence, our founders designed the Senate to give every senator the ability to be a Rules Committee of one and have powers nearly equal to the Senate majority leader should they choose to exercise them.

I told my staff our first mission was to learn the Senate rules as well as

Robert Byrd, the legendary Democrat of West Virginia. Instead of using the rules to grow government, however, we were going to use them to downsize and dismantle government. I kept a copy of the fifteen-hundred-page *Riddick's Senate Procedure* by my bedside and read it through several times. I also brought in top experts in Senate procedure, like Marty Gold, who had thirty-five years of legislative experience and had served as Majority Leader Frist's top floor adviser. I had Gold brief my entire staff on procedure; he regaled us with stories of how past masters, such as Senators Jesse Helms (R-NC) and Howard Metzenbaum (D-OH), had used the rules creatively and effectively.

Gold explained that Helms, a conservative, and Metzenbaum, a liberal, were both known as "Senator No" in their time. Helms was more than happy to lose votes in order to frame issues in a way that would advance the limited-government movement. Metzenbaum was equally relentless and would camp out on the Senate floor and look for openings to use the rules to voice objections and pursue his agenda. Both senators used filibusters effectively and routinely blocked nominees who violated their principles. Gold explained that the mere threat of a Metzenbaum filibuster was enough to win concessions.

While we studied and prepared, our first legislative actions were low-key and bipartisan. After Hurricane Katrina in August 2005, I gave a speech on the floor calling for the appointment of a chief financial officer—preferably someone with real-world private-sector experience—to manage the disbursement of billions in recovery funds for the Gulf Coast.

Chris Lu, the legislative director for fellow freshman senator Barack Obama (D-IL), was watching the speech and called my legislative director, Roland Foster, to discuss the possibility of our offices jointly introducing a bill to put my idea into action. I had connected with Obama during orientation. Lu was also highly regarded in our office in part because of his previous experience with Henry Waxman. Even though Waxman and I couldn't be farther apart philosophically, he was a master strategist and always among the most prepared, patient, and aggressive House members. Waxman's incremental approach to expanding government had been very effective. I believed government would be scaled back using his same tactics and discipline.

Our bipartisan work with Obama on Katrina-related oversight produced some helpful legislation reining in no-bid contracts and set the stage for our later work on transparency. However, when an earmark-laden transportation bill came to the floor in October 2005, I saw my opening to begin what would become a permanent campaign against earmarks, wasteful spending, and big government.

Katrina shocked the nation and raised troubling questions about the fundamental competence of the government. We had spent billions on disaster preparedness, but to what end? New Orleans was in chaos.

The aftermath of Katrina triggered a healthy debate in Washington about a subject politicians like to avoid: priorities. The cleanup and recovery effort would obviously cost billions, and Congress owed it to taxpayers and victims to make hard choices between competing priorities.

When the transportation appropriations bill came to the floor, I fully intended to force a debate about priorities. I prepared three major amendments to the bill, all targeting individual earmarks, including a parking garage for an art museum in Nebraska, a sculpture garden in Washington State, and two bridges in Alaska.

The Alaskan bridges, in particular, were inviting targets because they were so outrageous. My goal was not just to strike funding for the projects but to set up a necessary but uncomfortable debate about priorities. In this case, it would be pork versus disaster relief. The $452 million for the two Alaska bridge projects—the Gravina "Bridge to Nowhere" and the "Don Young's Way" Knik Arm Bridge—would be redirected to a more pressing need: the reconstruction of the Twin Spans Bridge connecting New Orleans and Slidell, Louisiana, that had been damaged by Hurricane Katrina.

The merits of both of the bridge projects had been widely questioned across the country, including by Alaska citizens. One Ketchikan woman admitted, "I think it's a colossal waste of taxpayers' money." Another man said, "The short view is, I don't see a need for it. The long view is, I still don't see a need for it."[3]

The media had already been calling the Gravina bridge the "Bridge to Nowhere," thanks to clever marketing by Taxpayers for Common Sense investigator Keith Ashdown. The label stuck because the bridge would connect Ketchikan, Alaska (a town with fewer than 8,900 residents), to Gravina Island (population 50) for a total of $223 million. The cost of the bridge alone would be enough to buy every Gravina Island resident his own personal Lear jet. The bridge also would have been nearly as long as the Golden Gate Bridge and taller than the Brooklyn Bridge—all to replace a seven-minute ferry ride.

The second Alaska bridge, the Knik Arm Bridge, had received less attention but was equally egregious. The two-mile toll bridge "Don Young's Way" would have linked Anchorage to Port Mackenzie and an area called the Mat-Su, which was home to no more than a few dozen people. The bridge was extravagant and costly. According to the Knik Arm Bridge and Toll Authority (KABATA), the project would have cost between $400 and $600 million, but estimates from a decade earlier indicated the project would cost $1.5 billion when adjusted for inflation.

I argued at that time when our nation was $8 trillion in debt (we're now approaching $16 trillion as of 2012), and fighting a multifront war against terrorism, with Social Security and Medicare facing insolvency, and with Hurricanes Katrina and Rita having caused tens of billions of dollars in damage to the Gulf Coast region, that we did not have the luxury of misusing taxpayer dollars on extravagant, costly, and low-priority projects.

This amendment was supported by a coalition of groups across the political spectrum—Citizens Against Government Waste, Club for Growth, Free Enterprise Fund, National Taxpayers Union, Sierra Club, and Taxpayers for Common Sense.

I knew my amendments would irritate my colleagues. Senators, including John McCain (R-AZ), had effectively critiqued pork-barrel spending for years, but to my knowledge, no one had ever dared to target individual earmarks and put senators on the spot. I spelled out my intentions on the floor in what was remembered as the "rumble" speech, which described the Tea Party before it had come into existence.

All change starts with a distant rumble, a rumble at the grassroots level, and if you stop and listen today, you will hear such a rumble right now. That rumble is the sound of hard-working Americans who are getting increasingly angry with out-of-control Government spending, waste, fraud, and abuse. It is the sound of growing disillusionment and frustration of the American people. It is the sense of increasing disgust about blatant overspending and our ability to make the tough choices people on budgets have to make each and every day, our inability to make priorities the No. 1 priority rather than spending our children and grandchildren's future . . .

Politicians have been trying to buy reelection by sanctioning more and more spending for years. Since 2000, discretionary spending in this country outside of defense and outside of homeland security has grown by 33 percent, and that does not include any of the $400 billion in emergency designations that have been passed by the Congress and signed by this President. We have the very great prospect that the spending over the last 5 years and the next 3 years will be the greatest growth in

Federal spending ever in our history in terms of percentage increase and speed and velocity of spending increases. And we will have made it possible when we should have been fighting it every step of the way.

. . . What I am here to tell you is that the rumble against spending is getting louder. People are fed up. All across the country, Americans are rising up against Government overspending. They are tired of hearing about perpetual budget crises when tax revenues keep rising faster and faster . . .

They know that for every dollar of increasing tax revenues, we have— both Republicans and Democrats—found a way to spend another $1.25. That is the crisis. It is a spending crisis. It is a lack of oversight crisis. It is a crisis of our will. Do we have the willpower to stop overspending, to make the hard choices about priorities that the American people expect of us? If we don't, the people certainly do. That is why there is a rumble building across this country. The people are tired of waiting for us to do the right thing. They know it will not happen, so they are working at the grassroots level to get the job done themselves.

. . . We need to wake up. I say let us change first. Let us find our will. No more low-priority projects in the face of half-trillion-dollar deficits, no more exorbitant bridges to nowhere. Speaking of bridges, that is where this Congress will be, on a bridge to nowhere if we do not gain control of ourselves. And if the voters finally rise up and reject us as the Congress that spends too much, we will have gotten what we deserve. You don't need to take my word for it. Just take a minute and listen to the voices of the people we represent. They are ready to rumble. They are getting louder. Are we listening?[4]

The amendment would have shifted the $223 million dedicated to the Bridge to Nowhere and instead sent it to a bridge damaged by Hurricane Katrina. I wanted to put my colleagues in the position of making a choice between a wasteful earmark and Katrina recovery not because I wanted to embarrass them personally, but because we would never avoid national bankruptcy as long as we avoided debates about priorities. The "go along to get along" earmark culture, and the belief that every state—and senator—was simply entitled to hugely expensive earmarks, was part of a system that was rigged to spend. The target of my amendment wasn't so much the bridge but an entire way of doing business in the Senate that was bankrupting the country.

Ted Stevens (R-AK), the longest-serving Republican in the chamber, was livid that I had the audacity to even offer the amendment. As Stevens rose to speak, the look on his face made his position clear. This. Was. Not. How. The. Senate. Operated.

> I have been here now almost 37 years. This is the first time I have seen any attempt by any Senator to treat my State in a way differently from any other State. It will not happen. It will not happen . . .
>
> I am now President pro tempore of the Senate, the second oldest Member of the Senate, the fourth in service in the Senate, and I again say to my friend from Oklahoma I have never seen it suggested to single out one State and say, you pay for a disaster that happened 5,000 miles away . . .
>
> I come to warn the Senate, if you want a wounded bull on the floor of the Senate, pass this amendment. I stood here and watched Senator Allen teach the Senate lesson after lesson after something was done to Alabama that he didn't like.
>
> I don't threaten people; I promise people. I came here and swore to uphold the Constitution of the United States . . .
>
> This amendment is an offense to me. It is not only an offense to me, it is a threat to every person in my State . . .
>
> The Senate is warned. It is wrong to do this to any State. It is wrong to

put colleagues in a position where we have to go home and explain why we couldn't prevent an amendment in which what is being done to our State has never been done to another State—never.

This is not the time to start this process. I urge my friend from Oklahoma to reconsider this, reconsider what he is getting us into. The amendment may pass, but if it does the bill will never be passed. If it does, I will be taken out of here on a stretcher.

I yield the floor.[5]

Visitors to the Senate, the press gallery, and other senators were stunned. Most Senate speeches are very pedestrian and ponderous. This speech was passionate, spontaneous, loud, and threatening. I wasn't taken aback or offended by Stevens's speech. I was more concerned about his blood pressure and whether I would have to resuscitate him on the Senate floor. I did not want to take him out on a stretcher.

More important, however, Stevens's speech was revealing. He had pulled back the curtain and it would never fall back in place again. The system taxpayers resented and desperately wanted to change would from now on be seen as not so intimidating. The wizard behind the curtain was just a group of career politicians who rationalized parochialism and reckless spending with bombast and bad arguments that had no basis in the Constitution.

Stevens's speech inspired other senators to come to the floor and defend their earmarks. Lisa Murkowski, the junior senator from Alaska, was equally irate, but less colorful. Murkowski was also aghast at the suggestion that earmarks were not a sacred right, but should be prioritized, critiqued, and compared against other projects.

We are told not to take this amendment personally, but it is very difficult to stand here as an Alaskan and not take this personally.

... [W]hen we are singled out as one State, saying, your project is not worthy; of all the other projects out there we are going to go after yours, it is not the time to be sitting back and saying we can compromise on this, we can make a deal.

[T]he reference to the bridge in Ketchikan as being a bridge to nowhere is offensive. It is a bridge to the future for the people of Ketchikan, Alaska.

Some people are making the assumption that just because we happen to have a chairman on the House side chairing the Transportation Committee, that all of a sudden any great idea, any project that we want as a delegation we were going to be able to snap our fingers and get. This is something that has been in the works for 30 years.

Now to have a colleague come in and say that because there is something that has happened in another part of the country and because we need to find ways to pay for it, we are going to make a determination that we are going to pluck this money and we are going to take this project and anything that the community has put into it, anything the State has put into it, is now thrown out the window, that is not it.[6]

After Murkowski spoke, Senator Stevens again took the floor. He intended to offer an amendment shifting funds from all fifty states to the New Orleans bridge. Stevens did not want members to choose between the Alaska bridges and the New Orleans bridge. Plus, in his mind, prioritizing earmark spending was strictly off-limits. He wanted an across-the-board cut of everyone's earmarks to avoid, in his words, unfairly singling out a particular state. And by offering his amendment he would have made it easier for senators to vote against my amendment.

However, I had beat Stevens to the punch. I had studied the Senate rules and sought counsel from old hands from Helms's office for moments like this. My amendment was already filed as a second-degree amendment to another amendment, which meant it would receive a clean vote. I believed I was using the Senate rules exactly as the founders intended—to maximize my rights as a constitutional officer on behalf of taxpayers. Stevens, however, didn't appreciate being checkmated by a freshman.

MR. STEVENS: I find myself in a strange position, as I indicated to the Senator from Oklahoma. Earlier today, I indicated to the Senator that I would suggest a series of second-degree amendments. I had under consideration second-degree amendments. It is my understanding now the amendment of the Senator from Oklahoma is filed as a second-degree amendment to the Bingaman amendment, am I correct?

THE PRESIDING OFFICER: That is correct. It is a second-degree amendment.

MR. STEVENS: I will put the Senate on notice—and I don't kid people—if the Senate decides to discriminate against our State and take money only from our State, I will resign from this body. This is not the Senate I came to. This is not the Senate I devoted 37 years to. If one Senator can decide he will take all the money from one State to solve a problem of another, that is not a union. That is not equality and is not treating my State the way I have seen it treated for 37 years.[7]

Another memorable and revealing speech that day came from Senator Kit Bond (R-MO). Bond also believed that putting another senator's earmarks on the chopping block was a serious breach of decorum.

MR. BOND: Madam President, before I turn it over to the Senator from Washington, as I said to the Senator, we have a difference in philosophy . . . we have very different philosophies on how we serve our people.

If he has told the people of Oklahoma how he is going to serve Oklahoma that is fine. I have told the people of Missouri how I am going to serve Missouri . . . What I am saying is, I am not going to tell the people of Oklahoma how their Senator should behave. I expect the Senator from Oklahoma would not be telling the Senator from Missouri how to behave . . .

We will have an opportunity for our colleagues to determine which philosophy they agree with. Do you want the bureaucrats solely to make the decisions, or should Senators be able to influence a small portion of those? That is the question, quite simply. It is not about saving money[;] it is about who makes those decisions. We have two very different philosophies.

I have great respect for my colleague from Oklahoma. He has offered a different philosophy to his people in being elected than I have offered to my people in Missouri who have elected me.[8]

I appreciated that Senator Bond didn't take my approach as personally as others had, yet he still faithfully defended the philosophy of career politicians. Bond wanted our views to coexist, but the problem was, we had irreconcilable mandates. Plus, I was convinced it wasn't Bond versus Coburn but Congress versus the country. Taxpayers in Oklahoma didn't need to pay for earmarks in Missouri or anywhere else.

Senator Patty Murray of Washington State followed Senator Bond. Murray was feeling less charitable because I was also targeting a sculpture park in Seattle.

MRS. MURRAY: Mr. President, I rise today to join Senator Bond in strongly opposing the Coburn amendment and the numerous other amendments he has filed with the same type of philosophy, as he calls it, in the Senate.

I join with my colleague from Missouri, the chairman of this committee. I, like him, go home every single weekend to Washington State, which is 2,500 miles away from the Nation's Capital. I, like the Senator from Missouri, do not believe the bureaucrats sitting in Washington, DC, know what is happening on the ground in my home State 2,500 miles away from here . . .

The Senator from Oklahoma now comes to the Senate with a series of amendments targeting a few States to pick out individually named projects and eliminate those projects' funding. We are not going to go down that road . . .

I don't care if it is my project, Senator Bond's project, Senator Nelson's project, Senator Chafee's project, or the other projects that the Senator from Oklahoma has randomly picked to target, the Senators that have EDI [Economic Development Initiative] projects in this bill—and that, by the way, is almost every Senator in this Senate—are going to have to stand together. We are not going to watch the Senator pick out one project and make it into a whipping boy.

Now, it is true that Senator Bond and I allow Senators to allocate EDI funds to those projects in their States that they think make best use of the funds. We do not make any apology for that practice . . .

I hope the Senate will not go down the road of cherry-picking individual projects that Senators have come to us and have championed on behalf of their constituents who do not live here in Washington, DC. I hope we do not go down the road deciding we know better than home State Senators about the merits of the projects they bring to us.

As the old saying goes: What is good for the goose is good for the gander. And I tell my colleagues, if we start cutting funding for individual projects, your project may be next.

So, Mr. President, when Members come down to the floor to vote on this amendment, they need to know if they support stripping out this project, Senator Bond and I are likely to be taking a long, serious look at their projects to determine whether they should be preserved during our upcoming conference negotiations.

We must not and we will not go down the road of picking on one Senator or another on the floor of the Senate. I urge a no vote on this amendment.[9]

So, their philosophy was that if you wanted your project you had to support all projects. This thinking seemed logical to most senators but was offensive to most taxpayers. When it came time to actually vote, the outcome was predictable. I lost the Bridge to Nowhere vote by a 67-vote margin—82 to 15.[10] But I saw the effort as a resounding success.

The Bridge to Nowhere debate was our Doolittle raid. The bridge was a low-value target in budgetary terms, but it had enormous strategic value. The debate showed millions of Americans, who were deeply disturbed about spending, that their voices mattered, and change was possible. If one elected official could launch a commando raid against the earmark favor factory and survive unharmed, it just might be possible to go after bigger targets, get spending under control, and take back our country. The lopsided vote tally against us didn't matter. The mission itself was the success. Taxpayers had sent a message to the careerists that we were coming, and there was nothing they could do to stop us.

Thanks to the reaction—and overreaction—of senators to my amend-ments to gut earmarks, our effort continued to gain steam throughout 2005 and beyond. The bridge even landed on the cover of *Parade* magazine in November 2005, which was a turning point in our effort. Republican pollster Frank Luntz told me that after the 2006 elections, the Bridge to Nowhere had higher name identification among voters than their own members of Congress. The bridge never would have become so famous if Stevens had not threatened to resign. Because of Stevens's speech, and other speeches that day, millions of Americans saw how far the Senate had drifted from the founders' vision of limited government.

There were many other battles in the years ahead—amendments to eliminate earmarks for the Woodstock Museum in New York, a rail-road in Mississippi, a teapot museum, and many more[11]—but the bridge endures as a symbol of congressional excess and corruption.

Still, some of our strongest supporters doubted whether earmarks could ever be eliminated. Columnist Bob Novak, who wrote approvingly of our cause, called the quest to eliminate earmarks quixotic, a noble but probably futile tilting at windmills. Still, every year we made progress—the vote losses narrowed—and the Senate moved closer and closer to an earmark moratorium.

We were also helped by a 2010 study from Harvard Business School that showed earmarks are bad economics because they displace pri-vate investment and hurt local economies.[12] This finding was a total contradiction of Washington's conventional wisdom that said power-ful committee chairmen benefit their states with parochial spending. As Joshua Coval, one of the study's authors, said, "It was an enormous surprise, at least to us, to learn that the average firm in the chairman's state did not benefit at all from the unanticipated increase in spending."

By the end of 2010, with the Tea Party mobilized, Congress finally saw the writing on the wall. On November 15, 2010, a few days after the elections, Senate Republican Minority Leader Mitch McConnell, who had unapologetically fought for earmarks for his state and campaigned on his ability to bring home the bacon two years earlier, delivered what I thought was one of the most important and eloquent speeches of his career.

I have seen a lot of elections in my life, but I have never seen an election like the one we had earlier this month. The 2010 midterm election was a "change" election the likes of which I have never seen, and the change that people want, above all, is right here in Washington.

Most Americans are deeply unhappy with their government, more so than at any other time in decades. And after the way lawmakers have done business up here over the last couple of years, it's easy to see why. But it's not enough to point out the faults of the party in power. Americans want change, not mere criticism. And that means that all of us in Washington need to get serious about changing the way we do business, even on things we have defended in the past, perhaps for good reason.

If the voters express themselves clearly and unequivocally on an issue, it's not enough to persist in doing the opposite on the grounds that "that's the way we've always done it." That's what elections are all about, after all. And if this election has shown us anything, it's that Americans know the difference between talking about change, and actually delivering on it.

Bringing about real change is hard work. It requires elected officials—whether they're in their first week or their 50th year in office—to challenge others and, above all, to challenge themselves to do things differently from time to time, to question, and then to actually shake up the status quo in pursuit of a goal or a vision that the voters have set for the good of our country.

I have thought about these things long and hard over the past few weeks. I've talked with my members. I've listened to them. Above all, I have listened to my constituents. And what I've concluded is that on the issue of congressional earmarks, as the leader of my party in the Senate, I have to lead first by example. Nearly every day that the Senate's been in session for the past two years, I have come down to this spot and said that Democrats are ignoring the wishes of the American people. When it comes to earmarks, I won't be guilty of the same thing.

Make no mistake. I know the good that has come from the projects I have helped support throughout my state. I don't apologize for them. But there is simply no doubt that the abuse of this practice has caused Americans to view it as a symbol of the waste and the out-of-control spending that every Republican in Washington is determined to fight. And unless people like me show the American people that we're willing to follow through on small or even symbolic things, we risk losing them on our broader efforts to cut spending and rein in government.

That's why today I am announcing that I will join the Republican Leadership in the House in support of a moratorium on earmarks in the 112th Congress . . .

This is no small thing. Old habits aren't easy to break, but sometimes they must be. And now is such a time.[13]

At a key moment, McConnell could have done what politicians typically do and buried his head in the sand and dug in. He didn't. I had many conversations with him about the corrosive effect of earmarking. And as he said, he not only listened to his members, but more important, to the American people. And then he acted. And just like that it was over.

At least for a time, the horrendous distraction of earmarks would be set aside while we focused on other areas of the budget. Sure enough, with the gateway drug of earmarks in disuse, the conversation shifted from cutting billions to trillions. Congress is still not cutting spending, but we are moving closer to acknowledging the true magnitude of our challenges. Most importantly, the earmark battle showed that change is possible when the American people say enough is enough. Together, we showed that if you tilt at windmills long enough, sometimes they fall over.*

I wish Ted Stevens were around to provide his perspective on this chapter. I'm sad to say, he was killed in a plane crash in 2010. Uncle Ted, as he was affectionately called, brought a lot to the Senate. One aspect of his legacy that isn't fully appreciated is how he raised the level of debate in the Senate.

We live in a time in which there is a lot of confusion about what it means to be civil. Civility does not mean being nice or being politically correct. It means *having the debate so that the best ideas might prevail.* It means honoring the other person by listening to him or her, understanding that individual's perspective, and then responding. It means communicating in a way that generates the best policies and the best results. It means focusing on ideas, not individuals.

Few may describe Tom Coburn and Ted Stevens as paragons of civility, but I can't recall a more enlightening, informative, and spontaneous debate in the Senate about the proper scope of government than our heated debate about the Bridge to Nowhere and earmarks.

---

* The American people have to stay vigilant. Congress is trying to undo this progress with practices like "phone-marking"—the practice of phoning in earmark requests—and creating slush funds in appropriations bills. If we let up the pressure, earmarking will resume.

Ted brought his A game to the floor to defend his earmark. He would often go to the Senate floor in an Incredible Hulk tie, which was designed to invoke memories of the trademark line from the TV show—"Don't make me angry. You wouldn't like me when I'm angry." I knew this was an act and shtick, of course, but Ted was always prepared and honored the public and his colleagues with his preparation.

Stevens gave the Senate and country what they deserved on earmarks—a full-throated debate about two competing visions of government. I can still hear his thunderous "No!" on the Senate floor as his hand smacked the podium in defense of earmarks for Alaska. Ted understood my perspective and disagreed with it vehemently. I felt equally strongly. We had a debate, and the country was better for it.

And when we were done with our debates that stretched over many years, and when the American people rendered their judgment against the earmark process, there was no bitterness between us. In the years before Ted's defeat in 2008, we enjoyed a warm rapport and friendly rivalry. I would occasionally give him a box of cigars. He would call me periodically from his patio office in the Capitol, overlooking the mall and the country he loved, to say hello. "Tom," he would say, "I'm here smoking one of your cigars, on the beach."

THE PROBLEM

Earmarks are the gateway drug to Washington's spending addiction. As the number of earmarks increased, so did spending.

Earmarks represent the erosion of the constitutional limits on Congress's power. Nowhere do the enumerated powers give individual members the power to build swimming pools, parking garages, and Woodstock museums.

The temporary end of earmarks has helped shift the conversation in Washington to the big-dollar problems like entitlements.

The credit for this progress goes to ordinary people like you who told Congress enough was enough.

Congress will try to restart the earmark favor factory if we let down our guard. If we allow earmarks to once again become a distraction at this moment of peril, we will never reduce our debt.

5

Getting to No

I sincerely believe . . . that the principle of spending
money to be paid by posterity under the name of
funding is but swindling futurity on a large scale.

—THOMAS JEFFERSON, LETTER TO JOHN TAYLOR IN 1816[1]

EARLY IN MY TERM IN THE SENATE, I RECEIVED A PACKAGE FROM
a man who introduced himself as a liberal from upstate New York. It
contained a note encouraging me to "keep doing what you're doing" and
a large framed picture of one simple word: *No.*

That stark image of two white letters—*N* and *o*—on a black background hangs over my desk to this day. It is a constant reminder to me
and all who visit my office that Washington's conventional wisdom is
often exactly the opposite of what is in the best interest of the country.
What is distasteful according to politicians—blocking spending bills—
really is progress according to much of the country, even liberals from
upstate New York, who may have little in common with this Okie from
Muskogee.

THE GRIDLOCK MYTH

Many in the media claim Democrats and Republicans in Washington cannot agree on anything.

They could not be more wrong.

Over the past decade, presidents of both parties and Congresses controlled by both parties approved massive new entitlement programs, tax breaks, pork projects for special interests, and trillions of dollars in new debt. What the American people understand to be gridlock, however, is quite different from what the media and political establishment want them to believe.

When ordinary Americans complain about gridlock, I hear them express a sense that politicians in Washington can't put aside short-term political concerns and come together to solve big problems. The American people are right. Washington has been unable to even consider, in a serious way, solutions to our long-term fiscal crisis.

What the media and political establishment describe as gridlock, however, bears little semblance to how Washington actually works. The argument goes like this: Washington is paralyzed because ideological extremes—of which I am sometimes accused of being a part—are too powerful and prevent political leaders from coming together around big ideas and solutions. The facts, however, show that this argument is a smoke screen.

Over the past several decades, in fact, Washington has hardly been a city immobilized by gridlock. Instead, Congress has been an assembly line of new programs and a favor factory for special interests. Our economy is on the brink of collapse not because politicians can't agree, but because they have agreed for decades. For years, a bipartisan supermajority in both parties has agreed to borrow and spend far beyond our means.

We began the twenty-first century with an annual budget surplus.

Over the ten years that followed, bipartisan cooperation erased this deficit and added $10 trillion in debt to our nation. There have been lots of excuses, such as unforeseen wars and economic hard times, yet none of these events explains Congress's bipartisan agreement to create or expand nearly forty entitlement programs, carve out tax advantages for special interests, and build bridges to nowhere and earmark tens of thousands of other pork projects.

Still, the American people are fed a steady diet of rhetoric about the imagined perils of gridlock because it serves the interests of the politicians who got us into this mess in the first place. The coverage of Senator Evan Bayh's (D-IN) retirement in early 2010 illustrates the desire of the media and political establishment to both consciously and subconsciously create a narrative that justifies and defends our unsustainable status quo. While I harbor no animus toward my friend and former colleague, his own statements and the media's coverage of them speak volumes about why Congress can't agree to defuse the debt bomb.

On February 15, 2010, Bayh stunned his supporters at a press conference in Indianapolis and announced he was leaving the Senate: "After all these years, my passion for service to my fellow citizens is undiminished, but my desire to do so by serving in Congress has waned . . . There is too much partisanship and not enough progress—too much narrow ideology and not enough practical problem-solving. Even at a time of enormous challenge, the peoples' business is not being done. I love working for the people of Indiana. I love helping our citizens make the most of their lives, but I do not love Congress."[2]

Bayh expanded on these thoughts in various interviews and writings. He told Ruth Marcus, a columnist with the *Washington Post*, "There are some ideologues in the Senate. There are some staunch partisans. The vast majority are good, decent people who are trapped in a system that does not let that goodness and decency translate itself into legislative accomplishments."[3]

In an op-ed piece in the *New York Times*, Bayh also wrote of his father, former U.S. senator Birch Bayh: "One incident from his career vividly demonstrates how times have changed. In 1968, when my father was running for reelection, Everett Dirksen, the Republican leader, approached him on the Senate floor, put his arm around my dad's shoulder, and asked what he could do to help. This is unimaginable today . . . Today, members routinely campaign against each other, raise donations against each other and force votes on trivial amendments written solely to provide fodder for the next negative attack ad. It's difficult to work with members actively plotting your demise."[4]

The response from the media was fawning. Ruth Marcus lamented: "The Senate, with its endless holds and 60-vote points of order, may be the epitome of a place that knows neither victory nor defeat."[5] Howard Fineman with *Newsweek* extolled Bayh as a centrist and explained, "But this is not an era of centrism; it is an era of philosophical extremes."[6] *Time* magazine offered similar coverage, as did CNN, which ran an entire series called Broken Government.[7] The *Wall Street Journal* was one of the few outlets to question the conventional wisdom. It argued that Bayh was resigning due to a failure of liberal governance (and the health care bill), not a failure of governance per se.

I don't question the sincerity of what Bayh said, and I do appreciate his sentiments about civility, but it's important to look at why the conventional Washington wisdom is wrong.

The argument that the Senate is being held hostage by extremists and ideologues is false on two counts. First, as I've explained, Washington has been in agreement for years about expanding the size of government. Second, the so-called extremes in Congress are sometimes those who get along best and are most likely to forge compromises. In 2005, I was on the opposite end of the spectrum from a young senator named Barack Obama, but we worked together on many issues, such as Katrina oversight and transparency, which he highlighted in his presidential campaign. I've also worked closely with liberals, such as Russ Feingold (D-WI) and, when I served in the House of Representatives, Henry Waxman (D-CA). On the other side, senators like Ted Kennedy (D-MA), the liberal lion of the Senate, had a legendary ability to form friendships and compromises across the aisle. From my experience, members motivated by ideas and a clear vision for government tend to work well across the aisle, while those motivated by partisanship are less able to come together. For the centrists, there is actually little room for compromise because they already agree.

Bayh also, perhaps unintentionally, offered a defense of political careerism by suggesting that senators should not campaign against one another or otherwise plot each other's demise. What Bayh and the media fail to understand is that the American people don't see being a senator as a lifetime appointment. Our founders would be appalled by the vast majority of politicians who stay in Congress as long as they can, and especially those, like Arlen Specter (R-PA), who switch parties to try to guarantee their own political survival.

What the American people want are political leaders who understand that it's not about the leaders but about ideas. Senators shouldn't take opposition so personally. My opponent in 2004, Brad Carson, and the Democratic Senatorial Campaign Committee, then led by Chuck Schumer (D-NY), ran a vicious campaign and accused me of being an "abortionist" because I had performed abortions to save the lives of two individual mothers. Am I supposed to refuse to work with leading Democratic senators like Chuck Schumer of New York, and others who plotted my demise, or should I do my best to work with them? Senators need to get over themselves and get on with the work of defending the country, not lengthening their political careers.

A CONSTITUTION OF NOES

In Washington we hear a lot about the founders' intent to keep the three branches of government balanced, but far less about their intent to keep the powers of those branches limited. Members of Congress like to complain about the imperial presidency and activist judges. The executive branch complains about Congress infringing on executive privilege. The judicial branch complains about the other branches politicizing judgeships, and so on. Yet few in Washington are concerned about maintaining the balance of power between government and "We the People."

In this age of big, imperial government, we have three branches—the Imperial President, the Imperial Congress, and the Imperial Judiciary—that are eroding individual freedom. According to our founders, the relationship between government and the people is far more important than government's relationship with itself. In Federalist No. 45, James Madison wrote: "The powers delegated by the proposed Constitution to the Federal Government are few and defined," not infinite and limitless. Restoring individual freedom means electing people who believe in the Constitution and the rights of the people more than their right to be here.

While today's bent in official Washington is toward saying yes to new spending, the attitude at our founding was precisely the opposite. My colleague Jim DeMint puts it succinctly: If President Obama's slogan is "Yes we can," the Constitution's is "No you can't."[8]

The most important constitutional principle is limitation, or saying no. If the Constitutional Convention were held today, it would be derided as a hotbed of obstruction. There is little doubt that if asked whether government should perform many of the functions we now take for granted, our founders would have likely said no. The

Constitution is full of noes. Could Congress establish a religion? No. Abridge free speech? No. Confiscate firearms? No. Manage state government? Place traffic lights? Force Americans to buy certain products? No. No. And no.

Much of what Congress funds today has little basis in the Constitution. Still, efforts to question the way these programs are structured are lambasted as obstructionism.

HOTLINES: DEATH BY A THOUSAND SPENDING INCREASES

One of the shocking facts about the modern Senate is that nearly all bills that pass every year are approved essentially in secret, with no debate, no amendments, and no recorded vote. In the Senate this process is called the "hotline" and it is a favorite tool of the "party of yes" to spending. The hotline process allows bills to call up and pass by "unanimous consent," which means passage by automatic voice vote, if all one hundred senators either say yes or fail to signal dissent.

Here's how the process works. Throughout the legislative day, and particularly near the end of a legislative session just before a vacation, a phone will ring in all one hundred Senate offices, with an automated message announcing something like: "The majority leader, in consultation with the minority leader would like to call up and pass by unanimous consent the following bills . . ." If no senator calls in to object, the bill passes without any public debate, votes, or amendments. All of this happens over the phone and e-mail. The public is not alerted and no debate occurs or is recorded.

The hotline was created to quickly dispatch innocuous and non-controversial motions, such as naming post offices or moving along perfunctory resolutions. Eighty percent of hotlined bills fit this mold.

However, the process has expanded to pass not just mundane bills but an enormous amount of costly and significant legislation.

In the 110th Congress, for instance, 95 percent of all bills that passed were hotlined. In other words, of the 1,211 bills the Senate approved, only 59 received a roll call vote. I asked the Congressional Research Service (CRS) to track how many bills had been hotlined in the past twenty years. CRS found "in the last ten Congresses (110th–101st) [20 years], an average of 93 percent of approved measures did not receive roll call votes."[9]

Other than the lack of transparency involved in the process, there are three other aspects of hotlines that are troubling.

One, very few senators read or even look at the thousands of bills that are hotlined every year. In other words, the elected officials who were hired by voters to be responsible for the legislative process, in many cases, have no idea what they are being asked to approve. In some cases, hotlined bills were never even read by the bill's author but were written by a staffer and a lobbyist only to be signed off by the senator.

Two, the hotline process assumes that the Senate's work is so vital that it must find a way to expeditiously pass more than a thousand bills every year. Yet, if none of the hotlined bills passed, very few Americans could tell the difference. Americans are hardly sitting on the edge of their seats, waiting to read about hotlined bills in the Congressional Record. The hotline process represents Big Government on autopilot.

Three, the hotline process perverts the democratic process—and, I would contend, the founders' vision of limited government—by presuming bills should be passed unless someone calls to object. The hotline process has it backward. Bills should pass only when elected officials agree, not when senators fail to object to a process rigged to succeed by lobbyists, special-interest groups, and unelected staff.

The presumption of consent for costly and significant legislation is one of the more subtle and insidious aspects of modern government. If a senator simply wants to do his or her job and review a bill destined to be hotlined, that person is labeled a troublemaker and an obstructionist. Failing to grant consent immediately, even if a senator just wants to read the bill, is considered a "hold" in Washington's backward rule book.

The presumption of consent also gives "party of yes to spending" politicians an opportunity to argue that principles of democracy and fairness are on their side. I'm often asked what right I have to stand in the way of ninety-nine senators who want to pass noncontroversial legislation. It's easy. I'm standing with 91 percent of Americans who don't approve of how Congress is doing its job. What's noncontroversial in Washington—spending money we don't have on things we don't need—is very controversial in America, and for good reason. Millions of Americans are irate we are saddling the next generation with debt.

As I came to understand how broken the hotline process had become, at the beginning of each Congress I began sending my colleagues a letter explaining my intention to not grant unanimous consent or "hold" bills that are unconstitutional or spend new money that is not offset.

To *offset* simply means to pay for new spending by cutting spending somewhere else. Normal people make these decisions every day. If you need to buy a new refrigerator, you have to offset the cost elsewhere in your budget and spend less on other priorities. For members of Congress, however, offsets are a novel concept. An institution that can simply borrow new money when it pleases has little use for offsets.

The purpose of the letter isn't to antagonize my colleagues but to clearly announce my intentions. Still, the reaction to my decision to "hold" items on the hotline calendar illustrates the tension between today's "party of yes" and the Constitution's doctrine of no.

RAGING BULLS

In late December 2007, at the end of a long, arduous session, Senator Ted Stevens of Alaska requested a meeting with me to discuss four bills I was holding because they were not offset. At that time, Stevens was the ranking member on the Senate Commerce Committee. As a past chairman, he used his influential position to push expensive bills related to the National Oceanic and Atmospheric Administration (NOAA) that would primarily benefit Alaska. I knew Senator Stevens desperately wanted the bills to pass before the holidays. I had no intention of letting the bills add to the deficit, but I told him I'm always happy to discuss my concerns with him.

When my lone staffer arrived in the ornate Strom Thurmond room in the Capitol, he was soon greeted by no fewer than five professional Commerce Committee staffers.

Senator Stevens and I arrived shortly thereafter, and we took our places at the long conference table. Senator Stevens began the meeting by highlighting the merits of the four bills in question. At the end of his measured and cordial presentation, Stevens asked me why I was blocking his bills.

I responded by respectfully reminding him that I had sent a letter to all senators early in the session, announcing my intention to block bills that were not offset. I explained to Stevens that while I didn't object to the merits of his proposals, if he wanted them to pass, they would have to be offset. I told him I would, of course, be delighted to work with him to identify appropriate offsets.

Stevens then asked me directly if I would lift my hold. I repeated my concerns and said, given the financial condition of the country, I could not let the bills go. When it became clear to Senator Stevens that I was not going to withdraw my objection without offsets, the meeting deteriorated.

"Tom, I need these bills. I have an election!" Stevens said.

With Stevens's frustration bubbling over, I tried to reassure him that I was willing to work with his office in good faith to pay for and pass his bills.

"I'm not going to work with him; I'm a senator!" Stevens responded curtly, believing my offer meant I wanted him to only work with my young staffer.

Stevens then let loose an expletive-filled tirade that culminated in a threat. "Tom, I'm not allowing any of your bills ever to pass. Not one, Tom. Not one."

With the meeting all but over, I politely repeated my pledge to work with his office to find offsets and wished everyone a happy holiday. Stevens, however, wasn't finished. As I got up out of my chair to leave, he repeated his threat. "Not one! Not one of your bills!"

I walked out and began the trek down the long corridor in silence with my staffer, only to hear the door swing open behind us and Stevens still swearing, "Not one! Not one of your bills, Tom!"

With Stevens still following us, I finally wound myself through the intricate corridors of the Capitol and out of earshot of the senior senator from Alaska.

Needless to say, I never did hear back from Senator Stevens or his office. As was so often the case with these "negotiations," had the senator and his staff entourage spent half as much time identifying offsets as complaining or issuing threats, many more of his bills would have passed.

My encounter with Stevens was also noteworthy because he was a Republican senator, a point I liked to remind the media of the next year when my colleague from the other side of the aisle, Senate Majority Leader Harry Reid, picked a high-profile battle with me after I blocked more than a hundred bills from being hotlined.

THE "COBURN OMNIBUS"

In the summer of 2008, Reid had grown weary of my holds and decided to roll all the bills I was blocking into one package his staff liked to call the "Coburn Omnibus" but officially, and pompously, titled the Advancing America's Priorities Act. As the title suggested, the country was waiting on the Senate majority to tell it what its priorities were. The bill rolled thirty-five of the more than one hundred bills I was holding into one package costing more than $10 billion.

Reid designed the package for maximum political effect. I believe he wanted to portray my stance as unreasonable obstruction of popular and important legislation. As a result, the Coburn Omnibus had something for everyone, especially victims of some misfortune or injustice. The bill included legislation for victims of racially motivated crimes, victims of torture, breast cancer patients, ALS (Lou Gehrig's disease) patients, paralyzed Americans, and even trafficked chimpanzees.

Reid's attempt to create a caricature of my opposition was obvious. He didn't care that I supported paid-for versions of much of the legislation in his package, such as the Emmett Till Unsolved Civil Rights Crime Act, a bill that was named after Emmett Till, a fourteen-year-old African American boy from Chicago who was brutally murdered in Mississippi after allegedly whistling at a white woman. I wanted to see these perpetrators brought to justice, but Reid was more interested in trying to score political points and mobilize public opinion against the "party of no" than actually passing many of the bills in his package.

The Emmett Till bill was the majority's preferred political weapon. Senators Dodd (D-CT), Leahy (D-VT), and Durbin (D-IL) lambasted me at a press conference for "delaying justice" for victims of unsolved civil rights crimes because of my hold on the Emmett Till Unsolved Civil Rights Crime Act. Leahy said, "It is disgraceful that it has taken us so long to take this basic step to pursue justice too long delayed. It is incredible that some continue to obstruct these efforts."[10]

Breast cancer was another flash point. Fran Visco, the head of the National Breast Cancer Coalition, said my hold on the unnecessary and unscientific Breast Cancer and Environmental Research Act meant I was essentially telling breast cancer patients to "drop dead."[11] Never mind the fact that I am a three-time cancer survivor, have family members who died of breast cancer, and as a practicing physician, have lost patients to the disease. Visco didn't care that the bill was redundant and empowered politicians rather than scientists to conduct research. My hold, she wrote, was "play[ing] politics" with her life.[12]

Still, even in a package that was compiled for the sole purpose of demagoguing my holds, senators couldn't resist adding in a host of parochial and less-than-vital priorities that cheapened the Emmett Till bill. If senators wanted to stand for civil rights, they also had to support the "Star-Spangled Banner and War of 1812 Bicentennial Commission Act," the "Beach Protection Act," the "Paul Simon Study Abroad Foundation Act," and the "Captive Primate Safety Act" that was designed, in part, to prevent the mistreatment of chimpanzees and protect them from human owners who lack the common sense to not keep large primates as pets. I wasn't for mistreating the primates. I was against mistreating our children, which we were doing by not paying for the bill with cuts elsewhere.

After several days of debate, Reid attempted to move the package through the Senate, but the chamber had grown weary of the exercise and failed to agree to pass "America's priorities." Reid vented his frustrations on the Senate floor.

We would be off this as long as it would take to adopt the motion to proceed, which would take 15 minutes for the vote. Then we could move immediately to the bill. We could do that immediately. We could finish it quickly. The only effort that my friend, the distinguished junior Senator from Oklahoma, wants is to throw a monkey wrench into proceedings around here. That is what this is all about.

I do not know why people on the other side of the aisle would join in this. You go home and explain to your constituents about Lou Gehrig's disease. You go home and explain about the stroke legislation. You go home and explain to your folks about the Emmitt [*sic*] Till legislation. You go home and explain to everyone there about the paralysis bill.

Next time you see someone in a wheelchair at home, explain to them how you voted against moving forward on something that may get them out of that wheelchair.[13]

There it was. Not since John Edwards had promised that paralyzed people would walk again if John Kerry beat George Bush[14] had a national leader so openly professed the "party of yes" faith in the messianic powers of big government. According to Reid, my actions were keeping people in their wheelchairs. If I would only lift my hold, they would walk again.

In hindsight, the Coburn Omnibus debate had two takeaways. One, the debate caused the media to refer to me more consistently as Dr. No. I didn't mind the title, but it revealed the media's bias toward more spending and government expansion. The name was ironic, and unearned, because at any given time I was blocking no more than 10 to 15 percent of all bills the Senate wanted to hotline. In other words, instead of allowing 1,152 bills to pass by hotline, I only allowed 1,000 bills to pass by hotline. Still, this was enough to earn me the title "Dr. No."

Two, the debate showed that the Senate was more interested in vapid and partisan political debate than solving real problems. One of the bills I did help pass in the Coburn Omnibus was a modified version of the Emmett Till bill that would not add to the deficit. Throughout the debate, I worked very closely with an incredible man named Alvin Sykes, who was a boyhood friend of Till and had been pursuing justice in the case for fifty years. I wanted Sykes to succeed and believed the majority was more interested in holding press conferences than doing the hard work of funding investigations and solving cases.

The Emmett Till Unsolved Civil Rights Crime Act was signed into law on October 7, 2008, and authorized the appropriation of $10 million annually from 2008 to 2017 for the Department of Justice (DOJ) to investigate and prosecute unsolved civil rights murders committed prior to 1970. Yet, as I suspected, Congress authorized money for the program but never funded it.

In 2009, I brought this to the Senate's attention and attempted to fund the Emmett Till bill by redirecting $10 million within the DOJ. My amendment was defeated by a vote of 37 to 58. The next year, 2010, Congress seemed to finally be serious about funding a program they created two years earlier. That year Congress appropriated $54 million for the DOJ's civil rights enforcement. Congress expected some of these funds would be used to investigate unsolved civil rights cases.

Yet, two months later, before a dime of the new federal funds was even spent, the *Washington Post* reported that the FBI was closing "all but a handful" of the unsolved civil rights murders. "There's maybe five to seven cases where we don't know who did it," according to the FBI special agent heading the bureau's effort.[15]

The Emmett Till debate showed that the disgrace was not my desire to pay for the bill but Congress's willingness to use the issue and people like Mr. Sykes for partisan political purposes. All the rhetoric and drama about the bill in 2008 was a charade. As I argued at the time, the new program was unnecessary, as these activities were already ongoing under a Bush administration initiative. Also, the program was authorized to spend $13.5 million with no more than seven unsolved cases to investigate. Even then, the Senate Democratic majority never funded the program, and eventually, the Obama administration closed down the initiative. A report to Congress from the Department of Justice admitted that "most of these cases will not result in prosecution."[16] The report also showed that instead of spending money trying to solve cases, DOJ was spending taxpayer funds attending conferences, meeting with community activists, and screening documentaries. In time, the whole debate proved to be a cynical partisan game to the bill's backers: let's demonize Republicans for being racists while never pursuing the actual substance of the legislation.

In the end, the Coburn Omnibus debate did nothing but remind Americans why careerists in Congress can't be trusted to make hard choices and solve real problems. Congress almost always refuses to pay for new priorities without a battle, even as we are facing a spending-and-borrowing-induced debt crisis. And in many cases, these new priorities are purely partisan political exercises. Bills that will supposedly decide the fates of lives and nations are really written as press release bills designed to help a politician win reelection.

Partisan Democrats in the Senate continue to invest an enormous amount of time and energy, pushing the phony narrative that "obstruction" and filibusters are the great enemies of democracy. Earlier this year, for instance, the senators from New York, Chuck Schumer and Kirsten Gillibrand, cried foul when I refused to immediately grant unanimous consent to pass a bill that would earmark $20 million to a 9/11 memorial and museum in New York.[17] I had two concerns with the bill. One, I wasn't convinced the museum needed federal funding when it was sitting on more than $500 million in assets and when other memorials, such as the Oklahoma City Bombing Memorial and Museum, were operating just fine without federal assistance. Two, I thought that if the sponsors believed this was a federal priority they should at least pay for it by reducing spending elsewhere.

Yet, the sponsors weren't interested in discussing the merits of their proposal or my arguments. It was pure politics. They clearly wanted political credit for supporting the measure. The fact that the museum was already receiving ample funding was not enough. It had to receive more *federal* funding. When I asked Senator Schumer how he was coming with identifying offsets he said he would get back to me. He clearly was not in a hurry to sit down and negotiate. The debate was a classic example of what's wrong with Washington and the hotline process. Career politicians dare other senators to "block" emotionally charged legislation and then refuse to do the hard work of making choices and setting priorities.

It's time for politicians in Washington to say no to these tactics. Saying no, after all, can be a great defense of life and liberty. When your three-year-old tries to cross the street you yell, "No!" When your teenager asks to stay out late on a school night you say, "No." No is a word we need to hear more often from politicians in Washington.

No is also a word the founders would have associated with the Senate. The founders created the Senate to force debate, deliberation, and consensus to make it *very* difficult to change course. Again, the problem is not that we have said no. The problem is we have said yes and agreed to run up a $15 trillion debt.

Yet, many in Washington aren't ready to stop saying yes to unsustainable spending. Early in 2012, Senate Majority Leader Reid once again blamed the Senate's lack of accomplishments on Republican "obstructionism on steroids."[18] A more accurate medical description of the Senate would be to describe the body as heavily sedated. From a practical standpoint, it is hard to argue holds and "obstructionism" are the problem when there has been little real legislation in the Senate to block. The number of votes in the Senate has declined steadily in recent years. For instance, the Senate held only 235 votes in 2011,[19] a nearly 47 percent decline in the number of votes held in the last year before a presidential election, 2007, which saw 442 votes.[20] At the same time, Reid has increasingly moved to cut off debate. He has done this through filing cloture—cutting off debate—more than in previous Congresses and through a tactic calling "filling the tree," in which the majority leader uses his privileges to fill all possible ways to modify a bill with shell amendments. This tactic essentially blocks other senators from offering real amendments. I believe our founders would call this practice obstruction or the tyranny of the majority.

Filling the Tree

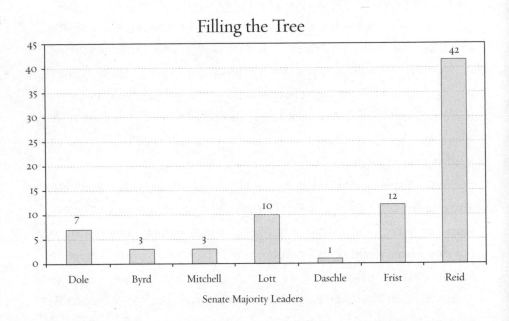

Senate Majority Leaders

The key point, though, is to look at the legislation Reid has *not* pushed. He has been AWOL in the deficit reduction debate. He hasn't put forward a single piece of serious legislation that would reduce the deficit, save entitlements from bankruptcy, reform the tax code, or eliminate a single program. Instead, he has pushed bills that grow government and are popular with the "party of yes," or he has pushed bills designed to score partisan points. Meanwhile, under his leadership Senate Democrats have not produced a budget for more than one thousand days even as our debt is slowing our economy by 25 to 33 percent and preventing the creation of a million jobs a year.

Fortunately, the American people have seen through these partisan arguments. They understand that it is impossible to obstruct something that isn't happening.

While Washington's faith in the power of government to solve all problems may be unlimited, the American people's patience is not. We the People are saying no, and it's time for Washington to listen. In a political culture that elevates the virtues of getting to yes, the American people—from liberals in New York to conservatives in Muskogee—understand that defusing the debt bomb depends on politicians in Washington getting to no.

THE PROBLEM

The problem in Washington is not "gridlock" or an inability to agree. The problem is both parties have agreed to borrow and spend way beyond our means.

In the real world, families have to set priorities and make hard choices. Labeling efforts to force Congress to do the same as "obstruction" is an excuse to continue spending.

The obstruction in our system that is hurting our country is our debt and Congress's refusal to act.

The Senate's productivity is declining because Senate leaders are afraid of debating and addressing the critical issues facing the country, not because some of us are trying to force Congress to make hard choices and live within our means.

6

Government Is Still the Problem

In this present crisis government is not the solution
to our problem; government is the problem.

—President Reagan's first inaugural address, 1981

Thirty years after President Reagan famously labeled
government "the problem," progressives are still offended. Some on
the left mark Reagan's comment as the beginning of a dangerous anti-
government movement that eventually gave rise to the Tea Party.

Progressives misunderstood Reagan's sentiment three decades ago
and still do today. Reagan was not offering an anti-government message
or fomenting a new hostility to government. Reagan believed government was a force to be limited, not an evil to be eradicated.

Reagan was echoing the wisdom of our founders who knew from history and experience that *government itself was limited in what it could
effectively do in a free society.*

In the past few decades, we have unlearned that lesson. The challenge
today is to remember what we have forgotten and reapply the principles
of limited government to our debt and economic crisis. If America is

going to survive and thrive for the next generation and beyond, the American people have to ask themselves whose vision is best, the framers of the Constitution or today's progressives?

Our answer will determine whether America recovers and thrives, or becomes a second-rate power with lower standards of living and less security.

President Obama posed a similar question after he was elected. In his inaugural address he said, "What the cynics fail to understand is that the ground has shifted beneath them, that the stale political arguments that have consumed us for so long, no longer apply. The question we ask today is not whether our government is too big or too small, but whether it works—whether it helps families find jobs at a decent wage, care they can afford, a retirement that is dignified. Where the answer is yes, we intend to move forward. Where the answer is no, programs will end."[1]

That's the debate we need to have. What works?

WHY GOVERNMENT SPENDING RARELY WORKS

Our founders were heavily influenced by the eighteenth-century economist Adam Smith, who described the market as an "invisible hand" in which the forces of self-interest, competition, innovation, and supply and demand work together to more or less self-regulate the market and create wealth. Smith wasn't offering a new idea but attempting to explain how people had always behaved and always will in economies. Our founders also understood that the visible hand of government would be clumsy, dumb, and destructive unless tightly controlled by free people.

Nobel-winning economist Milton Friedman, like Smith before him, had a gift for explaining complex systems in commonsense terms. No tool better explains why government tends to be terribly inefficient and wasteful than the Friedman table that follows.[2]

On Whom Money Is Spent

	Yourself	Someone Else
Yours	The Free Market at Maximum Efficiency Free Individuals Shop for Themselves and Exercise Choice	The Free Market, but Less Efficient Free Individuals Buy Gifts for Someone Else Still Efficient but the Best Price Is Not the Highest Value
Someone Else	The Government Economy at Its Best Agency Travel, Junkets	The Government Economy at Its Worst Most Federal Spending, Including "Stimulus"

Whose Money Is Spent (vertical axis label)

Box I

You spend your own money on yourself: In this box category, you have a very strong incentive to get the best value possible at the lowest price you can get. When you go to the supermarket, shop for new clothes, or purchase a new car, you tend to be very careful with your own money. The same is true of business owners. As a physician and as the executive of an optical company, I was very, very careful about buying new equipment and making new hires. Bad decisions would harm not only my bottom line but the well-being of people who worked for me.

Box II

You spend your own money on someone else: We like to think that when we shop for a gift, we are being every bit as careful as we would if we were buying something for ourselves. For some people, that may be true. But in many cases, no matter how pure our intentions, we just aren't as careful about what we spend on others. For example, you may be more likely to spend a few extra dollars on a gift for your fiancée than on yourself. Giving gifts expresses other important values that should be encouraged. Still, spending your money on someone else is not as efficient as spending it on yourself.

Box III

You spend someone else's money on yourself: This box is the expense account. If you're on a business trip, you are much more likely to order steak for dinner if it comes out of the company account rather than your own pocket. This box reminds me of the time I went on a Senate-sponsored trip and was handed cash for per diem spending. When I didn't spend all of the allowance and tried to return the money, the government said I couldn't do that. I was supposed to spend someone else's money on myself. I eventually wrote a check to the Treasury Department to reimburse the government.

Box IV

You spend someone else's money on someone else: Instead of managing your own budget or the budget of your business, in this category, you are a grant officer at a federal agency. You work hard and are well-intentioned, but you are not going to spend money as carefully as you would if you were spending your own money on yourself or someone else.[3]

Anyone who has ever run a business or worked and lived in the real world would find it hard to disagree with this description. Friedman's table describes the world in which we live, not the world politicians would like to imagine. Unfortunately, many politicians in Washington have little real-world experience and, therefore, do not even have the frame of reference to understand why most government spending doesn't work very well and is rarely efficient.

A STIMULUS TOO BIG TO SUCCEED

When President Obama took office, he developed a habit of blaming our bad economy on former president George W. Bush and ignoring the preceding eight decades of big government policies and excessive spending and borrowing that started with former president Franklin Delano Roosevelt. (See chart on page 26.) Nevertheless, the economy was now President Obama's to fix.

His first big solution was to spend $840 billion on a massive "stimulus" spending program, which would become one of the largest laboratories and test chambers for economic ideas in our history. On one side you had the founders, limited-government conservatives, and economists like Adam Smith, Friedrich Hayek, and Milton Friedman. On the other side you had today's career politicians, progressives, Vice President Joe Biden, *New York Times* columnist Paul Krugman, and 1930s economist John Maynard Keynes.[4]

Keynes himself predicted his importance in the debate surrounding the stimulus. As he wrote in his book *The General Theory of Employment, Interest and Money*, "The ideas of economists and political philosophers, both when they are right and when they are wrong, are more powerful than is commonly understood. Indeed the world is ruled by little else. Practical men, who believe themselves to be quite exempt from any intellectual influences, are usually the slaves of some defunct economist."[5]

The key tenet of Keynesian economics is that government spending on massive public works projects can stimulate economic growth and create jobs by stimulating demand. In a recession, the Keynesians argue, government can step in where the private sector is floundering and "prime the pump" with direct government spending. Obama's economic team believed their stimulus would work based on this Keynesian assumption. They believed each dollar of stimulus spending would have a multiplier effect of about $1.50. The term *multiplier effect* is a fancy word for measuring "bang for the buck."

Keynesianism is so popular, and dangerous, because it is so compatible with the congressional politics of instant gratification. For career politicians, there is no greater pleasure in life than spending someone else's money to promote their own reelection campaigns. And it's far easier to send a press release promoting a new grant or spending initiative than to investigate which programs are working. In practice, Keynesianism gives career politicians a pseudo-intellectual justification for being lazy.

Our founders wanted to limit government because they knew that if politicians were ever given the power to spend in Friedman's Box IV, the republic would be doomed. They knew politicians would fight to protect that spending because it would enhance their power base. That's why President Reagan often quipped that the closest thing to eternal life on earth is a government program—precisely because Box IV spending would be difficult to curtail.

The major failing of Keynesians is their refusal to acknowledge that every dollar spent on "stimulus" is a dollar taken out of the economy. In other words, every dollar spent on a big stimulus project is a dollar that cannot be spent by a private citizen, business, or investor. This is important because government does not innovate. Private citizens and businesses innovate.

Keynesians pay lip service to the power of the invisible hand, but then suggest government really does know best. For instance, Keynesians routinely argue that unemployment checks and food stamps are "stimulus" because they give low-income Americans money to spend, and that spending keeps businesses open and jobs in place. It is true those Americans will spend money they may not have otherwise spent. Yet, if food stamps are wonderful stimulus, then why not put everyone on food stamps and in the unemployment line so we can achieve more stimulus? Helping those who truly cannot help themselves is a worthy goal, but it is not real stimulus.

But the debate isn't about food stamps. It's about big projects. And, on that note, the Keynesians' grandest claim—that FDR's New Deal "stimulus" programs in the 1930s got us out of the Great Depression—is just plain wrong. As economists such as Amity Shlaes have noted, government intervention made the Depression great and stretched it out until the 1940s. The clumsy, heavy hand of government prevented the invisible hand of the market from healing the economy. A large percentage of the dollars taken out of the economy in the 1930s for stimulus spending would have been spent more efficiently and productively had they never left the private sector. In spite of grandiose stimulus programs, unemployment was still at 15 percent by 1940, and the stock market would not regain its 1929 peak until the 1950s.[6]

Keynesians are not entirely wrong, however, just 95 percent wrong. Keynesianism works in a few very limited circumstances. For instance, when President Dwight Eisenhower called for the creation of the interstate highway system in the 1950s, there was little doubt the dollars spent on the roads would be worth the investment. Even though businesses large and small would receive an enormous economic benefit from the roads, it was obvious the free market would not create the system on its own. More important, government had the constitutional authority to step in and create the system.

This decades-long debate about Keynesian economics, which is but a chapter in the timeless debate about the proper role of government, was the backdrop for the stimulus debate in 2009. Obama's economic team was unabashedly Keynesian in their outlook. Instead of rebooting our founders and the Constitution, Obama's goal was to reboot the New Deal.

NOT-SO-SHOVEL-READY SPENDING

When the stimulus debate kicked off, it was immediately obvious that many so-called shovel-ready projects were on the shelf precisely because they were never enough of a priority to move off the shelf. The president later admitted "shovel-ready was not as shovel-ready as expected." I and other conservatives argued that serious deficit reduction, spending cuts, lower tax rates, and tax reform would be the best stimulus for the economy. John McCain put forward a $430 billion stimulus bill that accomplished these goals and mixed in a little commonsense stimulus spending Keynesians might support, such as replacing military equipment that had been worn out in Iraq and Afghanistan and repairing our aging infrastructure system.[7] Both approaches would have forward-funded priorities that would have received funding anyway in future years, but the Keynesians complained the McCain alternative didn't spend enough.

I was working to make the case that now was the time to eliminate the more than $300 billion in wasteful spending I had already identified in dozens of oversight hearings and reports. When times are tough, most Americans tighten their belts and cut back on lower-priority spending. Yet, the Keynesians argued that you can't cut spending during a downturn, even if it's wasteful spending.

This was a ridiculous argument. Wasteful spending is a drag on the economy because it has a negative multiplier effect. As Reinhart and Rogoff argue, excessive debt burdens slow economic growth and stunt job growth. Borrowing money to spend on "stimulus" was generational theft. Eventually we would have to pay back what we were borrowing through higher tax rates, higher interest rates, or a debased currency.

Robert Barro, an economics professor at Harvard University and a senior fellow at Stanford University's Hoover Institution, offered a brilliant and scathing critique of the stimulus in the *Wall Street Journal*:

> [The administration assumes] added government spending is a good idea even if the bridge goes to nowhere, or if public employees are just filling useless holes. Of course, if this mechanism is genuine, one might ask why the government should stop with only $1 trillion of added purchases . . .
>
> The usual Keynesian view is that the World War II fiscal expansion provided the stimulus that finally got us out of the Great Depression.[8]

Unfortunately, none of these arguments impressed the president or congressional leaders. Democrats had little interest in negotiating. They rammed through a massive $840 billion stimulus bill that was larded up with earmarks they denied existed, such as $1 billion for the "FutureGen" clean coal plant in Illinois.[9] In defense of their spending orgy, then House Speaker Nancy Pelosi said, "Yes, we wrote the bill, we won the election."

On February 10, 2009, the package sailed through the Senate. I blasted the legislation and warned it would lead to great embarrassment to its authors:

> Instead of writing a bill that will work, Congress passed a bill that puts the ideological interests of one party ahead of the economic interests of the nation. The foundational principles behind this bill were tried and

failed in the 1930s. This bill represents the worst act of generational theft in our history . . .

[The] bill authors made zero effort to eliminate any wasteful spending to help pay for this package even though Congress wastes at least $300 billion every year. Few families in America have the luxury of avoiding tough economic choices. Yet, career politicians in Congress refused to make any tough choices . . .

If history is any guide, a bill of this magnitude will lead to considerable waste and embarrassment to its authors.[10]

The bill had other major flaws. For instance, it included a grossly irresponsible bailout to states that refused to live within their means. This effectively punished states such as Oklahoma that planned ahead and set up rainy-day funds to make it through economic downturns. The bill created a precedent that said states no longer needed to live within their means because the federal government would be there to bail them out. At all levels of government, the stimulus catered to the worst habits of politicians: Why make a hard choice today when you can borrow a dollar and make a hard choice tomorrow? The stimulus gave states such as California, Illinois, Nevada, and Michigan an excuse to delay hard choices that only became more difficult the next budgetary year.

The bill was also a wish list for forty years of pent-up progressive ideological demands. The stimulus laid the groundwork for the Soviet-style Federal Health Board that was a precursor to Obamacare's Independent Payment Advisory Board. The purpose of the board was to put bureaucrats and politicians in charge of our nation's health care system. In other countries, such as the United Kingdom, such boards had led to health care rationing and greatly reduced cure rates for diseases like prostate and breast cancer.[11]

Once the bill became law, I gave my staff the ambitious task of scouring every stimulus program for waste and abuse, which we would expose for the American people. Our first report was ready in June 2009, and we later released two more reports.[12]

Two of our best examples are from my own state of Oklahoma. In one case, Oklahoma was awarded more than $1 million to build a new guardrail next to "Optima Lake" near Woodward, Oklahoma—a lake that was planned in the 1960s but had never filled with water. A former city manager of Woodward, Alan Riffel, had called the lake "one of Oklahoma's greatest boondoggles." Thanks to the stimulus, this boondoggle was set to receive a new guardrail. Fortunately, our oversight helped kill the project.

In another case, the town of Boynton, Oklahoma, was awarded nearly $90,000 to replace a quarter-mile stretch of sidewalk—replaced only five years earlier—leading to a ditch.

The Boyton sidewalk after being repaved with stimulus funds

The same sidewalk in 2011—hardly a pedestrian thoroughfare

"It's 100 percent a waste of money," Boynton resident Ray Allen said of the sidewalk to nowhere, which was receiving funds ahead of a cash-strapped school in town. "They're absolutely throwing money away right now. If they're doing it in a town this size in Oklahoma, they're doing it everywhere."[13]

Allen was absolutely correct. Our office had little trouble identifying wasteful and ill-conceived stimulus projects across the country. We found a $3 million turtle tunnel "eco-passage" in Florida, an $800,000 grant to repave a backup runway at a little-used airport in Pennsylvania, and a $700,000 study asking why monkeys respond negatively to inequity. The stimulus also spent $1.8 million for a road project in Ohio that threatened a pastor's home, $760,000 to help Georgia Tech study improvised music, $5 million to provide geothermal heat to a mall in Tennessee that was virtually empty, and $1 million in "terrorism prevention" money for a dinner cruise company.

Across America the stimulus had become a punch line—the stimulus even gave Northwestern University $700,000 to create a joke machine— but taxpayers were not laughing.

As stimulus dollars flowed to questionable projects and recipients— even the dead received stimulus checks—the president and others fell back on standard Keynesian arguments.

"Some of the criticisms really are with the basic idea that government should intervene at all in this moment of crisis," Obama said. "Now, you have some people, very sincere, who philosophically just think the government has no business interfering in the marketplace. And, in fact, there are several who've suggested that FDR [President Roosevelt] was wrong to intervene back in the New Deal. They're fighting battles that I thought were resolved a pretty long time ago."[14]

Obama was using his favorite straw man. The "some people" was no one. Very few argued that we couldn't have an ounce of Keynesian thought in the stimulus. Our compromise—that we target funding only for vital infrastructure and defense—wasn't even considered.

Three years later, the Keynesians' view was proved almost entirely wrong. The stimulus failed to create the number of jobs it promised.

Even before the bill passed, the Congressional Budget Office delivered what I viewed as a devastating critique. CBO, which tends to be overly optimistic, said, "In the longer run, the legislation would result in a slight decrease in gross domestic product (GDP)."[15]

In hindsight, CBO *was* overly optimistic. For instance, in CBO's worst-case scenario, unemployment would be 8.5 percent at the end of 2009, 8.1 percent at the end of 2010, and 7.2 percent at the end of 2011.[16] The results speak for themselves. In the real world, unemployment was at 10 percent at the end of 2009, 9.4 percent at the end of 2010, and 8.6 percent at the end of 2011.[17]

The administration's own estimates were also overly optimistic. In early 2009, the administration said, with the stimulus, they would create 3.5 million jobs[18] and unemployment would be at 7.25 percent by the end of 2010, while without the stimulus unemployment would be at 8.8 percent.[19] In their worst-case scenario, they estimated the unemployment rate would not go beyond 9 percent with the stimulus.[20] However, using the administration's own estimates, the economy was worse off by the end of 2010 *than it would have been had we not passed the stimulus at all*. By the end of 2010, the unemployment rate was 9.4 percent,[21] which was worse than their own estimate of what it would have been if they had done nothing.

Then, near the end of 2011, CBO came out with another assessment that proved to be a devastating critique. CBO concluded the stimulus may have created or saved as few as 700,000 jobs and that the plan will be a net negative on the economy in the long term. CBO said the additional debt resulting from the stimulus will slow economic growth "by between zero and 0.2 percent after 2016."[22]

Regardless of the facts, progressives continue to argue that the stimulus prevented us from entering another Great Depression. It would have been so much worse had we not passed the stimulus, they argue. But simple math makes their case a hard sell. If the total cost of the stimulus was $840 billion and it created 700,000 jobs, each job was created at the staggering cost of *$1.2 million per job*. Even using the most optimistic estimate[23] of total jobs created would put the cost at about $250,000 per job. We would have been better off sending out checks for that amount. Individuals and families would have spent this money far more efficiently than government.

Conservatives were not at all surprised by the stimulus's failure. We understood that the government can't create jobs. The idea that government can direct an economy is a "fatal conceit," according to noted economist Friedrich Hayek. Hayek says, "The curious task of economics is to demonstrate to men how little they really know about what they imagine they can design."[24]

Hayek was especially critical of government believing it can do effective central planning or "stimulus." In his landmark book *The Road to Serfdom*, Hayek writes, "The effect of the people's agreeing that there must be central planning, without agreeing on the ends, will be rather as if a group of people were to commit themselves to take a journey together without agreeing where they want to go; with the result that they may all have to make a journey which most of them do not want at all."[25]

By the middle of 2011 it was clear the stimulus had taken the country on a journey it did not want. Then the nation learned the Obama administration had steered $535 million in loans to a solar company known as Solyndra that was supposed to create 4,000 jobs only to see the company go bankrupt. Solyndra was troubling because it appeared the loan was made for political rather than economic reasons. One of the administration's key donors also had a financial stake in the company.[26]

In an election year the principle of the Solyndra case will tend to get lost in the politics of the case. The principle is very simple: government does a lousy job of picking winners and losers in the market. The real scandal was the belief that government and people like Energy Secretary Steven Chu—a brilliant physicist who had zero business experience and had to outsource his decisions about how to invest—were more capable of allocating scarce resources than the private sector. Remember, every dollar government wastes on a bad idea is a dollar not available to invest in a good idea. If we want to achieve real innovation and energy security, Solyndra should serve, first and foremost, as a cautionary tale of the need to limit government.

INNOVATION IS THE THING

In a piece titled "Innovation Is the Thing," Rich Lowry at *National Review* argues, "This is the miracle of the modern world: In advanced economies, real income per capita is at least 16 times what it was about 200 years ago."[27]

What enabled that surge in wages and buying power to occur was not state-sponsored stimulus but old-fashioned capitalism, a belief in the free market and a realistic understanding of what motivates people. Government, of course, played a role by providing for a common defense and establishing a limited regulatory framework in which markets could work, but government was not the thing. Innovation spurred by creative individuals and enterprises was—and is—the thing.

Innovation also gives free people the opportunity to pursue not merely material wealth but the happiness that comes from knowing they have worked hard, applied themselves, and created something of value. Arthur Brooks, president of the American Enterprise Institute, put it well: "The government can redistribute money until the cows come home, but they can't redistribute earned success."[28]

The stimulus reminded America that the redistribution of wealth doesn't create much of anything. The commonsense skepticism of people like Ray Allen of Boynton, Oklahoma, who scratched his head at the sidewalk to nowhere, is well-founded. If money was being wasted in Boynton, it was being wasted everywhere.

The central challenge of our time is not to remember what government can do, but what it cannot do very well. We are on the edge of an abyss not because we had too little faith in government but because we had too much faith.

In the debate between the founders and today's career politicians and progressives, the stimulus rendered a resounding verdict in favor of our founders.

So what works?

A government that works is a government that is limited.

THE PROBLEM

The idea that politicians can grow the economy by growing government has been refuted repeatedly throughout history, most recently by the Obama administration's failed stimulus effort.

The best way to make something expensive is for government to make it affordable. That is true in any area of the economy, from housing to health care to education.

Today's government is too big to succeed. Excessive government spending crowds out private investment and misallocates scarce resources.

Highlighting government's innate incompetence and limitations is not anti-government extremism. It is an observation based on fact and evidence.

The problem today is not a lack of faith in government. The problem is, we have put too much faith in government.

PART 2

The Solution

Defusing the Debt Bomb

7

In the Arena

It is not the critic who counts; not the man who points out how the strong man stumbles, or where the doer of deeds could have done them better. The credit belongs to the man who is actually in the arena, whose face is marred by dust and sweat and blood; who strives valiantly; who errs, who comes short again and again, because there is no effort without error and shortcoming; but who does actually strive to do the deeds; who knows great enthusiasms, the great devotions; who spends himself in a worthy cause; who at the best knows in the end the triumph of high achievement, and who at the worst, if he fails, at least fails while daring greatly, so that his place shall never be with those cold and timid souls who neither know victory nor defeat.

—President Teddy Roosevelt, from the speech
"Citizenship in a Republic," delivered at the
Sorbonne in Paris, France, on April 23, 1910

MORE THAN ONE HUNDRED YEARS AFTER TEDDY ROOSEVELT'S speech, a group of United States senators serving on the Senate Finance Committee met in a private session. The world economy seemed to be unraveling, unemployment was rampant, and our debt was already slowing our economy.

The end-of-the-year meeting in 2011 was held to discuss how to handle what had become the annual holiday train wreck in Washington when important bills were put off until the last minute. Not long after Chairman Max Baucus (D-MT) began to go through the agenda, the meeting turned into an intervention—with ourselves.

Senator Olympia Snowe (R-ME) had enough of the delays. "Are we even going to fix this?" she asked. "We should have this meeting in January. We've known all this was coming. The committees of jurisdiction should be doing these. Are we just going to keep doing this year and after, in lurches? It's preposterous. We should use this occasion to do something right so we aren't embarrassed we wasted the last two years of America's life."

It was an important point. The Senate Finance Committee is in many ways *the* committee of jurisdiction in the Senate. We oversaw the largest portions of the budget—health care, entitlements, and taxes—in the wealthiest nation in the history of the world. Interestingly, the Senate Finance Committee included four senators who served on President Obama's National Commission on Fiscal Responsibility and Reform (the Simpson-Bowles Commission), three senators from the Gang of Six, and three senators from the supercommittee. Any solutions would come through us and should begin with us.

"We have to do something, not just say we are doing something," Senator Mike Enzi (R-WY) said.

"I'd like us to be senators again and do what we are supposed to be doing. Instead we keep kicking the can down the road," Baucus agreed.

Senator Kent Conrad (D-ND) leaned in and whispered to me, "This is a very critical meeting." It seemed the committee was waking up and accepting responsibility.

Senator Ron Wyden (D-OR) added, "If this committee really came together I believe we could do tax reform."

He was right. The fact that we had not done tax reform in *25 years*— since 1986—was a pox on both houses. Neither party wanted to let go of their favorite loopholes, exemptions, and deductions, even though doing so could lower rates and spur tremendous economic growth and job creation. Each side had a schizophrenic approach to tax reform that said, "Support simplification, give me complexity."

I added, "Most of us know what needs to be done, and significant reform on entitlements is needed. We need to reform the code, lower rates, generate revenue, and address our deficit."

Our discussion showed that many in Congress—and the administration—understood the severity of our problem. We all knew that we could not continue to borrow more than 40 cents for every dollar we spent. Yet, few were willing to risk their political careers to solve the problem. Most politicians were content to sit in their partisan bunkers and cling to the illusion that they were holding a line, when the reality was, there were no more lines left to hold. Both parties had betrayed their core beliefs and positions. We were under siege and surrounded on all sides, not by a foreign army but by foreign creditors.

Still, even in their bunkers, Republicans and Democrats could sense the political landscape shifting beneath their feet. The Tea Party had mobilized. Republican politicians who had long since gone AWOL in the fight to preserve our founding principles of limited government were terrified of losing reelection. Washington was at last ready to make a concerted effort to at least *look* serious about dealing with our fiscal crisis.

Some of us, though, *were* serious. We were ready to risk

everything—including our reputations—to come up with a solution. The island-hopping campaign—the battles on earmarks, the holds, the oversight hearings and reports, countless amendments to cut spending—had brought us to within striking distance of the real problem: unsustainable spending, especially in entitlements.

THE SIMPSON-BOWLES COMMISSION

Washington's method for putting our nation on a sustainable fiscal course was, not surprisingly, a commission. The problem with this approach was we already had a debt commission. It was called Congress.

Commissions are popular in Washington because they are a natural expression of the double-minded careerism that rules the city. On one hand, politicians say they want to do the right thing: cut wasteful spending and reduce the deficit. On the other hand, they don't want to anger special interests and be punished for cutting spending. A commission is the perfect solution for career politicians: it gives them all of the benefits of appearing responsible without actually having to take responsibility for any decision.

Commissions also expose the lack of integrity behind many of the so-called constitutional justifications for spending money on things that are not constitutional. Politicians love to invoke the constitutional power of the purse when it involves protecting their earmarks and pet priorities. Yet, when it comes to cutting spending and actually solving the country's fiscal problems, they are more than happy to give away that power to a commission. If members approached spending cuts with the same zeal they chased earmarks, we would have balanced the budget long ago.

The first commission was President Obama's deficit reduction commission. At the outset, the president was doubled-minded. He wanted to brandish his deficit reduction credentials heading into the 2012 election after spending trillions on a failed stimulus and a doomed health care plan. Yet, he also understood the danger of our debt and wanted to solve the problem.

In 2010, the president assured me he would go farther than anyone expects in terms of deficit reduction. He was signaling that when the moment of truth arrived, he would go for a grand bargain that would put everything on the table and include enough savings to at least start the process of putting the country back on course. Still, he didn't want to solve it badly enough to offer a plan on his own or push it from the bully pulpit.

In spite of my skepticism, when Senator McConnell asked me to serve on the commission, I could not say no. If the commission process and the president were not going to be serious, then I was. I was going to tip every sacred cow in sight and describe in painful detail the disastrous consequences of doing nothing.

Going into the commission, which was chaired by former senator Al Simpson (R-WY) and former president Clinton's chief of staff, Erskine Bowles, many observers on both sides misunderstood my goals and intentions. The liberals on the commission assumed I would simply block whatever was proposed. After all, I was "Dr. No" in their eyes. To them, my caricature was my character.

Meanwhile, many conservative observers assumed that because President Obama obviously hoped to benefit politically from forming a commission, the more conservative members of the commission would deny him an opportunity to look serious when he wasn't being serious. However, I didn't care the slightest bit who would be helped or hurt politically by the commission. Our economic condition was so dire that I was committed to using the process to advance the national debate about how we can save trillions of dollars and recommit ourselves to the founders' vision of limited government. If we didn't begin that process soon, the choices would become much more painful. We'd be facing a lost decade—or worse.

In the commission's early months, while little more was happening then a series of public hearings on the debt, I laid the groundwork with other commission members for real spending cuts. And I made it clear no area of the budget would be sacrosanct. From defense spending to the tax code, to health care and Social Security, I was determined to provide as many ideas for deficit reduction as possible.

In April, before even the first commission meeting, my staff compiled a three-inch binder, complete with more than four hundred pages outlining more than $150 billion in government waste and duplication, across every agency in the discretionary budget. This extensive menu of options was affectionately termed by some as the Coburn Bible. Yet, despite my effort to include all areas of federal spending, some of my colleagues dismissed this effort as partisan or not very serious. One staffer of a Republican commission member called to ask us if this was "just a bunch of earmark stuff" and if they really needed to look it over. Still, some saw the value of being specific. Executive Director Bruce Reed read every word of the binder, thanked me for the ideas, and even asked for more.

I told him he need not worry. I had more on the way. On May 18, 2010, less than one month after the commission's first meeting, I sent to each commission member a detailed, ten-page memo outlining the significant spending and mismanagement problems currently plaguing the Pentagon and adding hundreds of billions of dollars to our deficit every year. The memo suggested significant reforms and spending reductions at the Department of Defense. I hoped to find a way to signal to each member of the commission that I was willing to sacrifice what some in my own party believe to be untouchable areas of the budget in hopes we could find some areas of agreement in addressing the fiscal crisis.

I also was not afraid of going for a grand bargain and being accused of compromising. As much as I wanted Washington to be run by a governing majority of constitutional conservatives like me, there simply wasn't time to elect enough constitutional conservatives to get us out of danger. Congress was far out at sea in a perfect storm. We didn't have time to sail back to port and change out the crew. We would have to sober up, and quickly.

In the spring of 2010 when the commission first met, I believed a downgrade and even a depression were real possibilities in the near future. Japan and several European countries were on the brink of defaulting, and the euro itself was not likely to survive.

If conservatives waited to fix the problem until 2012, as many wanted, we would have to win the White House, maintain a solid majority in the House, and win about sixty-five seats in the Senate to control the national agenda. In the Senate, nothing can move without sixty votes, and even that is not enough, because a few moderate Republicans will often vote to violate the principles of limited government and their oath. There simply wasn't time to elect sixty or more constitutional conservatives to the Senate. We'd sink first.

Even if by some miracle Republicans reached this magic number, the culture of careerism in Washington would almost certainly undermine a conservative solution. This is precisely what happened when Republicans took control of Congress in 1994 and last controlled the White House under President Bush. Instead of cutting spending and reducing the size of government, Republicans embarked on an orgy of pork-barrel spending and expanded the welfare state. If we waited until 2012 or 2014, we would hear the same excuses for inaction that conservatives heard throughout the 1990s and Bush presidency. Our majority would never be secure enough to act.

I knew my openness to a grand bargain would anger some in the

Republican establishment and phony K Street conservatives in Washington. I had no interest in catering to the special-interest groups and professional activists—community organizers—on the Republican side who wanted to establish the rules of appropriate compromise. In fact, I was eager to challenge their false purity tests and perverse defenses of Republican careerism. Some of their warnings about negotiating with Democrats were valid, but in many cases their certitude was not matched by their experience. Most Washington operatives had no real-world experience. Their practical knowledge of negotiating was limited to deciding who spoke when at lunches and where to hold conferences. I had run a business and had negotiated with unions and wasn't terribly impressed by their lectures. Having served in the 1990s, I also knew that the only thing more dangerous than negotiating with Democrats was negotiating with Republicans.

The Simpson-Bowles Commission met for several months, starting in April 2010. For the typical American, our closed meetings would have been both inspiring and disturbing. At its best, the commission had a spark of the grand bargain that created our Constitution more than two hundred years ago. You had eighteen people who, for the most part, were willing to debate real issues and negotiate in good faith. On the other hand, it was obvious many of our key national leaders were well-intentioned but out of their depth. They lacked the frame of reference to judge the severity of our problems, much less craft solutions. Few commission members, and few members of Congress for that matter, had any significant experience outside of government. Even worse, most had already convinced themselves of what could not be done.

I'll never forget, before one commission meeting, discussing productivity gains in business with David Cote, a commission member and CEO of Honeywell International, a Fortune 100 technology company. As we traded stories, another commission member came by and asked what we were discussing. This member, despite having spent decades in Congress, had never heard of productivity gains in business. It took thirty minutes to explain how the goal in the private sector is doing more with less—in other words achieving productivity gains. It was a stark reminder of how separated Washington had become from the real world. Doing more with less truly is a foreign concept in Washington, which is why the commission had been formed in the first place.

After months of meetings, the commission settled on a proposal that would reduce the deficit by about $4 trillion over ten years. The plan would cut spending by about $3 trillion and generate $1 trillion in revenue through reducing tax rates and eliminating spending in the tax code.

The plan—called the Moment of Truth[1]—was a breakthrough in some ways, but it had many deep flaws. Most important, it did not save or reform Medicare, which was by far the biggest driver of our long-term deficits. Health care had essentially been taken off the table at the beginning. Washington was suffering from Obamacare fatigue, and the Democrats on the commission would not agree to reopen that contentious debate.

When it came time to vote on the plan, I urged the other members to at least make a down payment and put the country on a path toward dealing with the enormous challenges before us.

I made my appeal before the commission members in a crowded hearing room on December 1, 2010:

> As a physician, I'm trained to find the real problem, not the symptoms but the real disease. The real disease is we've abandoned the concepts of our founders. We've created reliance instead of depending on self-reliance. We've created government programs that are unaffordable. We've abandoned limited government. We've abandoned the enumerated powers. Now we're in trouble and nobody is looking at what the real problem is. And the real problem is us.

We're rotting. We're rotting as we sit here and speak today . . . we have way too much government and not enough of the thing that made America great, which is independence, personal responsibility, and self-reliance . . . We're out of control as a government. We've abandoned the principles that made America exceptional, which wasn't the government. It was the people. It was us relying on ourselves, not saying I can take a pass and depend on the government . . . Those who can't fix their situation any other way, we ought to help them, but that's not what we've created in our country.

This plan is a plan . . . I have heartache with tons of it, but I know we have to go forward. This is just the down payment.

Will we come together and put something out—even though probably 50 percent I'm not happy with—as a down payment that makes a statement that says this problem is so real, Tom Coburn can't have what he wants. And I can't. I'm going to have to sacrifice. My family is going to sacrifice. But I want to make sure my grandchildren have some of the same opportunities and freedoms I've experienced.

The potential for us to re-embrace the real character and success of America only will come if we embrace the principles our founders embraced. When Benjamin Franklin was asked—you've all heard this—what did you do, he said I gave you a republic if you can keep it.

Well, I think we ought to be cheating history. History says we're not going to make it. The way we cheat history is for all of us to give up something. Everybody at this table, give up something and then say the way forward for America is for everybody to start sacrificing so we create a future that honors the tremendous sacrifices that came before us.[2]

The House Republicans privately supported the tax-reform component of the plan—lowering rates and broadening the base—but because the entitlement reforms were not significant enough, they refused to go along. This was a disappointment because the problem was too big not to do something. Voting no was a missed opportunity to help force the debate in Congress.

More than anything I wanted to put these issues on the Senate floor and force both Democrats and Republicans to act and avert a crisis. I was convinced that if the plan ever did make it to the floor, it would either move significantly to the right or it would die. There was no chance the plan we were putting forward would become law as it was. Still, rather than offer a milquetoast endorsement that only said we wanted to debate the recommendations, the Senate Republicans on the commission— Mike Crapo, Judd Gregg, and me—decided to unambiguously support the commission's recommendations.

We all knew we would be shot at from all sides and have our motives questioned by interest groups. The problems before us were so enormous that I was more than willing to face those questions and attacks.

Mike Crapo and I decided to offer a joint statement. We went to the Senate Radio-TV gallery and released this statement:

Our debt crisis is a threat to not just our way of life, but our national survival. History has not been kind to great nations who borrowed and spent beyond their means. Doing nothing will, sooner rather than later, guarantee that this nation becomes a second-rate power with less opportunity and less freedom. The plan developed by the debt commission, while flawed and incomplete, will help America avoid this fate and secure freedom for future generations.

The time for action is now. We can't afford to wait until the next election to begin this process. Long before the skyrocketing cost of entitlements causes our national debt to triple and tax rates to double, our economy may collapse under the weight of this burden. We are already near a precipice . . .

This plan will not just avert a disaster, but help drive the kind of economic recovery we need to create jobs and spur growth. The plan's provisions to lower tax rates while creating fairness in the tax code are similar to pro-growth policies supported by President Reagan. The plan also reduces discretionary spending and takes meaningful steps to preserve Social Security. Taking steps now to reduce our debt burden and slow unsustainable entitlement spending can help prevent massive and debilitating tax increases in the future. Finally, all of these steps will send a clear signal to investors that America is serious about getting its fiscal house in order.

Still, the plan does not do nearly enough to address the crisis in health care spending. Eighty percent of our debt problem comes from Medicare . . . We also have to repeal the misguided health care law we passed last year, which will make our debt crisis even more severe.

The real choice facing Congress and the American people, however, is not whether to support the commission's recommendations, but whether we will rediscover the wisdom of our founders and apply the principles of limited government written into our Constitution. The debt problem is almost entirely the consequence of growing government far beyond our founders' intent. This plan is merely a down payment that will begin the process of reforming government at all levels.

. . . This challenge is a matter of national survival but we know America has faced great challenges before and emerged stronger and more prosperous. The good news is all of these problems can be solved. If we act now in the spirit of service and sacrifice that built this country, we can create a future that honors the tremendous sacrifice that came before us.[3]

In the end, eleven of the eighteen commission members supported the plan, three votes short of the fourteen required to report our findings.

We reported our findings anyway. More important, winning a majority vote set three critical precedents that would shape future talks.

First, we showed that both sides—progressives like Durbin and conservatives like me—were willing to cross the Rubicon and challenge the party orthodoxy on their respective sides. Second, while a few Republican activists howled it was a "tax increase," many free-market conservatives, such as Stephen Moore of the *Wall Street Journal*, recognized the importance of having a liberal like Durbin embrace tax reform[4] that reduced tax rates and did away with tax earmarks that misdirected capital. Simpson-Bowles was much more like Reagan's 1986 tax reform than President Obama's rate-hike proposals.

Finally, we set the precedent of forcing a down payment on spending cuts to avoid the bait-and-switch trap in which Washington enacts tax hikes but not spending cuts. This "trust but verify" approach would be key to any grand bargain.

Unfortunately, President Obama refused to embrace the recommendations and offered almost no feedback. His decision, I believe, will be remembered as one the greatest failures of presidential leadership in American history. As the year unfolded, Simpson-Bowles would remain the high-water mark of bipartisan deficit reduction efforts.

Gang of Six

As the Simpson-Bowles meetings were ongoing, another group of bipartisan senators, led by Saxby Chambliss (R-GA) and Mark Warner (D-VA), had been meeting throughout the year to rally support for a deficit reduction plan, which would hopefully be Simpson-Bowles.

After the Simpson-Bowles report was released, four of the remaining six senators who served on the commission joined forces with the Warner-Chambliss group and became known as the Gang of Six. Our hope was to put the Simpson-Bowles report into legislative language. The task would prove immensely difficult.

We spent months negotiating and made good progress in some areas, but we got so bogged down in process and procedure that we never truly improved upon the framework we started with. Like Simpson-Bowles, we agreed in principle that any deficit reduction package should be heavily weighted to spending cuts. The ratio of cuts to revenue would be about 3 to 1, and the revenue would come through economic growth generated by tax rate *reductions* and the elimination of tax earmarks and deductions that distorted the economy.

We also negotiated a strong down-payment mechanism that would force Congress to enact some spending cuts before tackling tax reform and further spending cuts. Had the Gang of Six plan ever made it to the floor, the most likely outcome would have been the enactment of this down payment and nothing else.

The plan had a four-step process. First would have been a down payment of about $500 billion dollars. This was perhaps the best aspect of the plan. It required real cuts to be implemented before anything else could happen. In the worst-case scenario we would cut spending by $500 billion and advance the moral imperative of cutting spending before revenue increases would be considered.

Step two of the plan would have required Congress to come up with additional spending cuts and tax reform. Step three would have been Social Security reform. Finally, step four would have merged steps two and three in one package. The group decided that steps three and four would stand or fall together.

In early drafts, one of the plan's main flaws was that too many of the key decisions would be left to committees. We decided this was unavoidable. Even if the six members could have agreed on the perfect tax reform plan, for instance, it would have been dead on arrival once it arrived in the Senate Finance Committee, which had jurisdiction over tax reform and would defend its turf. As a result, we simply punted tax reform to that committee, though I had little confidence in the committee's ability to get its act together and tackle real tax reform.

President Obama's decision to deliver a polarizing speech in April 2011 about his supposed "budget framework" in the middle of our negotiations also did not help matters. The president had invited House Budget Committee Chairman Paul Ryan (R-WI), who had offered a detailed plan of his own, only to lambaste Ryan's effort. The irony was that the president's proposal was so thin that Congressional Budget Office Director Douglas Elmendorf told Congress, "We don't estimate speeches . . . We need much more specificity than was provided in that speech for us to do our analysis."[5]

Democrats who wanted our effort to succeed were disappointed with the White House because they knew the president's speech would complicate our negotiations and take us a few steps backward from the work the commission had started a year earlier. Also about this time, third-party groups funded by liberal donors started running ads featuring a Paul Ryan look-alike pushing a senior off a cliff. The Democratic establishment's decision to demagogue Medicare sent a clear signal that the party was not remotely serious about entitlement reform.

In June 2011, I told the group we needed to balance what we were giving up through revenue changes with real entitlement reform. Even though we would be embracing tax rate reductions, we still had to convince our colleagues that doing away with spending in the tax code really would be used for deficit reduction and not funding for broken entitlement programs. Again, the fact was our starting point— Simpson-Bowles—addressed the need for comprehensive tax reform, as well as Social Security reform, but fell short on reforming health care entitlement programs. Without serious entitlement reform, there was no way the plan would get any traction with Republicans in Congress.

The agreement had other problems. For instance, we delegated most of the real spending cuts and reforms to Senate committees that were all controlled by Democrats, few of whom had expressed interest in entitlement reform. As a result, Social Security and Medicare reform would never happen.

A couple of weeks after I made my pitch for more courageous steps toward entitlement reform, it appeared we had a breakthrough on Medicare and Medicaid. However, overnight, the deal fell apart. Democrats seemed to be concerned with how the deal would look politically. They argued that our Medicare cuts would be greater than the cuts in Paul Ryan's budget. This was false but they backtracked anyway.

I then told the group, "Okay, then give me $130 billion in [entitlement] cuts somewhere else."

Through the next two weeks, Durbin complained about how much he had given up. "Anything I give you will cost me so you can get support," he said. Durbin was irritated that he would lose support from his liberal base for anything he gave up that might satisfy conservatives.

When I finally realized we weren't going to put a grand bargain together, I called Durbin. "I think we're at an impasse," I said.

"We have been at an impasse for two weeks, so I agree," he replied.

Later that day I told reporters I was taking a sabbatical from the Gang of Six talks. I was open to returning, but only if the plan would actually solve the problem instead of just pretending to. Yet for me, this would be a working sabbatical. I would spend the next several weeks on the most ambitious oversight project my office had undertaken. We would go through the entire federal budget and identify trillions in waste to show it is possible to identify major savings if Congress would muster the will and courage to act.

Still, the bottom line with the Gang of Six was, we negotiated a framework that was less aggressive than the deficit commission plan—and the commission plan did not effectively deal with Medicare and Medicaid.

LEVERAGING THE DEBT-CEILING DEBATE

During meetings of the Gang of Six, one deadline looming over our heads was the coming debate about raising the debt ceiling. The day after the 2010 elections, I told a reporter with the *Daily Caller* that I would block a debt-limit extension that was not paid for with spending cuts. When they asked if I was willing to let the country default, I said, "Sure, and that's the whole point. That's why the leverage is there to actually make the changes that need to be made for the country . . . We're in deep trouble, and you don't get out of that with timid solutions."[6]

I had never voted for a debt-limit increase because there is no debt limit in practice. We always raise it. Even so, Tea Party freshmen were as eager as I was to use the debate to push for real cuts. The debt-limit debate would be a rare moment when conservatives might have leverage to force real spending cuts. It would also be the mother of all offset battles and would apply the "dollar for dollar" test (if you want to spend a dollar you have to save a dollar) to a bill that would spend trillions rather than millions or billions.

President Obama and most Democrats were furious that the debt limit would not be raised automatically, as in years past. The president argued that raising the debt limit was simply paying the bill for something you already purchased and that it was irresponsible to engineer a crisis over what should be a routine vote.

The president, however, was wrong about the economics. If we didn't enact a serious deficit reduction package soon, we would face a downgrade or worse, regardless of whether we raised the debt limit. Again, we had already maxed out the credit card and were ordering another card just to pay off the interest on the other cards.

Still, the president was correct that there was a fair amount of partisan hypocrisy in the debt-limit debate. Every Republican still serving in the Senate in 2011 except for yours truly voted for President Bush's debt-limit extension in 2006 when our long-term economic outlook was also bleak and when we were on the eve of the collapse of the housing bubble.

As the summer dragged on without an agreement to pay for an extension of the debt limit, members went into crisis mode and started to look for alternatives. It was around this time, in July 2011, that I decided to release my own list of recommendations. I instructed my staff to review the entire federal budget by going agency by agency, line by line, and look at what was and was not working. I didn't start with an arbitrary target. Instead, I wanted to look at how much waste we could uncover in a government that was so monstrous it was nearly impossible to see all of it at once. After weeks of research we outlined $9 trillion in savings from across the entire federal budget in a 624-page report entitled *Back in Black*. The report was the product of a thorough and exhaustive review but it also showed my colleagues how easy it is to find major savings when we have the will to try. Congress, however, did not yet have the appetite for the kind of reforms I was suggesting, but they will sooner rather than later.

Also in July 2011, the Democrats in the Gang of Six were eager to roll out their updated plan. With time running out before a default, the president stepped up his involvement. On July 19, 2011, during our weekly staff meeting, my scheduler walked in at 10:30 a.m. and said, "It's the president." I sent my staff out of the office and talked to the president for a few minutes. This was the third time we had talked in four days. Both the president and Speaker Boehner were using the Gang of Six process as a back channel and sounding board to move the negotiations toward a grand bargain. The president also knew from our friendship that I was not pushing for cuts to play a political game or to try to embarrass him.

Even though the Gang of Six plan had not improved substantially since I left (I did win additional cuts to health care spending but not explicit entitlement reform), I decided now was the time to rejoin the group. When I announced my decision to a meeting of senators, the room broke out in applause. It seemed a serious deficit reduction plan may not be so impossible after all.

At 1:30 p.m. on July 19, 2011, the president went to the podium to brief reporters on the status of deficit talks.[7] I didn't know what he was going to say. Shortly after he started he essentially embraced our plan. Even though the Gang of Six never intended to attach our plan to the debt-limit increase, a compromise based on our outline was suddenly the best hope of avoiding a downgrade or default.

The little momentum we had, however, soon dissipated. The release of our plan was chaotic. All we had were three pages describing a framework but no bill, which left the product open to interpretation and criticism. The summary, for instance, used three different budget baselines to illustrate our points, which gave detractors endless ways to criticize our work. Some said it was a tax cut, while others said it was a $2 trillion tax increase. Some said it didn't touch entitlements; still others said it gutted entitlements. The truth was, we were sticking by our 3 to 1 agreement, but, without a bill, we could not back that up and explain why a stalemate was the surest way to see financial repression.

Then, on Friday, July 22, the Gang of Six effort was derailed when the president essentially used our work as a bargaining chip in a dueling press conference with Speaker Boehner. The president claimed we wanted to raise taxes by $2 trillion when I had not agreed to that number. Republicans were already irritated that my decision to rejoin the gang diverted attention from the "cut, cap, and balance" vote in the House. I had no intention of stepping on their vote and had actually stepped on my own plan, *Back in Black*, which I thought was vastly superior to the Gang of Six framework.

With no hope of a major breakthrough, the Year of the Commission ended as it began, with a deal that would create another commission. This time it would be a "super" committee. The deal essentially allowed the president to raise the debt ceiling by as much as $1.5 trillion in exchange for an alleged $917 billion in cuts and the creation of a "super" committee that would try to reach a broad deficit reduction agreement like Simpson-Bowles. If the supercommittee failed to come to an agreement $1.2 trillion across-the-board cuts ("sequestration") would go into effect.

On Saturday, July 30—two days before the debt-limit deadline—I had dinner with John Boehner and Saxby Chambliss, who had been close friends since serving together in the House. I shared my concerns with the Speaker, and he asked how I'd get to a better outcome. I couldn't give him a good answer. I had argued to my Republicans the week before that a default triggered by refusing to lift the debt ceiling really would be the best outcome if we would stick together and weather the storm. I was convinced our deficits had become so severe that our national credit rating would be downgraded anyway and our economy would continue to flounder. The shock therapy of a default could be the thing that awakened Congress. Unless we could stick together, however, it made little sense for me or one of the new members to mount a kamikaze mission to delay the vote and force a default.

Sure enough, the deal passed. But I was convinced it would not work. The caps in the bill would easily be evaded. The whole process was a farce and a missed opportunity to reach a breakthrough.

The minute after the bill passed, I wrote in a *Washington Post* op-ed:

The good news out of the debt debate is that Washington is now debating how much we can cut instead of how much we can spend. The American people deserve all the credit for forcing that change. Unfortunately, it's still all talk in Washington . . .

In spite of what politicians on both sides are saying, this agreement does not cut any spending over 10 years. In fact, it increases discretionary spending by $830 billion.

I voted against this agreement because it does nothing to address the real drivers of our debt. It eliminates no program, consolidates no duplicative programs, cuts no tax earmarks and reforms no entitlement program. The specter of default or a credit downgrade will still hang over our economy after this deal becomes law.[8]

DOWNGRADE ARRIVES

A few days later, my warning came true. We were downgraded. It was a humiliating moment for our country. Not surprisingly, politicians lashed out at the Tea Party when they only had themselves to blame.

I called the downgrade announcement "long overdue" and said, "For decades, political careerism has trumped statesmanship in Washington. Both parties have done what is safe for them, not what is right for the country. The dysfunction in Washington is the belief that we can live beyond our means forever. We can't. The moment to make the hard decisions we have long avoided has arrived. There is nowhere left to kick the can."[9]

Virtually everyone in Congress would privately admit that the only answer was to strike a deal that combined entitlement reform with tax reform. We refused to take that risk and were paying the price for our embrace of careerism over country. We were reaping what we had sown long ago and had refused to confront over the past thirty years.

THE BIG LIE OF 2011

As many predicted, the supercommittee failed to reach a broad deficit reduction deal late in 2011. The process ended with not even a whimper. It was another triumph of politicians and the culture of careerism. Even the promise of spending cuts through a process called sequestration—which was supposed to go into effect if the supercommittee failed—was a farce. Spending over the next ten years was set to *increase* by $1.65 trillion even with sequestration. And defense spending, which is supposedly facing massive cuts, is set to increase by 16 percent *with* sequestration.[10]

In November 2011, I went to the floor to expose what I was calling the big lie of 2011—the idea that we were cutting spending when we were not. I said:

> We need to quit lying to the American people about what we are doing. A 9 percent approval rating is well earned as long as we are dishonest with the American people about what we are actually doing. They understand the problem. We're broke.
>
> We have taken a stupid pill and now we sit bankrupt, physically bankrupt and fiscally bankrupt at this moment except we just haven't recognized it yet. What's happening in Europe is going to happen to us.[11]

I had also learned House Republican leaders were not passing appropriations bills because they could not get conservative votes. My thought was, *Why not make the bills conservative? Then they will pass.* This logic, of course, was too simple. The inability of alleged budget cutters to cut spending, along with their willingness to lie about it, was an eerie reminder of the Republican dysfunction of the late 1990s, when our leaders rationalized overspending for short-term political gain.

Even with Sequester, Federal Budget
Expands by Nearly $2 Trillion from 2012 to 2021[12]

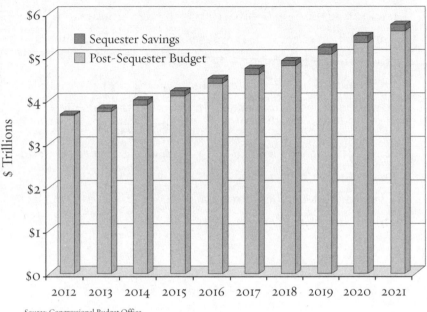

Source: Congressional Budget Office

I wasn't about to let this happen again. Even if Congress was not willing to accept deficit reduction measures along the scope of Simpson-Bowles or *Back in Black*'s $9 trillion savings, I had no doubt events and simple math would force these choices on us.

THE SOLUTION

Dismantling the debt bomb will require a solution that will be a combination of revenue increases, spending cuts, and, most of all, entitlement reform.

Republicans and Democrats who argue otherwise are lying to the American people and pandering in order to win reelection.

Doing nothing would be the act of betrayal for both sides. Doing nothing will lead to both massive tax increases and benefit cuts in entitlement programs.

We need to solve these problems today, not wait for a perfect moment that will never arrive.

8

Duplication Nation

Lord, the money we do spend on Government, and
it's not one bit better than the government we got
for one-third the money twenty years ago.

—WILL ROGERS[1]

WHEN WASHINGTON DECIDES OR—MORE LIKELY—IS FORCED TO confront our unsustainable fiscal course, the scope of deficit reduction required to solve the problem will be much closer to $9 trillion over ten years than the $1 trillion or so in phony cuts that have been considered in Washington.

A reasonable breakdown of those savings will be: $3 trillion from entitlements, $3 trillion from discretionary and other accounts, $1 trillion in defense, $1 trillion from ending some spending in the tax code, and about $1 trillion through avoiding interest costs.

This approach will gradually balance the budget within ten years, avert a crisis, and promote real growth. Doing half of what I propose (in the ballpark of Simpson-Bowles) would be a down payment. Anything less than $4 to $5 trillion isn't serious, and anyone who proposes no

Savings Breakdown in *Back in Black*

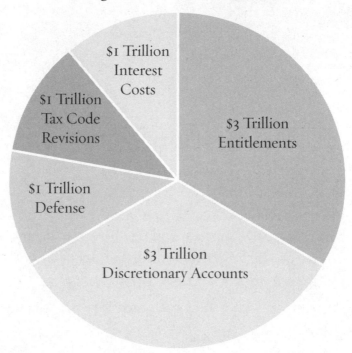

solutions should be fired. Let me pause to make an important point about Washington math.

Deficit reduction and spending cuts are not necessarily the same thing. Spending cuts shrink government while deficit reduction *reduces the anticipated growth in spending.* In other words, deficit reduction reduces deficits from what they otherwise would have been, but does not necessarily shrink government. Deficit reduction is still a critically important goal because high debt burdens kill economic growth, but it is not necessarily a spending cut. As a $9 trillion deficit reduction proposal, *Back in Black* seems radical to many in Washington. While it goes further than any other menu of options, it only cuts spending—or shrinks the real size of government—by $1 trillion over ten years. The House-passed budget—the Path to Prosperity—would actually increase spending by $2.1 trillion over ten years, but as a deficit reduction package it is still excellent because it would save $4.4 trillion more than the president's plan. Nine trillion dollars in *deficit reduction* is not radical at all. It's common sense. And it's a matter of national survival.[2]

So let's look closer at how we get to real savings. It's easier than it looks in a government as bloated and wasteful as ours.

Again, earmarks were the first target in the island-hopping campaign on the way to the ultimate goal of reducing the deficit by $9 trillion or so and putting America on a sustainable path. As I explained in Chapter 4, eliminating earmarks was an extremely important victory, and the credit really does belong to you—the American taxpayer—who said "enough is enough." As late as 2009, the goal of stopping carmarks seemed like a fool's errand to the Washington establishment. We the People proved them wrong.

The next step in our fight for survival should be ending duplication in the federal budget. When it comes to potential savings, the government is full of low-hanging fruit. And the fruit doesn't hang much lower than duplication.

A GOVERNMENT WITHOUT AN INVENTORY

When I came to the Senate, I routinely pressed agency heads to provide information about the programs they managed. After numerous failed attempts to get a clear inventory of overlapping federal programs, I concluded that the cause was something worse—and more dangerous—than agency heads simply trying to dodge the question. Agency heads literally had no idea of how many programs they were managing. I know because I asked them personally. Only the Department of

Education could tell me how many programs they administered. Agency heads were like store managers who didn't have an inventory.

The process was flabbergasting. Even the Congressional Research Service and, initially, the Government Accountability Office (GAO) said they couldn't tell me how many programs were in their agencies. Eventually I concluded the best way to get answers was to require it by the force of law. When Congress approved a debt-limit extension in 2010 (the year before Republicans finally decided raising the debt limit without cutting spending was a bad idea), I successfully attached an amendment requiring the GAO to conduct a study of duplication in federal spending.

I was convinced that if the American people could see a glimpse of the vast amount of duplication and sheer stupidity in the federal government, they would demand the changes we desperately needed.

When the report was finally ready in February 2011, the GAO confirmed my suspicions. I told a group of reporters the findings will make "all of us look like jackasses."[3]

"Read the report that comes out tomorrow from the GAO," I said. "It will show why we are $14 trillion in debt . . . Anybody that says we don't look like fools up here hasn't read the report."[4] This report, titled *Opportunities to Reduce Potential Duplication in Government Programs, Save Tax Dollars, and Enhance Revenue*, is available for anyone to read at http://www.gao.gov/new.items/d11318sp.pdf.

The report, which only covered a third of the federal government, revealed a staggering amount of waste and duplication. We estimated we could save at least $1 trillion over ten years—that's real money. The report confirmed not only my assumptions but what many Americans assumed about their government. We are spending trillions of dollars every year, and nobody knows what we are doing. The executive branch doesn't know. Congress doesn't know. Nobody knows.

In its landmark study, the GAO identified a mother lode of government waste: 9 federal agencies spend approximately $18 billion annually to administer 47 separate job training programs (it was unclear if *any* worked); 20 separate agencies run 56 different financial literacy programs (why Congress believes it is qualified to teach financial literacy is beyond me); 10 agencies run 82 teacher training programs, while 15 agencies monitor food safety. One agency manages cheese pizza (FDA), but if you buy a pepperoni pizza, that's another agency (USDA). In many areas the GAO found little evidence these programs were effective. And in the understatement of the year, the GAO said, "Considering the amount of program dollars involved in the issues we have identified, even limited adjustments could result in significant savings."[5]

DUPLICATION IN FEDERAL PROGRAMS[6]

Type of Program	Number of Programs
Science, technology, engineering, and mathematics education programs	209
Surface transportation	100+
Teacher quality	82
Economic development	88
Transportation assistance	80
Financial literacy	56
Job training	47
Homelessness prevention/ assistance	20
Food for the hungry	18
Disaster response/ preparedness—FEMA	17

So why do we have so much duplication? It's simple. Each career politician wants the credit for solving the same problem. On several occasions I have seen members introduce bills that duplicated *exactly* programs that already existed. This reveals two things. One, members are generally lazy. And two, they often do what special-interest groups tell them to do. Had they done their own homework, they would not have offered the bills. These habits explain why multiple agencies have their own monuments to the good intentions of politicians.

Duplication is an unforgivable problem because it is so careless. The economics of the problem are obvious. When Congress creates a duplicative program, it creates a whole new set of administrative costs and overhead that not only adds no value, but often makes existing programs less effective. Overlapping bureaucracies create massive confusion and turf battles between agencies that are enormously wasteful.

Let's look at a few examples.

The Problem with Job Training Programs

Few instances of duplication illustrate the futility of Washington's good intentions more than federal job training programs. These programs are immensely popular with career politicians because they give them the opportunity to be for job creation while absolving them of the hard work of creating an economic environment in which jobs are actually created.

Federal job training programs are fundamentally flawed in two ways. First, they are unconstitutional.

Second, they don't work very well. The GAO found no evidence that the programs actually work, and those closest to the programs have found them to be hopelessly confusing. Greg Korte, a talented investigative reporter at *USA Today*, followed up the GAO report and talked to people in the field working on these programs. One person was Sherry Marshall, a manager of one of the nation's forty-seven job training programs.

Marshall said, "Most employers find it [the web of job training programs] incredibly complicated. It's mind-boggling to me, and this has been my profession for the last 12 years."[7]

Sherry Marshall is like the millions of Americans who work with or for the federal government. They work hard. They play by the rules. And they are motivated by a desire to serve their country and their neighbors. Yet, in spite of their best efforts, they are trapped in a system that is rigged for failure.

Virtually all federal employees operate in what Milton Friedman described as Box IV—"spending somebody else's money on somebody else"[8]—even though they want the efficiency of spending one's own money on oneself. (See chart on page 131.) With few exceptions, the programs they operate are confusing, ineffective, and duplicative.

Agencies and federal employees, however, are not the real problem. The real problem is the career politicians, who would rather send a press release announcing a *new* program than hold an oversight hearing to determine whether *existing* programs are working. The economic results speak for themselves. Joblessness is still high in spite of Washington's "investment" of billions in job training programs.[9] The GAO also found that "little is known about the effectiveness"[10] of the programs. Only five programs had ever truly examined their effectiveness by looking at whether job seekers in the programs do better than job seekers who are looking on their own.[11]

The examples of waste and mismanagement found in many job training programs were disgraceful. A few examples:[12]

- *Grants to an Admitted Thief*: In West Virginia, Martin Bowling—
  an admitted thief with a long rap sheet—was the primary

beneficiary of a $100,000 federal worker training grant and was put up for another federal job training grant worth $1 million by his mother, a state official at the time.

- *Tampa Bay Binge*: The Tampa Bay WorkForce Alliance in Florida used federal job training funds for self-indulgent binges on food and other extravagances, including: lunch at Hooters, valet parking for lunch at the Cheesecake Factory (topped with $9 dollar [*sic*] slices of cheesecake), $20 delivery fees for cupcakes, $443.99 on flowers, 300 koozie drink holders and more.

- *Luring Youth to Remove Asbestos*: A now-defunct California company benefiting from federal funding "knowingly exposing high school students to the cancer-causing agent asbestos under the guise of involving the students in work experience and job training programs."

- *State Job Training Executives Scheme Bonuses, Frequent Casinos During Work*: Iowa workforce executives conspired to enrich themselves with $1.8 million in bonuses—paid for with federal funds—while engaging in sexual relationships and frequenting casinos during work.

- *Job Training to Sit on a Bus*: In San Francisco, California, graduates of a federally funded job training program recalled receiving "little training" and having been paid to "sit on a bus."

Job training programs represent the foolishness and conceit of Washington. Job training is not a federal responsibility. It is ludicrous to believe the federal government can do more effective job training than the private sector, which has a vital interest in hiring and training competent and skilled workers. Government does not create jobs. Individual Americans create jobs through hard work, ingenuity, innovation, and economic risk taking.

Unfortunately, thousands of Americans may be putting their hope in duplicative job training programs that have very little, if any, benefit. Without question, in today's economy millions of Americans may need to learn new skills to succeed. But they are not going be helped by career politicians who are more interested in using emotion and good intentions to secure their own jobs than allowing innovators and entrepreneurs to create jobs.

Other examples of duplication are legion.

82 TEACHER TRAINING PROGRAMS

Nowhere do the enumerated powers of the Constitution give Congress the power to train teachers, but that hasn't stopped politicians from creating 82 duplicative and failing programs.

The GAO found that 53 of the 82 programs received less than $50 million, yet many had their own separate administrative processes. There is no government-wide strategy to minimize fragmentation, overlap, or duplication among these programs.[13]

Education officials agree fragmentation has hurt efforts to improve teacher quality. What's more, according to education officials, it is typically not cost-effective to allocate the funds necessary to conduct rigorous evaluation of small programs; therefore, small programs are unlikely to be evaluated.[14]

MORE THAN 100 SURFACE TRANSPORTATION PROGRAMS

Congress has not been able to rationally address our crumbling infrastructure and help repair unsafe bridges in large part because we have created overlapping cloverleaves of duplicative transportation programs and bureaucracies.

According to the GAO, Congress has created a "fragmented approach as five DOT agencies with 6,000 employees run 100 separate programs with separate funding streams for highways, transit, and rail and safety functions."

In an unintentional critique of Congress's parochialism, the GAO said, "The current approach to surface transportation was established in 1956 to build the Interstate Highway System, but has not evolved to reflect current priorities."

What evolved instead was the culture of earmarks, which displaced higher-priority projects with lower-priority projects. In 2009, I requested a GAO report along with Senator McCain that looked at how Congress's parochialism was displacing important projects. The GAO found that the U.S. Department of Transportation (DOT) obligated $78 billion between 2004 and 2009 for "purposes other than construction and maintenance of highways and bridges."

A few examples of those other purposes:

- Over $2 billion on 5,547 projects for bike paths and pedestrian walkways and facilities;
- $850 million for 2,772 "scenic beautification" and landscaping projects;
- $224 million for 366 projects to rehabilitate and operate historic transportation buildings, structures, and facilities;
- $28 million to establish 55 transportation museums.[15]

80 ECONOMIC DEVELOPMENT PROGRAMS

The GAO found 80 programs at 4 agencies costing $6.5 billion annually that do economic development work for the federal government, 52 of which help with entrepreneurial efforts and 19 with tourism. The

Economic Development Administration (EDA), which runs "8 of the programs GAO is reviewing continues to rely on a potentially incomplete set of variables and self reported data to assess the effectiveness of grants." The poor data "may lead to inaccurate claims about the success of the program."

These are just a few examples. GAO is preparing a second report that should be released around the time of this publication.

SPUTNIK MOMENTS BECOME SPACE JUNK

Duplication continues to run rampant in government because politicians simply cannot resist calling for new spending. For instance, in his 2011 State of the Union address, President Obama made a pitch for more "investments" in stimulus spending, particularly in science, technology, and education. The president said, "This is our generation's Sputnik moment."

Sputnik, of course, is the satellite the Soviet Union launched into orbit in 1957. It was the first object ever released into orbit, initiating the space race.

The connection the president wanted to make was that today we face great economic competition from emerging powers such as China, India, and Brazil, and we can't afford to be complacent. A "Sputnik moment," is really a wake-up call.

The problem is all of our Sputnik moments from government have created little more than space junk. Politicians launch program after program with great fanfare but never bother to check their progress. Then they are surprised when their past efforts crowd out and threaten future innovation.

For instance, in January 2012 a report from the GAO revealed there are at least 209 federal programs supporting science, technology, engineering, and math education, costing $3.12 billion.[16] Yet, industry continuously sounds the alarm that we don't have enough highly trained workers in these areas. Duplication itself is a barrier.

Our unsustainable debt is the real wake up. It should prompt us to stop spending money we don't have on things we don't need. We can start by clearing away duplicative programs instead of creating new ones.

DUPLICATION DENIAL

The only thing more remarkable than the vast amount of duplication in government is the lengths career politicians will go to avoid solving the problem. For decades, Congress has known there was a crisis of government duplication and inefficiency. In 1984, the Grace Commission reported to President Reagan that as many as one in three taxpayer dollars was lost due to waste, inefficiency, and duplication.[17] Government has hardly become more efficient in the intervening years.

If Congress was serious about living within its means and reviving our economy, eliminating duplication would have been at the forefront of its agenda long ago. Again, that should be the easy part. Restructuring entitlements, reforming the tax code, and rethinking defense are far more complicated and controversial tasks.

When the GAO report was initially released, both sides of the aisle viewed it as an unbiased and authoritative call to action.

Republican Minority Leader Mitch McConnell said the report represented the "virtual incompetence" in the federal government and said it underscored the need to cut spending.

Senate Majority Leader Reid agreed. "I commend my friend, Dr. Coburn, the senator from Oklahoma. He got a GAO report that shows all kinds of redundancies and overlapping. Those are places we can cut money. Let's do it."[18]

Newly elected senator Jeanne Shaheen (D-NH) offered some

refreshing nonpartisan common sense: "We need to address our long-term deficit. We all know that. We need to make some hard choices to balance the budget . . . The right way is to first look at things such as eliminating the billions of dollars in duplicative programs that were identified just this week by the GAO."[19]

Senator Mark Kirk (R-IL) agreed: "[W]e need to incorporate what we just learned from the Government Accountability Office about inefficient and duplicative areas of the Federal budget. GAO's recommendations for consolidations and eliminating programs should be fully reviewed and, in many places, implemented for next year's budget."[20]

Senator John McCain (R-AZ) ridiculed duplication in food safety. "GAO estimates that the USDA would spend about $30 million in taxpayer dollars to implement the agency's new catfish inspection program and that we would be further fragmenting our federal food safety system by having catfish regulated twice by both USDA and FDA."[21]

Even Nancy Pelosi (D-CA) applauded the report. "Again, we all agree we have to get rid of waste, fraud, abuse, duplication, obsolescence, and the rest. The GAO [report] has given us a blueprint for that, and we subscribe to that. We all agree that we must reduce the deficit and the fiscal commission has given us a road map for that. We can agree or disagree with some of it. But the fact is, it gives us a blueprint for how to go forward. And we should take heed of that."[22]

Senator Pat Roberts (R-KS) summed up the congressional reaction. "[I]t is also essential we focus on removing redundant programs within the various Federal agencies. Listen up. Every upset taxpayer should know this and, more importantly, demand action from this Congress."[23]

For a time, Senator Reid's "let's do it" sentiment prevailed.

On April 6, 2011, a few weeks after the report was released, the Senate voted 64 to 36 to eliminate $5 billion in duplicative spending that was highlighted by the GAO. The amendment I offered with Senator Mark

Warner (D-VA) came as Congress was facing possible government shutdown because of its failure to pass a budget. We had reached an impasse in part because the Senate was essentially AWOL when it came to eliminating wasteful spending. The vote for our amendment showed if the Senate would simply take the time to go through the budget, set priorities, and make cuts, we could get our economy and country back on track.

Unfortunately, the legislation to which our amendment was attached was pulled from the floor by Majority Leader Reid. Democrats and Republicans blamed one another for the impasse, but there was nothing preventing Congress from eliminating duplication. Even though Reid said he agreed with the GAO, he has not brought a single bill to the floor to eliminate duplication.

As our cutting amendment languished, I tried to pass a simple requirement forcing Congress to review all bills before they are considered by the Senate to prevent the creation of duplicative and overlapping government programs. I argued that no family makes a new purchase or goes grocery shopping without first checking to see what they already have. Congress, however, routinely buys the same thing, or creates similar programs, two, three, or dozens of times without ever checking. My amendment would have forced Congress to at least take a simple inventory. However, by this time, the Senate's "let's do it" sentiment had become "let's do it some other time." My amendment fell 4 votes short of the 67 it needed to pass. I was troubled that 3 of the deciding votes against this commonsense measure came from Senators Warner, Durbin, and Conrad, my Democrat counterparts in the Gang of Six.

At the end of the day, the double-minded careerism of politicians once again prevailed over common sense. Everyone knew the duplication problem, and our economy was worse than the GAO described. My office alone counted a staggering seven hundred examples of duplication across all federal agencies.[24]

Hearings Held in the Senate and House of Representatives by Congressional Session:
96th – 109th Congress

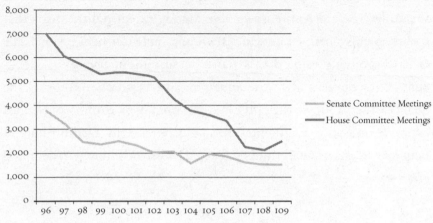

Source: Brookings Institution

Instead of reducing our debt burden, the Senate voted to continue the dysfunctional habits that had brought us to the edge of a fiscal abyss. Senators *knew* we were wasting billions through duplication but refused to solve the problem. Even worse, they refused to even review what government was already doing before creating new programs.

The most audacious rejection of the GAO's work, however, occurred in September 2011 when the members of the Senate Appropriations Committee—the appropriators—decided to exact revenge on GAO and cut its budget for putting out such an embarrassing report. It was pure payback and incredibly petty. If the appropriators would have done their oversight work (see chart above), the GAO would not have needed to prepare this report. Plus, every appropriator voted for the amendment that required the GAO to publish the report in the first place.

In response, I issued a report titled *Shooting the Messenger: Congress Targets the Taxpayers' Watchdog*[25] that detailed the decline of congressional oversight, and the relationship between the decline of oversight and overspending.

Ultimately, Congress refuses to eliminate duplication because politicians find it much easier to propose new spending than to cut wasteful spending. The conventional wisdom among career politicians is that spending cuts hurt people while spending increases help people. The GAO thoroughly refuted this flawed assumption. Spending cuts—eliminating duplication—can actually be the best way to improve the quality of services. As the GAO said, "Reducing or eliminating duplication, overlap, or fragmentation could potentially save billions of taxpayer dollars annually and help agencies provide more efficient and effective services."[26]

DISCRETIONARY SPENDING—A WASTE ODYSSEY

Eliminating duplication is only a first step in the battle to restrain our bloated discretionary spending. Defenders of Big Government like to suggest that these examples of duplication are anomalies, and the rest of government is operating quite efficiently. Progressives will even sometimes argue that discretionary spending is somehow quite low historically.

These arguments are simply false. Nearly every agency of government has seen generous, and sometimes massive, increases in funding since 2001. The Departments of State and Labor have seen their budgets triple. The budgets of the Departments of Energy and Homeland Security more than doubled, while the Department of Education's budget nearly doubled.[27] In other words, while real wages for working families have flatlined, government has given itself a big raise. In total, nondefense discretionary spending increased 46 percent in the past decade from $391 billion in 2001 to $569 billion in 2011.

Each year, I release a report called *Wastebook* that highlights whether government's raise to itself is justified. Some disgraceful examples from my latest report:[28]

1) Despite a federal budget crisis, taxpayers will spend $35 million this year for the Democrat and Republican conventions. These funds will "help pay for the stages, confetti, balloons, food, and booze" at the conventions.[29]

   In Roman Times, before their fall, Roman leaders used bread and circuses to try to pacify the public with spending. Today, we use booze and conventions.

2) Taxpayers have been forced to spend $65 million to study how to resurrect a Bridge to Nowhere in Alaska (the Knik Arm crossing) that could cost up to $4 billion to build.

3) Your money helped scientists study whether political candidates can get more votes by taking a "green" position. The study's groundbreaking conclusion, that "people who pay close attention to the issue [climate change] and consider it to be extremely important to them personally—are likely to base their votes on this issue," cost the scientists $200,000 in taxpayer funds to discover.

4) And, apparently, video game preservation is an enumerated power in today's Congress. The International Center for the History of Electronic Games (ICHEG) received over $100,000 in federal funds for video game preservation.

5) Finally, the University of Kentucky will spend $175,000 in federal funds studying the connection between cocaine and the sex habits of quail.

Here are a few other examples of wasteful spending I highlight in *Back in Black*.

We've given "Energy Star" certifications to gasoline-powered alarm clocks. We pay farmers billions to not grow crops. We send California winemakers on wine tasting trips to Europe and Asia. USDA spends millions promoting cheese consumption, then spends millions more fighting obesity. Meanwhile, we let tens of billions of dollars in unobligated funds sit in accounts while politicians demand tax increases or complain about how hard it is to find savings.

Politicians' disease-specific earmarks that go to the disease with the best celebrity lobbyists have siphoned dollars away from promising research. Meanwhile, we use federal funds to study energy fields and distance healing through the National Institutes of Health. (It's a shame we can't do distance budgeting.) We also study trendy baby names and sponsor fashion shows courtesy of NIH.

Americans are losing their homes, and the Department of Housing and Urban Development can't figure out why its vehicle fleet has increased 70 percent since 2004. "[W]e can't explain it," HUD says. Nor can HUD explain why the Philadelphia Housing Authority spent housing funds on lavish gifts for executives, $500,000 to settle a sexual harassment lawsuit claim against its director, and $17,000 for a party with belly dancers.

Meanwhile, politicians want to buy more federal land even though the federal government already owns 650 million acres and can't maintain what it already has (we have a $14 billion backlog).

At the same time, we send unemployment checks to millionaires. Maine, for some reason, spent $60,000 of federal unemployment insurance funds on a 36-foot mural containing images of labor union strikes. Speaking of jobs, we pay the National Labor Relations Board the same amount we did thirty years ago for only half the work.

Americans loathe flying, but beleaguered small airports receive generous subsidies. Kentucky's Williamsburg-Whitley County Airport received $11 million in federal money to build an airport with a 5,500-foot lighted runway, a Colonial-style terminal with white columns, and hundreds of acres for growth, even though it does not have any airline passengers and is used only by private airplanes. On a typical day, the airport has just two or three flights.

Finally, the next time you go to the movies to escape the stress of these challenging times, rest assured that the Hollywood studio that made the film you are paying $10 to see may have already been subsidized by you through one of the federal government's Hollywood liaison offices.

Several federal departments and agencies maintain these offices to help Hollywood communicate a positive message about the federal government. These agencies have at least 14 employees with a combined salary total of $1.2 million, including:

- The Department of Homeland Security, with one federal employee;
- The United States Air Force, with two employees;
- The United States Coast Guard, with three coast guard employees;
- The United States Marine Corps, with four employees; and
- The United States Navy, with four employees.

If Congress eliminates these offices, taxpayers could see savings of $34.4 million over ten years, and you could enjoy your time at the movies that much more.

These examples, and the massive amount of duplication in government, are just the symptoms of the deeper problem we face today—a Congress that refuses to set priorities and acknowledge how easy it is to get rid of massive amounts of waste. And in most cases it is not the grant recipients that are the problem but the politicians who love to spend money but refuse to do oversight. Throughout government we see this principle at work: those who are irresponsible with a little will also be irresponsible with much. Nowhere is this more apparent than with the biggest area of the budget—entitlements.

THE SOLUTIONS

We need to take a chainsaw, not merely a scalpel, to discretionary spending.

Eliminating the massive amount of wasteful spending in Washington, beginning with duplication, will save taxpayers $3 trillion over ten years.

Ending duplication should be the easy part. The more we cut from wasteful programs, the easier it will be to reform entitlements and the tax code.

9

The Entitlement Trap

We can't save Medicare as we know it. We can
only save Medicare if we change it.

—U.S. Senator Joe Lieberman[1]

The future of our economy and nation may hinge on
politicians in Washington accepting Senator Lieberman's advice. Nothing
is more likely to trigger a debt crisis than Washington continuing to
ignore the looming bankruptcy of our entitlement programs. The
American people have a choice as well. We can tolerate Washington's
refusal to tackle this challenge or we can demand action and real reform
that will preserve our safety net and our future. I'm convinced the
American people want their leaders to make hard choices and are ready
to have the adult conversation about the serious challenges we face.

Today, entitlement programs are the biggest drivers of our long-term
debt.

These programs—Medicare, Medicaid, and Social Security—are
driving our debt because their scope is so massive.[2] Medicare and
Medicaid provide health insurance coverage to approximately 100

What Drives Our Debt?[3]

(Government Spending as Share of Economy)

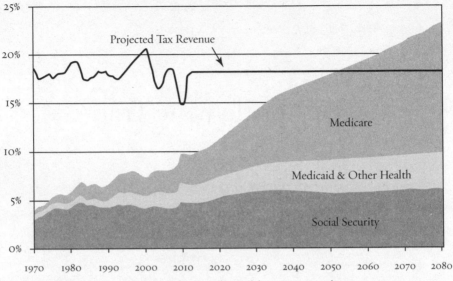

Note: This chart excludes interest costs, defense spending, and discretionary spending.

million Americans. Medicare alone covers 48 million Americans, most of whom are senior citizens,[4] while Medicaid covers more than 68 million low-income Americans.[5] Nine million Americans are enrolled in both programs.[6] Together, they give health care coverage to approximately one in three Americans and, along with Social Security, make up what has long been called the federal social safety net.

WHY ENTITLEMENT PROGRAMS ARE GOING BANKRUPT

Entitlement programs face two long-term challenges—unsustainable demographics and unsustainable benefits. In terms of demographics, there simply are not enough workers per retiree to sustain benefits at current levels. As the Simpson-Bowles report noted:

When Franklin Roosevelt signed Social Security into law, average life expectancy was 64 and the earliest retirement age in Social Security was 65. Today, Americans on average live 14 years longer, retire three years earlier, and spend 20 years in retirement. In 1950, there were 16 workers per beneficiary; in 1960, there were 5 workers per beneficiary. Today, the ratio is 3:1—and by 2025, there will be just 2.3 workers "paying in" per beneficiary.

Unless we act, these immense demographic changes will bring the Social Security program to its knees. Without action, the benefits currently pledged under Social Security are a promise we cannot keep.[7]

The same demographic problem applies to Medicare. We don't have enough working taxpayers to pay for the Medicare benefits of an aging population. The average couple at age 65 has put in about $120,000 toward Medicare during their working life, but takes out $350,000.[8] That is unsustainable.

The second problem with our entitlement programs is we have allowed benefits to grow far beyond our ability—and will—to pay them. The costs of health care entitlement programs are increasing so dramatically—they already cost $1 trillion a year—that the nonpartisan Congressional Budget Office (CBO) concludes, "The single greatest threat to budget stability is the growth of federal spending on health care."[9]

Medicare as we know it simply won't exist in four years because we won't be able to borrow the money to fund it. According to the 2011 Medicare Trustees' Report's worst-case scenario, which is very likely, the trust fund could be insolvent as early as 2016.[10] The Trustees' report also notes that the trust fund is expected to pay out more in benefits than it receives into its accounts from revenue in *all* future years. In other words, Medicare is already broke and running on empty.[11]

Looking farther into the future, the picture is even worse.

The Government Accountability Office (GAO) estimates the federal seventy-five-year funding gap—the difference between anticipated revenue and government spending—is a staggering $76.4 trillion. This is more than five times our current national debt and five times the size of our economy. Entitlement spending alone accounts for more than 80 percent of that debt.[12] Unless reforms are enacted, before today's twenty-five-year-olds are eligible for Medicare, *every dollar* the government takes in will go toward health care entitlements.

The math makes two points that are crystal clear. First, our debt problem really is largely a *health care entitlement* problem. Second, major health care entitlement reform, therefore, is a necessity, not a choice. One way or another, these programs will be transformed. We can do the foolish thing and let them collapse and bring down our economy. Or, we can reform them now.

Our founders, of course, saw this coming. They predicted out-of-control programs politicians did not want to pay for could bring about economic ruin.

In a letter to J. W. Eppes in 1813, Jefferson wrote:

It is a wise rule . . . "never to borrow a dollar without laying a tax in the same instant for paying the interest annually, and the principal within a given term; and to consider that tax as pledged to the creditors on the public faith." On such a pledge as this, sacredly observed, a government may always command, on reasonable interest, all the lendable money of its citizens, while the necessity of an equivalent tax is a salutary warning to them and their constituents against oppressions, bankruptcy, and its inevitable consequence, revolution.[13]

In other words, Jefferson expected us to pay as we go. If we wanted to create a new program, we should either raise taxes or cut spending elsewhere to offset the new spending.

Interestingly, Jefferson favored tax increases as we grew government for an important reason. As he wrote to Albert Gallatin in 1820, "I hope a tax will be preferred [to a loan that threatens to saddle us with a perpetual debt], because it will awaken the attention of the people and make reformation and economy the principle of the next election. The frequent recurrence of this chastening operation can alone restrain the propensity of governments to enlarge expense beyond income."[14]

In other words, Jefferson wanted us to raise taxes as we go so the American people would see what we are doing and throw us out of office. We have not done that. Instead, we have borrowed as we have gone and have tried to hide the fiscal impact of our careerist indulgences. For instance, Medicare Part D—the prescription drug benefit—was a new $16 trillion unfunded mandate with no new taxes or spending cuts to pay for it. Our borrowing habits have put the very survival of our nation at risk. The safety net has become a trap.

Our long-term entitlement debt is so massive that conservatives and liberals agree that we cannot raise taxes high enough to get out of debt. Tax rates would have to double at all income brackets to cover our entitlement deficit.[15]

Ezra Klein, with the *Washington Post,* put it well: "The problem with health-care costs is that they rise faster than wages, GDP or most anything else . . . You wouldn't just need to raise taxes. You'd need to raise them again and again and again, because every tax increase would soon be outpaced by Medicare's growth."[16]

THE LEADING MEDICARE SOLUTIONS

For most of the time I've served in Congress, conventional wisdom in Washington has said the debate about entitlements is over. The welfare state is here to stay, this thinking went, which is one reason why Republicans expanded the welfare state with the Medicare prescription drug benefit. In recent years, however, these assumptions have changed. The American people are asking hard and necessary questions about programs President Obama and others want to believe are "settled" matters.

Today, many Americans are realizing the safety net that was designed to protect seniors and the poor have institutionalized poverty and created unsustainable debt, deficits, chronically high unemployment, and a stagnant economy.

Going back to the causes of our entitlement debt, the problem of unsustainable demographics can be eased through an economic recovery. A growing economy that creates jobs and increases wages will ease the financial burden on our entitlement programs. Yet, growth alone will not be enough. It's also unlikely we'll have much of a recovery if we don't first reform these programs.

So how do we save Medicare? Because the problem of unsustainable benefits cannot be solved through tax increases, we have no choice but to change benefits. There are two basic ways to change the way benefits are structured: (1) adjust the eligibility and generosity of the Medicare benefit by relating benefits to income (i.e., forcing wealthier Americans to pay more) while raising the retirement age to reflect changing life spans, and (2) transitioning Medicare from a defined benefit to a defined contribution. The latter would be best accomplished by introducing real market principles that forced the government-run plan and private plans to compete and used consumer choice to help lower costs.

Let's look at a few plans that accomplish these goals in different ways:

1. Paul Ryan's Plans

Paul Ryan, the chairman of the House Budget Committee, deserves an enormous amount of credit for putting forward detailed plans to save Medicare from its inevitable collapse. Ryan has backed four plans: his

Roadmap for America's Future;[17] a plan with former CBO Director and Democrat Alice Rivlin;[18] the Path to Prosperity (2011 Republican House Budget);[19] and a plan with Democratic Senator Ron Wyden (D-OR) from Oregon.[20] He would be the first to say his plans are not perfect. But his blueprints have been specific, real, and at least one version—the Path to Prosperity—has passed the House of Representatives.

Under most versions of Ryan's plans, his approach preserves the existing Medicare program for those currently enrolled or becoming eligible in the next ten years (those 55 and older today), so Americans can receive the benefits they planned for throughout their working lives. For those currently under 55—as they become Medicare-eligible—he creates a Medicare payment, initially averaging $11,000, to be used to purchase a Medicare-certified plan. The payment is adjusted to reflect medical inflation and pegged to income with low-income individuals receiving greater support. The plan also provides risk adjustment, so those with greater medical needs receive a higher payment.

The strength of Ryan's approach is he uses forces that work in the real world and applies them to health care. I'll describe this more in the next chapter, but Ryan essentially saves Medicare by putting patients rather than politicians at the center of the decision-making process.

2. The Rivlin/Domenici Plan

The Rivlin/Domenici plan, a project of the Bipartisan Policy Center with former Congressional Budget Office director Alice Rivlin and former senator Pete Domenici, like the Ryan plan, uses the most important fix available to us in the health care debate—competition and consumer choice. Rivlin/Domenici uses a "premium support" model in which the government makes a defined contribution to a health plan of your choice. Their approach keeps traditional Medicare in place but uses the market to keep prices down by forcing traditional Medicare to compete with private plans. This encourages seniors to shop and use common sense. If seniors don't like traditional Medicare, they can shop for their own plans on an exchange. Rivlin and Domenici predict, "[c]ompetition among plans will improve the quality of care and increase efficiency."[21]

Rivlin and Domenici embrace what is the best way to improve choices, protect seniors, and lower federal spending—a competitive pricing model. Today, private plans in Medicare are paid in reference to traditional Medicare costs. The problem is that a traditional Medicare plan is full of cost distortions. The Rivlin/Domenici plan would fix this problem by making both traditional Medicare and commercial health plans bid to provide seniors with their Medicare benefit. Regardless of which plan seniors chose, they would have a basic fixed subsidy, with more for lower-income earners who need extra help.

There is good reason to believe that this model will be successful: essentially the same model has increased choices, protected beneficiaries, and kept costs lower in Medicare's prescription drug benefit and the federal employees' health benefit plan.

The Rivlin/Domenici plan builds on a long history of bipartisan support for a competitive pricing and premium support approach that goes back for decades, but was most noticeably championed by former senator John Breaux (D-LA) and former chairman Bill Thomas (R-CA) during their work in the Medicare Commission in 1998–1999.

3. The Coburn/Lieberman Proposal

Even though I'm convinced nothing will fix health care entitlements and our system more than consumer choice, most Democrats in Congress have so far refused to embrace those reforms. Sooner or later they will, because events will force them to embrace bold reform. Fortunately, a few members on the other side of the aisle are willing to consider serious entitlement reform.

One of the those statesmen is U.S. Senator Joe Lieberman, an Independent from Connecticut who caucuses with Democrats and, in 2000, came within a few votes of becoming Al Gore's vice president.

In the summer of 2011, Lieberman wrote in the *Washington Post*: "Medicare is hurtling toward its demise—our government is approaching a cataclysmic fiscal tipping point—while Washington is busy posturing for the next election."[22]

Lieberman was exactly right. Joe later told me he wrote the op-ed because he had voted against House Budget Committee Chairman Paul Ryan's plan and knew it wasn't enough to just oppose what Republicans wanted to do. As a leader, he knew he had to put forward a real solution.

Over the next few weeks we spent many hours together, along with our staffs, crafting a plan to prevent the collapse of Medicare.

We met in Senator Lieberman's office on Monday, June 27, 2011, to iron out the final details of our proposal.

"I think we're going to do something significant tomorrow," Lieberman said. "I hope it will get people thinking."

"I do too," I said.

The three key elements of our plan would raise the retirement age for Medicare, income-adjust premiums for wealthier and lower-income seniors, and remove the need for costly supplemental plans by creating a new maximum out-of-pocket deductible for seniors.[23]

The eligibility age for Medicare benefits is 65, although certain people qualify for coverage earlier because of disability. Since the creation of the Medicare program in 1965, life expectancy and the average length of time that people are covered by Medicare have risen dramatically. According to the Centers for Disease Control, when Medicare was passed in 1965, the average life span for Americans was about 70.[24] In 2007, the average American life span was 77.8—an increase of more than 10 percent. While lengthening lives is wonderful, increasing the length of an enrollee's Medicare coverage has significantly raised the costs of the overall program.

Our plan called for increasing Medicare's eligibility age by 2 months every year, beginning with people who were born in 1949 (who would turn 65 in 2014) until the eligibility age reached 67 for people born in 1960 (who would turn 67 in 2027). After that point, the eligibility age would remain at 67.[25] These increases are similar to those already under way for Social Security's full retirement age. For Social Security, the eligibility age increases to 67 for those attaining age 62 in 2027 or later.

Traditional Medicare has long been criticized for being a hodgepodge of co-pays and deductibles that can be unpredictable and costly for seniors. The reason is that, unlike most commercial insurance, basic Medicare does not offer seniors maximum out-of-pocket protection. As a result, too many seniors fear they may be exposed to unpredictably high costs when they get sick or stay in the hospital and feel forced to purchase costly supplemental plans. These supplemental "medigap" plans are a symptom of the problem—traditional Medicare's irrational cost-sharing structure—but they have been proven to increase utilization and costs to the program.

The Lieberman/Coburn proposal would address these problems by streamlining Medicare into a single combined annual deductible of $550 for both Parts A and B services. As we noted in our proposal, "streamlining the deductibles will make it easier for seniors to navigate Medicare while also directly addressing overutilization." Our proposal would also add a maximum annual out-of-pocket cap at $7,500—so no senior, except for the very wealthy, would pay more than $7,500 out of pocket in a given year. This means that every Medicare recipient would enjoy a cap on annual medical costs, which would protect them from financial hardship or bankruptcy in the event of a major illness. This would improve and modernize Medicare substantially, because Medicare enrollees do not have this kind of protection now. Coupled with these changes, we would prohibit medigap coverage for the first $550 of a senior's cost-sharing for services, and limit coverage to half of the senior's coinsurance up to the newly established $7,500 cap.

Our plan also included income-related benefits and embraced the "skin in the game" principle, which says when people have skin in the game, they're better shoppers. We would ask all seniors to pay a little more to keep Medicare afloat, with the burden weighted toward higher-income Americans. Still, we asked all seniors to pay a little more, and estimated the "dollar amount of the monthly premium increase per year would be, on average, approximately $15–20 a month."

Medicare Part B (which covers outpatient visits) allows retirees to purchase insurance coverage for physicians' services for a set monthly premium. In 2011, the majority of Medicare enrollees paid a premium of $96.40 per month. When Medicare began in 1966, premiums paid by seniors were intended to finance 50 percent of the costs of Medicare Part B. The remaining costs would be funded by the federal government. Today, however, the government is funding the remaining 75 percent of Medicare Part B, which puts enormous pressure on the federal budget. In other words, because career politicians wanted to look good and receive praise for providing "affordable" health care, we have expanded benefits—and lowered what we ask seniors to pay—but have not created a revenue stream to pay for these benefits. The careerists have done exactly what our founders like Jefferson and Washington warned against. They have allowed our nation to go deeper into debt to satisfy their short-term political desires.

With the major details of our plan worked out, I encouraged Senator Lieberman to adopt additional measures to crack down on Medicare fraud, which prompted a friendly debate about who had compromised more.

"Joe, I'm giving," I said.

"That's good, because I've been giving on most things," Lieberman responded.

"The next time we address this," I followed, referring to big changes in Medicare, "it will be in the midst of a debt crisis, so let's go as far as we can."

"You're so flexible," Lieberman deadpanned.

We met a final time the next day in Lieberman's hideaway in the Capitol before unveiling our proposal. What we were unveiling was by far the most specific "bipartisan" entitlement proposal that Washington had considered for many years. We knew we would be attacked on all sides and discussed what questions we might be asked by reporters. We then made the short but winding walk up and down stairs and through hallways to the Radio-TV gallery in the Capitol.

Lieberman stepped on the platform, stood behind the podium and before the cameras, and delivered one of the most moving and common-sense speeches I had heard about the need for Congress to make tough choices:

There are a lot of issues that Dr. Tom Coburn and I disagree on; but there are two bigger things we agree on that bring us here together today. First, we both love our country and can see that it is heading over a fiscal cliff unless people like us come together to get our government's books back in balance. Second, we both love our children and grandchildren and don't want to leave our country to them in such an economic mess that they won't have the same opportunities we had, growing up in America.

That's why Tom and I are making this proposal that will cut our national debt and preserve Medicare as a government program for current and future seniors. There is not much disagreement about the basic facts of America's current fiscal crisis.

Our national debt is over $14 trillion dollars and growing by more than a trillion dollars each year. The biggest, but not only, drivers of the debt are entitlements, including Medicare.

So if we don't deal with those entitlements we won't ever balance our budget. Almost fifty million Americans depend on Medicare now and about 20 million more people will go on Medicare during the next ten years, mostly because of retiring baby boomers. Each Medicare beneficiary will, on the average, take almost three times more out in Medicare benefits than they put in in payroll taxes and premiums. That's why we say that the status quo in Medicare is unsustainable. What we mean is that if we do nothing, Medicare will go broke and take our government down with it . . .

These facts lead to two painful but unavoidable conclusions:

First, we can't balance our budget without dealing with mandatory spending programs like Medicare. Second, we can't save Medicare as we know it. We can only save Medicare if we change it . . .

We know that each part of our proposal will make some group of people unhappy and provide easy targets for attack by those who understandably want to preserve the status quo, but the status quo will lead to the collapse of Medicare and fiscal disaster for our country. We're way past the point when we can save Medicare and cut the debt, while keeping all the interest groups satisfied and all our constituents happy.

If there ever was a time in American history for elected officials to stop thinking about the next election and start thinking about the next generation, it is now.[26]

I couldn't add much to what Senator Lieberman said, so we spent most of the remaining time answering questions. As we made our way through a gaggle of reporters and stepped into the elevators, I joked that we were brothers—the Brothers Karamazov, the characters in

Dostoyevsky's classic story. Our conversation about entitlement reform wasn't quite as lofty as the subjects of faith and ethics the brothers in Dostoevsky's story discussed, but it was a discussion that would shape and perhaps decide the fate of our republic. And like the author of the story, we were in our own ways both dissidents in a political culture that was more interested in reelection than hard choices.

Later in the summer I released an expanded version of our proposal (which also included ideas developed in the Simpson-Bowles Commission) in my *Back in Black* report that included $2.64 trillion in health care savings. One of the key reforms I proposed, which was included in the package I developed with Lieberman, was a series of measures to reduce health care fraud that I believed could save taxpayers up to $100 billion over ten years.

Medicare and Medicaid consume 1 in 5 federal tax dollars. Unfortunately, not every dollar is spent on health care. Taxpayers lose an estimated $100 billion a year to waste, fraud, and abuse.[27] To put that number in perspective, $100 billion is roughly the combined annual budget of three entire federal departments—Transportation, Homeland Security, and Housing and Urban Development.

Congress has known about the scope of health care fraud for years but has done little to address the problem. The GAO designated Medicare as a "high-risk" program in 1990, a designation reserved for a select group of programs particularly vulnerable to fraud, waste, abuse, and mismanagement.[28] Medicaid was added to the high-risk list in 2003.[29] Medicare's improper payment rate for fiscal year 2010 was $48 billion, while Medicaid's was nearly $36 billion. Last year, 1 in 10 improper payments in traditional Medicaid were due to a lack of any documentation whatsoever.[30]

Finally, I'm working with Senator Burr (R-NC) on a plan called the "Seniors' Choice Act" that brings together the best aspects of all of these plans. As we argue, it is clear that Medicare is on an unsustainable course, and the problem is rapidly getting worse. To do nothing and deny needed reforms is to embrace the status quo. And the status quo itself will certainly end Medicare as we know it.

How We Can Save Social Security

Social Security, the first major entitlement program, was created in 1935 in the midst of the Great Depression to prevent retired and disabled Americans from slipping into poverty and destitution. Today, Social Security is officially broke. Its disability program has become a cesspool of corruption, and the programs' ideological backers refuse to embrace reforms that will save the program from bankruptcy. Meanwhile, career politicians in Washington, especially those on the left, continue to misrepresent Social Security's finances and future, as they have for decades.

Again, while politicians may be entitled to their own opinions, they aren't entitled to their own math. The numbers are clear. In 2010, Social Security posted a deficit of $37 billion and is now permanently running cash flow deficits. Between 2010 and 2021, the program's cash flow deficits are projected to total $630 billion.[31]

Many career politicians and progressive fundamentalists argue that Social Security is "solvent" until 2036 when the trust fund balances run out. The problem is, there are no real dollars in the trust funds. They are as empty as Al Capone's vaults. Washington has spent every penny of the trust fund balances on other programs. Today, Social Security is kept afloat with money borrowed from future generations and foreign countries.

The deception of this argument is best captured by what Jacob Lew, White House Chief of Staff, has to say about Social Security. In a *USA Today* piece from 2011, when he served as director of the Obama administration's Office of Management and Budget, Lew wrote: "Looking to the next two decades, Social Security does not cause our deficits . . . Social Security benefits are entirely self-financing . . . The trust fund will continue to accrue interest and grow until 2025, and will have adequate resources to pay full benefits for the next 26 years."[32]

Lew, however, told a very different story back in 1999, when he served as President Clinton's director of OMB. In OMB's official commentary on President Clinton's budget for fiscal year 2000, he wrote on page 337 of Analytical Perspectives:

> These [trust fund] balances are available to finance future benefit payments and other trust fund expenditures—but *only in a bookkeeping sense.* These funds are not set up to be pension funds, like the funds of private pension plans. *They do not consist of real economic assets* that can be drawn down in the future to fund benefits. Instead, they are claims on the Treasury that, when redeemed, will have to be financed by raising taxes, borrowing from the public, or reducing benefits or other expenditures. *The existence of large trust fund balances,* therefore, *does not,* by itself, *have any impact on the Government's ability to pay benefits.*[33]

Lew was right in 1999, but not in 2011. The Social Security trust fund is an accounting gimmick and a fiction that is designed to shield career politicians from accountability, hard choices, and harsh words from demagogues.

DISABILITY FRAUD

In my years in public service, my office has uncovered countless examples of waste and stupidity. None may be more disturbing, and representative of the entitlement trap, than the case of Stanley Thornton Jr., whom you met in chapter 3. Thornton is a functional thirty-year-old man who collects Social Security disability payments while living a life engaging in role-play as an adult baby.

The Thornton case has drawn attention to the real problem—how common it is for people who are not truly disabled to receive disability payments. Again, there is no way 1 in 18 Americans are truly disabled.

OVERCOMING THE OBSTACLES TO REFORM

When Social Security was created in the 1930s, politicians in Washington understood that if Social Security was anything but a universal entitlement program that included everyone, it would be seen as a welfare program. As Wilbur Cohen, a former chief administrator of the Social Security Administration, famously said in a 1973 debate with Milton Friedman, "A program for poor people will be a poor program."[34]

For eighty years, politicians have defended this idea fiercely and turned Social Security reform into a third rail. Even Milton Friedman acknowledged the power of this argument in an interview twenty-five years after his debate with Cohen: "Now, if you stop and think about it, you ask yourself: 'Isn't that true? . . . You need to have a universal program to have the backing of society as a whole, in order that it can really be a part of the structure of society."[35]

Yet, today, the world has changed. The days of universal entitlements as we've known them are over. Maintaining the status quo is a mathematical impossibility. Telling seniors otherwise is dishonest and will delay needed reforms.

The compromise between today's unaffordable system and pure welfare is a true safety net. Social Security already adjusts for earnings but we need to go further. Does Donald Trump really need to receive a Social Security check when he turns 65? And if he does not receive a check, would that undermine his support for some kind of retirement safety net? I believe the answer to these questions is no. This is where progressives underestimate the generosity and enlightened self-interest of higher-income Americans. Not receiving a check but paying into the system helps everyone, including the wealthy, because doing so would avert a debt crisis and prevent the terrible social and economic costs of letting seniors slip into poverty.

Canada's system is closer to pure welfare than ours but they have shown that adjusting benefits to income works. In Canada, once a retiree's income exceeds $67,000 in Canadian dollars, his or her benefit payment is reduced until it is completely eliminated at approximately $150,000 in Canadian dollars. Samuel C. Thompson Jr., professor at Penn State's Dickinson School of Law, argues this should be adopted in the United States, stating, "This is a sensible approach that is consistent with the safety-net purpose of Social Security. Interestingly, this phase-out feature of the Canadian Social Security system is apparently one of the reasons Canada does not face the same long-term budgetary problems the U.S. faces."[36]

Commonsense reforms like adjusting benefits to income and raising the retirement age will help save Social Security and our safety net, not undermine them. While these measures will avert a debt crisis, the best solution for our nation's long-term health is to give individual Americans real control and ownership of their retirement accounts. The government has done a miserable job managing Social Security. If any private fund manager raided an employee pension fund in order to fund company operations, they would be thrown in jail. Yet, that is precisely what career politicians have done with Social Security. This is a useful point to remember when careerists on the left harp about "privatizing" entitlement programs. If the choice is between you owning your retirement and the government owning your retirement, I would trust the individual every time.

TAKING ON THE DEMAGOGUES

Politicians often complain they can't fix big problems like health care entitlements because it's just too hard. Once legislators start spelling out specific solutions, interest groups will find something to pick apart.

That simply is not true. It is not that hard to fix these problems. The truth is, we have a surplus of solutions, but a deficit of courage. For instance, the Breaux-Thomas Commission's ideas for saving Medicare have sat on a shelf for more than a decade.

Plans like that haven't moved because career politicians on the left have engaged in a relentless and dishonest campaign of demagoguery against anyone who would propose reforming—and therefore saving—health care entitlement programs.

The American people are growing tired of these arguments. They realize it is simply despicable for career politicians to use elderly and low-income Americans as rhetorical human shields in their war to maintain power at any cost.

In a *Commentary* magazine article titled "The Fog of Mediscare," former deputy secretary of Health and Human Services Tevi Troy explained why the so-called supercommittee of 2011 was not likely to achieve a breakthrough:

For [Senator Patty] Murray and other Democrats, the Medicare "advantage" means rekindling the politics of the 1990s, when Democrats in Congress teamed up with a Democratic president to turn a Republican attempt to reform Medicare from an honest debate into a decisive victory against conservatives in 1995. This "advantage," as Murray sees it, means ignoring the Medicare trustees who have warned that the long-term liability of Medicare is in the neighborhood of $30 trillion. It also means ignoring the lessons of Greece, Portugal, and Italy, whose unsustainable entitlement programs are sending shockwaves throughout the international monetary system.

Democrats have good reason to see Medicare-based attacks as a path to electoral success. Looking at the history of such attacks over the last 30 years reveals a landscape littered with the bodies of those who got on the wrong side of what the late columnist William Safire dubbed "Mediscare." He defined it, back in 1995, as a "shamelessly demagogic campaign to frighten older Americans into thinking that deficit reduction might soon leave them destitute in the snow, and to bamboozle them with pie in the medical sky." This sorry conduct also explains why and how Medicare ended up as a program in crisis that could sink the nation's economy.[37]

Again, we see the same problem in the Social Security debate. However, Social Security is much easier to fix with a combination of relating benefits to income, raising the retirement age to meet life expectancy, and other formula adjustments, which I describe in *Back in Black*.

The real question is, can a nation that has learned to vote money for itself from the Treasury step back from the abyss?

The Obama administration has been leading us closer to the abyss with its entitlement expansion and misinformation about our true fiscal condition. For instance, when President Obama warned that a failure to raise the debt limit would stop Social Security payments, he essentially admitted the trust funds are exhausted. As Obama told CBS News, "I cannot guarantee that those checks go out on August 3rd if we haven't resolved this issue. Because there may simply not be the money in the coffers to do it."[38]

If we needed to borrow money to fill the coffers, that was confirmation the trust fund was empty.

Meanwhile, the American people were led to believe that the payroll tax cut would be stimulus even though it is cannibalizing the Social Security program progressives view as sacrosanct. If Congress really wanted to give low-income Americans a tax break, we would ideally do tax reform that lowered rates or we could give Americans a tax credit that avoided weakening Social Security. The payroll tax debate is a classic example of short-term political expediency—the desire of Democrats to steal the tax issue for the next election—triumphing over the best long-term policy outcome for the nation.

In 1996, Pete Peterson, who wrote the landmark 2004 book *Running on Empty*, published a piece in the *Atlantic Monthly*, titled "Will America Grow Up Before It Grows Old?" The lead-in to this article could be written today: "The long gray wave of Baby Boomers retiring could lead to an all-engulfing economic crisis—unless we balance the budget, rein in senior entitlements, raise retirement ages, and boost individual and pension savings. Yet politicians of both parties say that most of the urgently necessary reforms are 'off the table.'"[39]

Sixteen years later we are stuck in exactly the same place. Congressional leaders sometimes believe they are demonstrating their progressive purity by taking Social Security and entitlement reform off the table. The problem is, you can't take demographics off the table. The wave of retiring Baby Boomers will wash away our economy if we don't reform the programs.

As Peterson wrote back in 1996, "We cannot sustain the unsustainable. Nor can we finance the unfinanceable. By 2013, when Baby Boomers will be retiring en masse, the annual surplus of Social Security tax revenues over outlays will turn negative."[40]

Today, the reality is worse than Peterson feared. Social Security revenues turned negative in 2010, three years earlier than he predicted.

It's time to say enough is enough. I'm confident individual Americans are willing to rethink the entitlement system and reconsider what government can really do for them. In order to help one person, politicians are willing to make one hundred dependent and bankrupt the country. There are better ways to help those who truly cannot help themselves.

Most of all, it's time to hold accountable the politicians who have created a system that is designed to help incumbents stay in power. I'm confident the American people prefer a safety net to an entitlement trap and are ready to restore the heritage of service, hard work, and sacrifice that has made our nation great.

THE SOLUTIONS

Reforming entitlements like Medicare, as Senator Lieberman says, is the only way to save them.

Doing nothing is the surest way to betray Americans who rely on these programs. If we don't save Medicare, it will go bankrupt as early as 2016.

The most important health care fix is to shift decision-making authority away from government and back to doctors and patients. Giving seniors and low-income Americans choices and allowing them to shop among plans and use market forces are the only viable ways to control costs short of rationing.

We have to reconnect the purchase of health care with the payment for health care. If no one is responsible for paying the bill, we will continue to see tremendous waste and overutilization.

Returning Medicare to its original purpose by income-adjusting premiums and raising the retirement age should be common sense. Applying the same commonsense reforms to Social Security will ensure the solvency of the program.

Back in Black suggests entitlement reforms that would save nearly $3 trillion. Five specifics:

1. Gradually raising the eligibility age for Medicare to 67 and then 69 in 2080 would save $124 billion over ten years.
2. Shifting management of Medicaid to the states and away from Washington will save $770 billion over ten years.
3. Asking seniors to pay $15 to $20 more per month for Medicare Part B (hospital insurance) premiums would save $241 billion over a decade. The problem is, when the program began the government was supposed to pay half and seniors half. Today, the government pays 75 percent. If government only paid 65 percent, as I suggest, we would see enormous savings.
4. Ending Medicare fraud would save $100 billion. Taking a chunk out of fraud with a bill like the Fraud and Abuse to Save Taxpayer Dollars Act, the FAST Act, could save billions.
5. Reforming our disability programs so they only serve those who are truly disabled would save about $17 billion over ten years.

10

The Case for Repealing and Replacing Obamacare

If you think health care is expensive now, wait
until you see what it costs when it's free.

—P. J. O'ROURKE[1]

AMERICA'S HEALTH CARE SYSTEM SEEMS HOPELESSLY CONFUSING. It isn't just everyday Americans who are confused, but Washington policymakers too. The truth is, most politicians mean well but are completely clueless about health care policy, which is one reason we have the system we have today.

The health care debate, though, need not be so complex. Here's the debate boiled down to three sentences.

The real problem is cost.

And why does health care cost so much?

Because government has tried to make it affordable.

As Friedman shows (see chart on page 131), spending someone else's money on someone else is a recipe for inefficiency that doesn't help anyone other than the politicians who want the credit for creating programs. Yet, in spite of their intentions, we see in the cases of Medicare and Medicaid that access to health care *programs* does not equal access to *health care*.

The real solution is to put most health care spending back in Box I—spending your own money on yourself. At the end of the day, that is the only way to fix the system.

PUTTING THE COMMON SENSE BACK IN HEALTH CARE

If you really want to understand health care today, ask the Amish.

I'll never forget debating Robert Shapiro at the American Enterprise Institute's World Economic Forum. Shapiro was ridiculing the idea that Americans were capable of shopping for their health care, which is a widely held assumption among many Washington politicians and "experts."

I couldn't wait to dismantle his argument.

"Let me tell you about Amish farmers in Oklahoma. None of them have a college education and some have just an eighth-grade education. But the Amish pay about half of what you and I pay for health care. Why? They shop for the best price."

To the audience at the World Economic Forum, this argument seemed quaint. Yet, I know firsthand that Amish farmers in Oklahoma know far more about our health care economy than most experts and politicians. They know more because they have skin in the game. For the Amish, health care is a Box I exercise. They are very discerning consumers because they are spending their own money, not someone else's.

It isn't just Amish farmers who know how to shop. Everyone in America knows how to shop. If you go to any American city today, you'll see people at all income levels and ages using apps on their iPhones and other personalized gadgets. When individual Americans are allowed to shop with their own dollars, they both reward innovation and spur further innovation. All Americans need is a market, which is exactly what they don't have in health care.

THE THREE FUNDAMENTAL PROBLEMS WITH OUR HEALTH CARE SYSTEM: COST, PERVERSE INCENTIVES, AND THIRD PARTIES

In many ways, Americans enjoy the best health care system in the world.[2] The problem is our system is far too expensive for what we get and costs are too high for too many Americans. This is an enormous challenge because health care is one of the largest sectors of our economy. Nearly 1 of every 6 dollars spent in the United States is spent on health care.[3] At the same time, nearly 1 in 3 health care dollars does nothing to help people get well or prevent them from getting sick.[4] In other words, our nation throws away about $750 billion every year—more than the size of the GDP of the Netherlands—on things like defensive medicine, fraud, and unnecessary paperwork. Again, this money is wasted because politicians have tried to make health care "affordable."

Today we see both gross inefficiencies and runaway costs. Over the past ten years, health care costs have more than doubled, increasing at three times the rate of wage growth.[5] Meanwhile, the government's role in health care has continued to expand. Today, more than half of health care is run by the government.[6] Under Obamacare, this percentage will grow. Medicare's unsustainable course is now the greatest threat to our long-term budget, and, by extension, our national security. And Medicaid runs as a close second, threatening states with massive financial mandates that they cannot afford.[7]

If more government spending and "investment" in health care were the solution, we would have the least expensive and most efficient health care system in the world. We don't. Again, we do have the best health care in the world, but our system is far too costly. That's because government has created perverse incentives that have driven up costs while empowering third-party payers and managers (health insurance and government bureaucrats), who have severed the doctor-patient relationship and shuttered the health care market.

Far too many patients feel trapped by health care decisions dictated by others. Meanwhile government interventions have effectively replaced the market and individual choice with a distorted system that drives up costs.

Decades of flawed health care policy have essentially conditioned Americans to accept a dysfunctional status quo they would never accept in other areas of the economy. We intuitively expect and demand transparency and choice in every area of the economy except for health care and education. Imagine, for instance, if you wanted to shop for a new car but no manufacturer had a website on which you could design your own vehicle and compare prices. Or, what if you wanted to buy a laptop or television but couldn't find reviews. The average consumer would be incensed.

Instead of a rational health care market based on transparency and choice, we have a bizarre system of perverse incentives that create the illusion that someone else is paying the bill. Because the third party is in the room, patients accept prices they would not pay on their own, and to keep up with the rising costs of insurance paperwork and malpractice insurance, doctors charge prices they would not charge if the consumer were directly paying the bill. At the same time, too many doctors are torn between serving their patients and protecting their practices from predatory trial attorneys trying to make a quick buck.

Doctors routinely order tests that are not necessary because they may go out of business if they don't. Nine in ten doctors acknowledge practicing defensive medicine in large part because they don't have time to listen to patients under today's government-distorted payment system. Defense medicine costs patients between $650 and $850 billion a year.[8]

I also know firsthand that many doctors have never been more frustrated than they are today. There is a coming doctor shortage in our country that will place a tremendous burden on patients and taxpayers. The Association of American Medical Colleges estimates that between 2010 and 2015 "the shortage of doctors across all specialties will quadruple" and their estimates show we will fall 63,000 physicians short, "with a worsening of shortages through 2025."[9] To compound the problem, many of the most experienced doctors are retiring early because they are tired of dealing with third parties who constantly interfere with their practices.

Some of the best doctors are beginning to practice concierge medicine, in which doctors agree to treat patients for a certain fee each year in order to avoid government and health insurance bureaucracy. Many doctors practicing concierge medicine believe the quality of their care has improved because they are able to listen to patients instead of complying with mandates, with a recent survey showing nearly two-thirds of doctors saying concierge is the ideal practice.[10] The conceit of Washington politicians who believe they can control the health care market without doctors and the market reacting against their heavy-handedness will cause health care to shift from primary care doctors to nurse practitioners and physician assistants.[11]

The Fatal Flaws of Obamacare

It's been said that the definition of *insanity* is doing the same thing over and over again and expecting a different result. Regrettably, the

Affordable Care Act (aka Obamacare) meets that definition. Instead of rebooting our health care system and helping Americans escape the entitlement trap, Obamacare took all the ideas about health care that had not worked in the past thirty years and put them into one bill. It's no wonder it hasn't worked, and won't.

Early on, it was clear Obamacare would not live up to its promise and expectations. One hundred days after the bill was passed, I, along with senator and fellow physician John Barrasso of Wyoming, released a report, titled *Bad Medicine: A Check-Up on the New Federal Health Law*, that detailed the failures of the law. We wrote:

> Unfortunately, when measured against the Administration's own stated goals, the new health law fails to address the top health care concerns of the American people . . .
>
> Independent experts have found that the new health law will increase the cost of health insurance and health care services. According to the nonpartisan Congressional Budget Office (CBO), premiums for millions of American families in 2016 will be 10–13 percent higher than they otherwise would be. This represents a $2,100 increase per family, compared with the status quo.
>
> And, according to a recent memo from the Actuary of the Centers for Medicare and Medicaid Services, the medical device and pharmaceutical drugs fees and the health insurance excise tax will "generally be passed through to health consumers in the form of higher drugs and device prices and higher insurance premiums, with an associated increase in overall national health expenditures . . ."
>
> This is not the only bad news. According to the same memo, the new health care law bends the cost curve upward and increases national health spending. In other words, health care will cost more because of this new law.

Contrary to the promise that Americans who like their current health plan can keep it, the Administration published a regulation regarding "grandfathered health plans"—plans that are exempt from the changes under the law. According to the published regulation, as many as seven out of every 10 businesses across the country will lose their "grandfathered health plan."[12]

Unfortunately, in the intervening time, all of our predictions have come true.

Obamacare has many flaws, but let me spell out five fatal flaws.

First, the law will increase costs and decrease access. Under the law, an estimated 16 to 25 million Americans will be forced into Medicaid and many Americans will lose their high-quality private coverage. Former Tennessee governor Phil Bredesen, a Democrat, explained why he thinks employers will drop health coverage: "For a great many employers, when they compare the total costs of dropping coverage with those of keeping it, dropping it will make good financial sense . . . dropping coverage will be a very attractive option."[13] As Reuters reported last year, "At least 30 percent of employers are likely to stop offering health insurance once provisions of the U.S. health care reform law kick in in 2014, according to a study by consultant McKinsey."[14]

Businesses looking at the law agree with Governor Bredesen and McKinsey. A survey from the National Federation of Independent Business found that more than half of small businesses are already considering dropping coverage.[15] Business consultants at Lockton found that one in five employers is considering completely dropping health coverage because of the law.[16] And Towers Watson's survey of large employers showed even some of the largest companies have incentives to drop coverage.[17]

The law has already caused insurance premiums to increase even before it has been fully implemented. Premiums shot up 9 percent, or $1,200 for the average family, after one year of Obamacare, according to the Kaiser Family Foundation's Health Benefits Survey.[18]

The second and more troubling flaw is the law's rationing provisions that I fear will save money by allowing patients to die sooner than they would otherwise. When I made this argument during the debate about the bill, supporters were outraged. Vice President Biden, who is a very nice man but has no experience in health care—or any field outside of politics—chastised me in a video message for daring to suggest that seniors would "die sooner" if the bill became law.

My goal, however, was not to be provocative but to highlight disturbing provisions in the bill. As I explained in a *Wall Street Journal* op-ed, in my twenty-five years as a practicing physician, I had learned that when government attempts to practice medicine, doctors begin to respond to government coercion and fear instead of patient cues. As a result, patients die prematurely.[19] That is precisely what will unfold with Obamacare unless it is repealed.

Regardless of what the administration says, the law explicitly empowers what is effectively a rationing board. The Independent Payment Advisory Board created in the law is composed of unelected, and therefore unaccountable, members whose job it will be to "reduce the per capita rate of growth in Medicare spending." Because this board of Medicare czars is barred from making commonsense changes to Medicare, like adjusting premiums or benefit design, the board's de-facto mechanism to reduce Medicare spending will be to reduce reimbursements to physicians and health care providers. As Medicare reimbursements plummet, many physicians will not be able to see Medicare patients, which will delay or deny patients' access to medical care. Putting unelected technicians in charge of Medicare is not the way to run a program and I fear it will hurt seniors.

The bill creates a new office called the "Innovation Center" that at best is a waste of taxpayer dollars. At worst it may prove to be an Orwellian enterprise with too few restraints and too much power. The Center—funded with 10 billion taxpayer dollars—is charged with "test[ing] innovative payment and service delivery models to reduce [Medicare] expenditures."[20] Giving bureaucrats a $10 billion slush fund and assigning them to "test" ideas is a poor substitute for implementing wholesale proven solutions that increase access, reduce costs, and improve outcomes. Instead of helping health professionals deliver care in a more efficient manner, the center gives the secretary of Health and Human Services—an unelected political appointee—the sole authority to determine if seniors' quality of care is negatively affected by the new payment models.[21]

The law also creates new "comparative effectiveness research" (CER) programs, which could give the rationing boards pseudoscientific justifications to ration care. CER panels have been used to ration care in the UK, for instance, where fifteen thousand older cancer patients die prematurely every year, according to the National Cancer Intelligence Network.[22]

Most physicians want to, and do, use comparative effectiveness guidelines developed by their own professional societies. What the law does, however, is effectively tell all commercial health plans to develop what could devolve into a kind of cookbook medicine that ignores the art of medicine, which is critical to diagnosis and treatment. For instance, millions of women will remember the controversial recommendations from the U.S. Preventive Task Force, which was responsible for advising women under fifty to not undergo annual mammograms, a recommendation that was roundly criticized by cancer groups. Even though Health and Human Services secretary Kathleen Sibelius denounced the recommendation, in more than a dozen places in the bill, the health law nonetheless empowers the very same board to make recommendations.

Moreover, the law itself says health insurance plans "shall provide coverage for" services approved by the task force, which effectively gives the task force's recommendations the force of law.

All together, these provisions take power from patients and physicians and hand it over to disinterested bureaucrats. This is an unconscionable "Washington-knows-best" approach that undermines individual liberty. Defenders of the law cite specific provisions that rhetorically promise to prohibit rationing or protect patients. But this ignores the clear experience of history. For example, the Medicare law itself contained a provision that prohibited the government from supervising or controlling "the practice of medicine or the manner in which medical services are provided."[23] Yet virtually every physician and health care provider today will acknowledge that because Medicare covers nearly 1 in 6 Americans and has a gargantuan payment structure that is larger than any commercial health plans, the Medicare program already dictates the practice of medicine in America.

So my fear over the law's negative impact on patients is not an abstract argument. It is an argument based on twenty-five years of real-world experience. I fear the law will impact millions of lives, especially older Americans, whose costly treatments and services unelected Washington bureaucrats may not deem valuable enough to cover.

In my own practice I've seen numerous patients who I believe would have died sooner had this bill been law.

One patient who comes to mind, whom I'll refer to as Sheila, was a young wife and mother with a lump in her breast. Traditional tests, including a mammogram, under the standard of care indicated it was nothing serious, just a cyst. However, because I knew her medical history, I wasn't convinced. For her, even a cyst was unusual. So I made the decision to aspirate, or drain, the cyst. I discovered she had a highly malignant form of breast cancer. Sheila fought a heroic battle, and her husband and daughters enjoyed twelve good years with her before Sheila finally succumbed to the disease.

Had another doctor in my position been practicing medicine under Obamacare, the government, following the cookbook guidelines of "comparative effectiveness research," would have likely said the test I ordered that detected Sheila's cancer would have been unnecessary, and they would not have paid for it. After all, everything about normal care suggested it was just a cyst. The cyst, therefore, would not have been inspected, and Sheila in all likelihood would have died much sooner and missed out on many precious years with her family.

Obamacare may be well-intentioned, but a system in which bureaucrats make coverage decisions on cost and overrule the judgment and insights of physicians is also foolish and wrong, and will be deadly to patients whose cases don't fit some Washington bureaucrat's cookie-cutter formula.

The law's third flaw is its provisions that will undermine health care innovation. The future of health care will be shaped in labs, not legislatures. Obamacare will do nothing but ensure that innovation happens outside the United States.

For instance, the law includes $500 billion in tax increases and a particularly harmful 2.3 percent excise tax on medical devices that will go into effect in 2013. This may not sound like much, but it is already killing medical innovation in the United States and outsourcing the future of health care innovation.

Richard Packer, chairman and CEO of Zoll Medical Devices, told the *Washington Examiner*'s Byron York, "We believe that the tax will cost us somewhere between $5 million and $10 million a year." He added, "Our profit in 2009 was $9.5 million."[24]

York noted: "That would be a devastating blow. Zoll employs about 1,800 people. Roughly 1,600 of them are in the United States, and about

650 of those are in Massachusetts. Once the new tax kicks in, that could all change. 'We can't run this company at a break-even or a negative rate,'" said Packer, 'so we will be forced to look at alternatives.'"[25]

The medical device tax will only compound the problems required by overregulation and slow approval times at FDA. Approval costs for new drugs and devices here are about three times higher than in Europe. In short, the FDA has caused the loss of thousands of jobs. Venture capitalists are following the regulatory path of least resistance, which isn't toward pharmaceutical and medical device companies in the United States. A survey of 156 venture firms found "dysfunction at the FDA" as the main reason for this shift.[26]

The FDA is also responsible for deadly delays, according to Sam Kazman of the Competitive Enterprise Institute.[27] As an example, he estimates that if the FDA's three-year approval process for a groundbreaking kidney cancer treatment had been accelerated, as many as three thousand people could have had their lives extended.[28] Unsurprisingly, physicians—who actually deliver health care to patients—share this concern. Surveys of physicians consistently demonstrate that more than two-thirds of physicians think the FDA approval process is too slow.[29]

Instead of reforming the FDA's broken approval process, Obamacare will outsource innovation.

The fourth flaw of the law is reckless expansion of Medicaid. At the same time Medicaid is going bankrupt, Obamacare foolishly expands Medicaid's enrollment when the program was not working well in the first place. Under the act, Medicaid's rolls will be expanded by 25 million patients, which will place an enormous burden on states.[30] A tally of individual state estimates showed that the Obamacare Medicaid expansion slammed states with at least $118 billion in additional costs over the next decade.[31] The timing could not be worse. A 2011 survey from the National Governors' Association found that just now are "states experiencing an improvement over one of the worst time periods in state fiscal conditions since the Great Depression."[32]

The fifth and final critical flaw with the unpopular health care law is the law's phony financing structure. In order to hide the law's massive spending—$2.6 trillion for the first ten years of full implementation—the law's authors used an accounting gimmick to get the answer they wanted from the Congressional Budget Office (CBO). As I explained in a health care oversight report with Senator Barrasso (R-WY):

> CBO usually evaluates the relative costs or savings under legislation within the specific timeframe of decade, or the immediate ten-year budget window. The new law takes advantage of CBO methodology and is designed to downplay the true cost of the legislation. While taxes under the overhaul have already begun, the major insurance market changes are not effective until 2014. *By effectively frontloading the tax increases and punting the largest insurance changes and spending increases to future years, the design of the overhaul masks the true costs of the health law.*[33]

Additionally, the authors pretend their plan was "paid for" with about $530 billion in cuts to Medicare and roughly the same amount in new taxes. The problem? Taking money from Medicare makes the already-shaky program even more unsustainable. In fact, the CBO and the independent actuary of the Medicare program have both explained that these reductions to Medicare themselves may be unsustainable. If the Medicare reimbursement cuts in the law were allowed to be fully implemented, the actuary warned that "Medicare prices would be considerably below the current relative level of *Medicaid* prices, which have already led to access problems for Medicaid enrollees, and far below the levels paid by private health insurance."[34]

In other words, if Medicare is really allowed to be arbitrarily cut enough to fund the law, seniors will have severe problems seeing a doctor who will take their Medicare insurance card. We will see more of the same. Access to a health care *program* will not lead to access to *health care.*

The outlook for the sustainability of the tax increases in the health law is not much better. Taxing health care only increases its cost and makes it more expensive for millions of Americans. A review of the data shows that taxes—and costs—will continue to rise. When the law passed, the CBO estimated the law would levy about $500 billion in tax increases on the American people. But just a year later, the CBO estimated repealing the law would reduce the tax burden on Americans by about $800 billion because health costs will rise. There is no way to raise taxes enough to pay for the bill.

The best fail-safe to prevent the tragically misguided Affordable Care Act from surviving is, ironically, the law itself. Even if the law is implemented fully, it will never work. Imagine what will happen, for instance, when healthy young people realize the penalty of not buying care ($750) is cheaper than the cost of paying annual premiums ($5,000). When that happens, the private health insurance market will collapse. Everyone else will be herded like cattle into a government-run health program run by bureaucrats who will decide who lives based on formulas. In fact, I believe the law was designed to fail, with the fallback position being government-run single-payer health care.

THE REPLACE SOLUTION

Repealing Obamacare is not a matter of if but of when. The law is already coming apart at the seams and simply will not work. The Obama administration itself abandoned a key provision of the law—the Community Living Assistance Services and Supports Act (or CLASS Act)—because it was unsustainable. Meanwhile, more than half of all Americans want the law repealed.[35]

In early 2009 a bill was introduced by Senator Richard Burr (R-NC), Representatives Paul Ryan (R-WI), Devin Nunes (R-CA), and me called the Patients' Choice Act,[36] which was a 180-degree departure from Obamacare. Where Obamacare kept government at the center of health care, we put individual patients at the center. Our proposal received short shrift in the mainstream press because it was never perceived as a serious contender with the Affordable Care Act. Now that Obamacare's failures have become more apparent, the contrast is even more important.

We started with the understanding that our health care system, which was wasting the equivalent of the Dutch GDP every year, needed a total reboot, not piecemeal reforms that pandered to special interests and catered to the fears of career politicians.

The problem in health care is its operating system was designed after the Second World War. In postwar America workers tended to stay in the same job for decades. That's why Congress created what has since been called an "employer-based" health care system. As the name suggests, the system encourages workers to obtain health care through their employer. Employers receive generous tax breaks from the government for providing health care through the workplace.

Employer-based health care also set up what is called the "third-party payer" model, in which insurance companies and the government pay the costs of health care. The third-party payer model has effectively severed the doctor-patient relationship and put government and health insurance bureaucrats in the exam room.

More important, this model has also separated the *purchaser* of health care from the *payment* of health care. Individual consumers operate under the illusion that someone else is paying the bill. As a result, we all pay more for less. It is the third-party payer model that has moved the economics of health care from Friedman's Box I—spending your own money on yourself—to Boxes III and IV—spending someone else's money on yourself, or someone else.

The problem with health care today is our operating system hasn't been updated since 1945. To put it in computing terms, we are effectively still running Windows 1945. That system worked fine in 1945, but today, it's clunky and outdated. Today's economy looks much different from that of nearly seven decades ago. Americans change jobs and move across state lines much more frequently. Our health care system simply has not kept up. Instead of upgrading the operating system, we keep adding service packs in the form of Medicare, Medicaid, SCHIP (the State Children's Health Insurance Program), Medicare Part D, and most recently, Obamacare, which is really Windows 1945 Service Pack 5.

The way we reboot health care in the Patients' Choice Act is to move the economics of health care back to Friedman's Box I, where you spend your own money on yourself. This would restore the doctor-patient relationship and reconnect the purchaser of health care with the payment of health care.

Unlike Robert Shapiro, we assume Americans from all walks of life—even the Amish—know how to shop. Innovation and competition are the only forces that have ever made scarce products less scarce and more common. Americans old enough to remember the first calculators and cell phones know what I'm talking about. Did a government program lead to smaller and more efficient electronic devices? No. The market and educated consumers made products that were once rare, expensive, and clunky, now affordable and common.

We have been conditioned by Washington to believe in choice and competition in every area of the economy but health care and education. Our plan is designed to change those assumptions using the following principles.

PROVIDING TAX FAIRNESS

The problem with today's treatment of health is that it discriminates against people who don't get their health care through their employer. The current system also discriminates against low-income citizens. A 2004 analysis found that wealthy Americans receive $2,680 in tax breaks for health care, while the poorest Americans get only $102.26.[37] In 2011, according to the Kaiser Family Foundation, the average annual premium for employer-sponsored health insurance in 2011 was $5,429 for single coverage and $15,073 for family coverage.[38] This means that wealthy Americans receive $4,974 in a tax benefit if they have employer health coverage for their family, while some of the poorest Americans get only $1,507 in a tax benefit—less than one-third the tax benefit wealthy Americans receive.

Also, the current tax treatment of employer-sponsored health insurance effectively depresses wages. Employers essentially shift dollars that would have gone to wages to overpriced health care.[39] Even John Gruber, a leading health care economist and Obama administration adviser, has said, "The costs of health insurance are fully shifted to wages."[40]

The ideal solution, as I'll discuss in the next chapter, is to do away with all tax credits and deductions in exchange for major rate reductions and a flatter, fairer tax code. That way, people would have more of their own money to use to buy health care.

However, as long as employers receive tax breaks for providing health care, the next-best option is to make sure we give all Americans buying power. Under our plan, Americans would get an individual tax rebate to purchase health insurance. The rebate, worth about $2,300 for individuals and about $5,700 for families, would help households shop for health care.

PROTECTING THE POOR FROM GOVERNMENT

Medicaid, as it is currently structured, is a disaster for low-income patients. Medicaid is a case study in the principle that access to a government health care *program* does not equal access to health *care*. Forty percent of doctors don't accept Medicaid patients because reimbursements are so low. As a result, Medicaid patients often end up in the emergency room for basic health care services simply because they cannot get access to a primary care physician.

This lack of access has resulted in poor patient outcomes in the Medicaid program relative to patients in private plans. The *Wall Street Journal* documents several examples of Medicaid harming the poor:

- "Medicaid patients were almost 50% more likely to die after coronary artery bypass surgery than patients with private coverage or Medicare."
- "Elderly Medicaid patients with unstable angina had worse care, partly because they were less likely to get timely interventions or be treated at higher quality hospitals."
- "Medicaid patients presenting with heart attacks or unstable angina received cardiac catheterization less often than Medicare or private paying patients. This procedure to open blocked heart arteries has become standard care, with ample evidence showing it improves outcomes."
- "Patients on Medicaid were two to three times more likely to die from [cancer] even after researchers corrected for differences in the location of the tumor and its stage when diagnosed."[41]

We can improve Medicaid and restore accountability by transitioning *away* from open-ended entitlement programs that offer little or no accountability to taxpayers and patients. A twenty-first-century, rebooted Medicaid program, under the Patients' Choice Act, would provide individualized, personalized care by giving patients real choice and equipping them with buying power.

Our plan includes a number of other commonsense reforms. For instance, we would help the private sector in its prevention efforts. Five preventable chronic conditions consume 75 percent of our health spending and cause two-thirds of American deaths.[42] Yet, most of what the government does in an attempt to help makes health care more expensive, not less.

The private sector is already leading the way on prevention. Supermarket giant Safeway Inc. saved 11 percent on health care costs during the first year of a results-based prevention program.[43] Johnson & Johnson's integrative prevention program saved as much as $8.8 million in one year and reduced health risks related to high cholesterol levels, smoking, and high blood pressure.[44]

Our plan also uses voluntary state exchanges to help consumers shop for the best plans. If plans treat patients unfairly, they can't participate. President Obama often argued that his exchanges were just the same as our state-based exchanges. The key difference, though, is he puts government at the center of the decision-making process, while we put *consumers* at the center. Moreover, the Obamacare exchanges are mandated by law, overrule state efforts, and are mini-regulatory bureaucracies that are part of the law's provisions that force Americans to buy insurance and dictate what kind of insurance they can buy.

The Patients' Choice Act, on the other hand, creates incentives for states to find a solution that fits their individual needs and the goals of empowering consumers with more transparent choices. Our bill text, which would create our voluntary state exchanges, fits on four pages of paper, while just some of the regulations and guidance implementing Obamacare exchanges are already hundreds of pages in length.

Finally, our plan would set up health courts that can resolve disputes fairly without encouraging today's lawsuit lottery that has driven up costs for everyone.

Fortunately, the courts have slowed the implementation of Obamacare by declaring its individual mandate provision unconstitutional. Never before has the federal government commanded free citizens to buy a particular product, in this case, health insurance.

The 11th circuit ruling majority opinion put it well:

> The individual mandate exceeds Congress's enumerated commerce power and is unconstitutional. This economic mandate represents a wholly novel and potentially unbounded assertion of congressional authority: the ability to compel Americans to purchase an expensive health insurance product they have elected not to buy, and to make them re-purchase that insurance product every month for their entire lives.[45]

The U.S. Supreme Court is expected to decide the fate of the individual mandate in June of 2012. If the Court decides Congress has the power to force consumers to buy health insurance and, by implication, eat their fruits and vegetables, the last vestiges of the Commerce Clause's limitations on government interfering with the market will be washed away. America will never be the same.

The health care debate, I believe, will be remembered as a historic missed opportunity for President Obama. The president was elected with a mandate to pursue real change. The great tragedy of his health care initiative was its lack of imagination and ingenuity. Instead of pursuing change and reimaging health care across party lines, he pandered to the status quo assumptions of politicians on his side of the aisle and made health care and our economic situation worse.

Hopefully, the law will be repealed and replaced before it can be fully implemented, and we won't have to see how bad it will be for patients. That's a change that can't happen soon enough.

THE SOLUTIONS

Turning patients into shoppers and equipping them with buying power will do more to bring down costs than any other reform.

Universal health care—the true mission of Obamacare—is a right goal, but not a right. We will get closest to that goal by using the only principles that have ever made scarce services common—competition, transparency, and choice.

The free market is not perfect but it is far better than any other option and vastly better than allowing elites in Washington to make our choices for us.

The free market has not failed patients; government has. The employer-based model is a government invention that makes little sense in today's economy. Updating the tax code so that it doesn't discriminate against the self-employed will let the market work to bring down costs and increase choices.

Repealing Obamacare is a necessary step to enacting true reform. Because rising health care costs are fueling the debt bomb, reducing those costs with real reform will go a long way toward getting us out of economic danger.

11

The Tax Reformation

Where is the politician who has not promised his
constituents a fight to the death for lower taxes—and
who has not proceeded to vote for the very spending
programs that make tax cuts impossible? There are
some the shoe does not fit, but I am afraid not many.

—BARRY GOLDWATER[1]

ASIDE FROM ENTITLEMENTS, NO POLICY DEBATE HIGHLIGHTS THE
dysfunctions of American politics more than taxes. Instead of viewing
the tax code as a way to raise revenue and enable government to perform
its essential functions, politicians on both sides of the aisle use the tax
code—and the debate about taxes—as tools to keep themselves in power
and to reward their friends and interest groups who put them there.

Both Democrats and Republicans have a rich heritage of intellectual dishonesty in the realm of tax policy. For years, Democrats have
used shameless class warfare rhetoric to advance the fiction that taxing the rich will solve our long-term debt problem. Republicans, on the
other hand, have desecrated the limited-government legacies of Reagan,

Goldwater, and our founders by embarking on spending orgies with borrowed money—a form of deferred taxation and financial repression—while hiding beyond false pledges of tax purity that have made tax reduction and simplification much more difficult to achieve.

THE PROBLEM WITH THE TAX CODE

Today's tax code is hopelessly complex. In fact, it is a permanent stimulus program for lobbyists on K Street and tax preparers across America. The code caters to politicians and interest groups at the expense of economic growth and job creation. At more than 3,800 pages, the code is a labyrinth of exclusions, deductions, exemptions, and credits, which make it nearly incomprehensible. The code is longer than the Bible, but without the good news.

Our tax code is also horrendously inefficient and discriminatory against middle-income Americans who make enough to have to pay taxes but can't afford to hire a tax accountant or lobbyist. Meanwhile, millions of low-income Americans don't pay any taxes at all.

The code's complexity has caused compliance costs to be absurdly high. For every dollar of revenue raised, Americans pay 30 cents just in compliance costs. The Tax Foundation estimates annual compliance costs to be $363 billion.[2]

The complexity and inefficiency of the tax code in part comes from the countless spending programs hidden within it. The code is loaded with spending programs masquerading as tax cuts. By most estimates, these special preferences add up to more than $1 trillion in annual spending, all administered by a Treasury Department that receives little oversight from Congress. Spending in the tax code is stimulus for the tax compliance industry that produces nothing of real economic value.

Finally, overall tax rates are too high. We're paying too much because government is doing too much, and what it is doing, it is doing terribly inefficiently and ineffectively. Individual tax rates could come down significantly if government were brought back within its constitutional boundaries. We also have the highest corporate tax rate in the world, which has encouraged our companies to move overseas and take American jobs with them.

Congress has also set up a worldwide tax system in which profits from American companies are taxed even if earned overseas. Moving to a territorial system—in which profits earned here are taxed here— would make our economy much more competitive and prosperous.

Washington's refusal and inability to tackle tax reform is the fault of both parties and, like everything else in Washington, is the result of careerism more than ideology.

LIBERAL DISHONESTY ABOUT TAXES

Liberals tend to make two arguments about taxes that have more to do with keeping themselves in power than with helping families.

First, liberals like to argue that taxing the rich will solve our debt and deficit issues. They ignore one major problem. There simply are not enough rich people to tax to make a difference.

Billionaire investor Warren Buffett wrote an op-ed in the *New York Times* last year that progressives used to validate their bad math. "While the poor and middle class fight for us in Afghanistan," he said, "and while most Americans struggle to make ends meet, we mega-rich continue to get our extraordinary tax breaks . . . These and other blessings are showered upon us by legislators in Washington who feel compelled to protect us, much as if we were spotted owls or some other endangered species."[3]

Buffett's criticism was actually an entirely fair broadside against career politicians in both parties. Yet, he proposed raising taxes on those making $1 million or more a year, and he proposed even higher rates for those earning $10 million or more.

President Obama seized on Buffett's argument in speeches and interviews. The nonpartisan Tax Foundation looked at this proposal, however, and found it lacking. They wrote, "Taking *half* of the yearly income from every person making between one and ten million dollars would only decrease the nation's debt by 1 percent. Even taking every last penny from every individual making more than $10 million per year would only reduce the nation's deficit by 12 percent and the debt by 2 percent. There's simply not enough wealth in the community of the rich to erase this country's problems by waving some magic tax wand."[4]

The Tax Foundation also found that the only way to solve the debt problem by "taxing the rich" is to confiscate *every penny* of disposable income earned by *everyone* making more than $200,000 a year.[5] Doing this would destroy our economy.

Plus, it is important to remember that Congress created a system in which 47 percent of Americans pay almost nothing in federal income taxes.[6] When those low-income Americans do decide to work, their new income is taxed at incredibly high effective rates because when they start making money, they lose benefits. Instead of being rewarded for making the transition from welfare to work, the government effectively punishes the working poor and gives the fruit of their labor to the others. That is hardly economic justice.

So why do liberals work so hard to create the perception that "taxing the rich" will solve our problems even though the top 10 percent of taxpayers already pay 70 percent of all federal income taxes and many low-income Americans pay no federal taxes at all? Because it's all about the politicians. Liberals believe that inflaming class envy will persuade the American people to elect Democrats over Republicans, who allegedly want to protect tax cuts for the rich. It would be hard to find a more tired and intellectually dishonest argument in American politics today than the idea that we can balance the budget by soaking the rich. Plus, as Margaret Thatcher said, the problem with socialism is you "always run out of other people's money."[7]

The second liberal deception in the tax debate is the suggestion that under-taxation is as much of a problem as overspending. Any American who wants to look at the numbers will plainly see that spending, especially health entitlement spending, is the primary driver of our long-term debt. Asking families to pay more in taxes without first making massive spending cuts and reforming entitlement programs essentially rewards incompetence in Washington and subsidizes the desire of career politicians to avoid hard choices.

As long as we have a government that builds bridges to nowhere, funds shrimp on a treadmill, and pays adults to engage in role-play as babies, the problem will continue to be overspending, not under-taxation.

Finally, the tax-the-rich argument is dishonest because liberals—and some so called conservatives—have no problem spending billions a year on subsidies for the rich and famous, mostly through the tax code. I released an oversight report on this topic that showed how people who earned $1 million a year were receiving $7 billion in tax breaks through the mortgage interest deduction every year.[8]

As I wrote for a CNN piece titled "End Welfare for the Wealthy":

Millionaires receive tax earmarks and deductions crafted by both parties that allow them to write off billions each year. These write-offs include mortgage interest deductions on second homes and luxury yachts, gambling losses, business expenses, electric vehicle credits and even child care tax credits.

Meanwhile, direct handouts for millionaires have included $74 million in unemployment checks, $316 million in farm subsidies, $89 million for preservation of ranches and estates, $9 billion in retirement checks and $7.5 million to compensate for damages caused by emergencies to property that should have been insured. Millionaires have even borrowed $16 million in government-backed education loans to attend college since 2007.

The goal of highlighting these excesses is not to demonize those who are successful. Instead, by highlighting the sheer stupidity of pampering the wealthy with lavish benefits through our safety net and tax code, I hope to make a moral and economic argument for real entitlement and tax reform.

The most troubling gap in America today is not an income gap. It is an integrity gap—and even intelligence gap—between Washington and the rest of the country. Families are struggling to make ends meet and are making painful economic choices as politicians in Washington borrow billions to provide welfare to the wealthy. Politicians on both sides refuse to fix big problems and defend stupid policies because changing those policies would involve upending a comfortable political status quo.[9]

REPUBLICAN DISHONESTY ABOUT TAXES

In politics, leadership means reforming your team. Partisanship means reforming the other team. It's time for real leadership on taxes. As Goldwater wrote, excessive spending makes tax cuts difficult to enact. Conservatives have to ask themselves, had Congress cut government spending to pay for the tax cuts of 2001 and 2003, where would our budget deficit and debt be now? I voted against extending the Bush tax cuts because we refused to cut spending to pay for them. If we had cut spending, we would still be facing the looming bankruptcy of Medicare, Medicaid, and Social Security, but our economy and employment numbers would be much stronger than they are today.

Republican duplicity about taxes needs to be challenged because Republicans are supposed to be the party for limited government. Sad to say, for the past twenty-five years, Republicans have used tax pledges as security blankets to make them feel secure and innocent while borrowing and spending beyond our means. Even worse, Republicans have turned the tax code itself into a shelter for spending and earmarks.

Like Democrats, Republican careerists enjoy manipulating the code because it keeps them in power. As one key Republican staffer confessed to my office, "I can't wait to play with the code [when Republicans take control of the Senate]."

"Playing with the code"—that is, using the code to pick winners and losers from Washington—should be anathema to conservatives. Yet, today's tax code has become a playground for politicians, special interests, and political fund-raisers, and a laboratory for social engineers who want to modify behavior through the tax code.

THE GROVER NORQUIST PROBLEM—AND MYTH

Anyone who has followed the debate about how to reduce our debt and deal with the tough issues of entitlement reform and tax reform has likely heard the name Grover Norquist. This delights no one more than Mr. Norquist, who has spent the last two decades managing and manipulating the insecurities of career politicians in order to cultivate his image as a power broker and secure well-paying clients who want to protect their tax earmarks.

Grover has been called the most powerful man in Washington and is routinely demonized by progressives and the media as the primary obstacle to deficit reduction. For instance, John Kerry blamed the failure of the supercommittee on Norquist by calling him the panel's "13th member."[10]

Meet the Press then bought into Kerry's spin by asking Norquist to represent the Republican perspective the Sunday after the super-committee failed.[11] Yet, the fact is, Norquist himself holds little to no sway over the decision makers in Congress. Understanding why Grover is seen as all-powerful while being functionally irrelevant is key to understanding the tax reform debate in Washington.

First, Norquist is a creature of Washington and consummate insider. He essentially functions as a career politician who has never been elected. Sadly, he and his organization have followed the path of many individuals and groups who go native in pursuit of the Inner Ring. (See chapter 2.) His group is not alone. Special-interest outfits in Washington on the left and right tend to go through the following stages of development: idealism to activism, activism to action, action to arrogance, and arrogance to self-protection. Interest groups and their leaders usually start with a clear purpose and have a positive impact, but then become enamored with their status as power players and make decisions based on how to protect their status.

On the surface, Grover makes a compelling argument with which I largely agree. He argues that if Republicans put revenue on the table, as Reagan did in 1982 and Bush did in 1990, Democrats will agree to fake spending cuts and the American people will only see their taxes go up. He's right that politicians will always try to take the easy way out. No one knows more about the lengths politicians will go to make fake cuts than I do.

Grover's helpful reminder about the risks of negotiating with people who want to grow government is fatalistic. Our nation, after all, was built on a grand bargain called the U.S. Constitution. More importantly, Grover's core economic argument is flat-out wrong and simply ridiculous. He argues that any deficit reduction deal that includes a penny of revenue—even a deal that reformed entitlement programs and saved $9 trillion—would be a "sellout" and a betrayal of conservative principles.

In other words, he would demand that Republicans and conservatives walk away from a deal that was $9,000,000,000,000 (that's $9 trillion) in cuts and $.01 (one cent) in revenue. That's pure stupidity and, fortunately, no one serving in Congress agrees with him. I know all the major negotiators on the Republican side and, regardless of what their public statements suggest, not a single one would automatically walk away from a deficit reduction deal that included revenue. Their concern is achieving a fair ratio of cuts to revenue with the end result of defusing the debt bomb and reducing spending far more than we increase revenue. The greater barrier to a grand bargain has been the left's reluctance to embrace entitlement reform. Plus, as I've explained, doing nothing and maintaining phony standards of tax or entitlement purity is the surest way to invite massive tax increases and bankrupt entitlement programs.

Yet, Grover's real argument has little to do with economics or conservatism and everything to do with careerism. For instance, Grover said the following to *60 Minutes*:

> Let's say you take that Coke bottle home, and you get home, and you're two-thirds of the way through the Coke bottle. And you look down at what's left in your Coke bottle is a rat head there. You wonder whether you'd buy Coke ever again. You go on TV, and you show 'em the rat head in the Coke bottle. You call your friends, and tell them about it. And Coke's in trouble.
>
> Republicans who vote for a tax increase are rat heads in a Coke bottle. They damage the brand for everyone else.[12]

In other words, Grover's chief aim is to protect the Republican *brand* rather than the *republic*. Ironically, the activities that destroyed the Republican brand in the 1990s and in the last decade—the K Street Project, earmarks, and overspending—were endeavors in which Norquist was unfortunately complicit. Grover deserves credit for helping fashion the Contract with America, but he also allowed Republicans to use his Taxpayer Protection Pledge as an alibi to borrow and spend way beyond our means. As long as those Republicans signed the pledge, they could chase earmarks and spend to their hearts' content. Remember, as Goldwater warned, those are the very politicians who would make real tax cuts difficult to achieve.

WHAT IS A TAX INCREASE?

One of the questions behind the Norquist problem and myth is, "What is a tax increase?"

That seems like a simple question. It isn't. As Doug Holtz-Eakin, a former CBO director and adviser to John McCain, jokes, "I can tell you how many angels can fit on the head of a pin, but I have no idea what a tax increase is."[13]

I would argue a tax increase is any policy that transfers wealth from individuals to the state. This can be done through direct rate increases but also indirectly through financial repression—government-induced inflation and the debasement of currency. This is why I argue that doing nothing and letting the debt bomb go off is the tax increase position.

Some tax lobbyists like Norquist, on the other hand, say eliminating any credit or deduction is a tax increase. They argue that all tax earmarks are sacred. Norquist even testified before the fiscal commission that all provisions in the code should be permanent, even the dumb ones.[14]

Norquist, for one, has been remarkably consistent in the application of this misguided principle. For instance, when I tried to eliminate a tax earmark for Hollywood movie producers in President Obama's stimulus bill, Norquist alleged that I was trying to raise taxes.[15] Similarly, when I moved to end the tax earmark for ethanol blenders, Norquist also said that was a tax increase.[16] Norquist's organization even opposed the repeal of a key part of Obamacare because doing so would be a "tax increase," this after he nearly opposed the Patients' Choice Act I authored with Paul Ryan because our bill might cause some wealthier Americans to pay higher premiums even as we established free-market, consumer-directed health care.

Grover's bizarre defense of ethanol created an opportunity for me and other free-market conservatives to ask the Republican Party to decide what it really believed about tax policy.

Ethanol, of course, is a fuel made from corn, and it has been widely discredited. It is ineffective and inefficient. Ethanol has also been shown to increase the price of food because it diverts the supply of corn to fuel production. These increases in food prices have also been shown to exacerbate global hunger, which we pay for with increased food aid and defense spending—both of which are financed with taxes and borrowing.

The ethanol blender's credit is a classic tax earmark because it is a cash payment hidden in the tax code to protect it from being cut. If it were in an appropriations bill, it would be spending. But because of effective lobbying, it is seen by some as a tax cut.

My decision to challenge Norquist publicly[17] had little to do with Norquist and everything to do with challenging the culture of careerism in the Republican Party that believed adhering to pledges to protect tax credits, however wasteful, somehow absolved them of the sins of over-spending and reckless borrowing. Michael Munger, a Catholic and director of the Philosophy, Politics, and Economics Program at Duke University, called this practice the selling of fiscal indulgences, after the Catholic Church's practice of selling indulgences for the forgiveness of sins. Munger wrote:

> We need a Reformation. We need a Martin Luther to speak out and tell the truth. The Catholic Church reformed itself after 15 centuries; why can't we fix our tax system?

The indulgence business is just too profitable, too useful, to the priestly classes of both parties.[18]

Munger was touching on the same problem identified by Goldwater. The desire of politicians to spend, and feel innocent about overspending, makes tax reform much more difficult to achieve. Every dollar borrowed is a deferred tax increase on the next generation.

In the spring of 2011, I decided to set up a choice for any Republicans who wanted to defend tax earmarks by forcing a vote on eliminating the ethanol tax earmark. When Norquist once again called my proposal a "tax increase," I sent him a letter instructing him to drop his support of tax earmarks and directed him to realign his organization with its own charter, which says: "We believe in a system in which taxes are simpler, flatter, more visible, and lower than they are today. The government's power to control one's life derives from its power to tax. We believe that power should be minimized."[19]

I continued in my letter:

Rather than demanding that Senate conservatives violate their consciences and support distortions in the tax code that increase spending and maintain Washington's power over taxpayers' lives, your organization should assist our efforts. Calling for the elimination of tax earmarks without qualifications would be a good start. Continuing to issue blanket defenses of all tax expenditures is a profoundly misguided embrace of progressive, activist government and a strategy for tax complexity, tax deferment, excessive spending and unsustainable deficits.[20]

When the measure finally came to a vote, my amendment won handily on a bipartisan vote of 73 to 27 margin. Democrats had been persuaded by senators like Dianne Feinstein who argued, "Ethanol is the only industry that benefits from a triple crown of government intervention. Its use is mandated by law, it is protected by tariffs, and companies are paid by the federal government to use it."[21]

Rank-and-file Democrats who voted for the amendment were also frustrated with majority leader Reid, who had insisted that Democrats vote against an identical amendment I offered two days earlier because Reid did not like the tough procedural tactics I used to force a floor vote. This was a classic example of Reid's incompetence, obstruction, and willingness to waste the Senate's and America's time on purely partisan grounds. Several Democrats switched their vote and voted as they had wanted to—against ethanol—after Reid insisted on reminding the chamber he was majority leader.[22] Meanwhile, nearly all Republicans who had signed Norquist's "Taxpayer Protection Pledge," which Norquist had decided to interpret inappropriately, joined me in supporting genuine tax reform.

After the vote, many Republicans criticized Norquist. Of Norquist's position, *National Review*'s Jonah Goldberg wrote, "I'm sorry but that's nuts . . . This is simply one of those areas where if the pledge is the law, and the law says you can't kill an ethanol subsidy, then the law is an ass."[23]

Elected officials were also more than happy to put Norquist in his place. Most free-market conservatives signed the petition forcing a vote on my amendment. After the vote, others piled on.

"Cutting out special subsidies hardly is the same thing as raising taxes," said Sen. John Cornyn (R-TX), who was in charge of the Senate GOP's campaign operations.[24] Sen. Richard Burr (R-NC) added: "Grover Norquist can say what he wants, but I would disagree with him on this."[25]

"I voted for lower food prices and less federal debt. I'd do that again if I could," said Sen. Lamar Alexander (R-TN), a member of the Senate leadership at the time.[26] Even freshman fiscal hawk Sen. Pat Toomey (R-PA), who called the pledge a useful tool in uniting Republicans, acknowledged having "subtle" differences with the ATR [Americans for Tax Reform] president. "I am not interested in raising taxes," he said. "But I am interested in ending ethanol subsidies."[27]

The Club for Growth, a leading free-market conservative group, announced that there would be key votes on my amendment. "Our position is that bad economic policy should be eliminated, regardless of other changes in the tax code," Club for Growth spokesman Barney Keller wrote in an e-mail. "Ethanol subsidies are a travesty, and we're looking forward to seeing their abolition."[28]

The conservative and center-right media piled on as well. The *Wall Street Journal* editorialized in favor of my position,[29] while the *Economist* ran a humorous cartoon depicting Norquist driving an ethanol-powered tank.[30] *National Review Online* also conducted a poll asking readers who was right about taxes: Coburn or Norquist. In spite of an intense lobbying campaign by ATR, conservative readers sided with me 60 to 40.[31] The poll was instructive because it raised an important question: How can an organization that supposedly controls Republican tax policy fail to win an online poll or a vote in the Senate?

The answer was, Norquist wasn't nearly as powerful as the center-left media made him out to be. The left had created the Norquist myth in order to portray Republicans as irrational on tax policy. To the press, Norquist was a quotable boogeyman and the perfect talk-show guest. When career politicians like John Kerry blame the failure of the super-committee on a lobbyist like Norquist, many in the media prefer to give the lobbyist (Norquist) a platform rather than asking the elected official with the power to legislate (John Kerry) why he failed to come to an agreement. Fortunately, some commentators like Charles Krauthammer picked up on this point and exposed the myth of Grover's power.[32]

Were Grover all-powerful, Pat Toomey never would have proposed a compromise that lowered rates but did put revenue on the table.

Republican members of the supercommittee also denied bringing up the pledge. I do know that on the commission on which I served—Simpson-Bowles—Norquist's bizarre definition of tax purity was never raised and defended by a single Republican.

As these talks continue it is important for members of Congress to understand that Norquist need not be feared. Washington is a menagerie of paper tigers. None roar louder than Norquist.

THE SIGNS OF A TAX REFORMATION

Real tax reform would embrace the following key principles:

Tax Fairness

The core problem with the tax code is it causes our nation to misdirect capital to less efficient uses. As a result, we all suffer. One inefficiency in the code is the ease with which the wealthiest Americans, who can hire lobbyists, carve out special exemptions and loopholes. The game of tax evasion takes money out of the economy and slows growth. As Paul Ryan argues, "Every dollar that businesses spend lobbying for a better tax deal, is a dollar they're not spending on making a better product."[33]

Ending the culture of fiscal indulgences in Washington will require going after these special deals, which is really spending in the tax code. In his recent *National Affairs* analysis of the tax code, "Spending in Disguise," former member of President Bush's Council of Economic Advisers Donald Marron explains how the code has become a tool for secret spending programs. He wrote, "Tax preferences are social safety-net programs. They are middle- and upper-income entitlements." Marron concluded, "The federal government is therefore bigger than we typically think it is. Conventional budget measures miss hundreds of billions of dollars that are implicitly collected and spent each year through spending-like tax preferences."[34]

The nonpartisan Congressional Research Service agrees, explaining how tax expenditures are "in many ways equivalent to entitlement spending.[35] That is, "tax expenditures are available to everyone who qualifies and federal budgetary costs depend on program rules (the tax code), economic conditions, and behavioral responses. Furthermore, they often remain in the tax code until changed or eliminated by congressional action."[36]

Martin Feldstein, a professor of economics at Harvard, and chairman of the Council of Economic Advisers from 1982 to 1984 under President Ronald Reagan, said it best when he called tax expenditures "spending by another name."

Feldstein wrote in the *New York Times*:

> Tax credits for buying solar panels or hybrid cars are just like government spending to subsidize those purchases. Similarly, the exclusion from employees' taxable incomes of employer payments for health insurance is no different from subsidizing the purchase of those insurance policies. The deduction for interest on residential mortgages, probably the best-known tax expenditure, amounts to a giant subsidy for homeownership.
>
> At their worst, such tax expenditures create incentives for wasteful borrowing and spending; they have been factors in the mortgage crisis and the rising cost of health care . . .
>
> Federal revenue must be raised to deal with our very serious fiscal problems. But it would be far better to do so by capping tax expenditures than by raising marginal tax rates.[37]

Congress's tax code spending spree has created an unfair system in which taxpayers with similar incomes and businesses with similar profits often do not pay similar rates. For example, a recent report found eleven major U.S. corporations with $163 billion in profits from 2008 to

2010 had effective federal tax liabilities averaging only 3.3 percent—far below the corporate rate of 35 percent. In the case of General Electric, the company had a *negative* income tax liability of 61.3 percent, receiving $4.7 billion from the federal Treasury over the last three years.[38]

Many tax preferences are little more than corporate welfare designed to compensate for our country's high tax rate. Inevitably, these exceptions tend to favor those companies and groups with close ties to lawmakers and access to the most experienced lobbyists. Without such access, small businesses and the middle class often bear the burden of the high standard tax rates while the wealthy and powerful receive a vast array of deductions, credits, and other preferences created by Congress.

Meanwhile, loose requirements for various tax write-offs allow clever taxpayers to reduce their taxable income for bizarre and dubious expenditures. One family was allowed to deduct the cost of cat food as a business expense, claiming cats were needed to keep animals out of their junkyard.[39] Meanwhile, others have allowed deductions including elective abortion services, toupees for some balding men, and breast augmentations for exotic dancers.[40]

Allowing deductions for everything from clown wigs to basketball jerseys,[41] the tax code not only misdirects federal funding but imposes a significant drag on the overall economy, hindering growth and slowing the recovery. As wages continue to stagnate, and many Americans are still unemployed, the sluggish economy has produced below-average levels of federal revenue in recent years. With Washington spending at an all-time high and record deficits, we simply can no longer afford the present code.

Competitive Rates

Ending tax earmarks and spending hidden in the code is the best way to exchange "revenue" with lower rates. This is what the Simpson-Bowles

Commission proposed.[42] The plan also lowered the corporate rate to 26 percent.[43]

SIMPSON-BOWLES TAX REFORM CALLED FOR LOWER TAX RATES

	Bottom Rate		Middle Rate		Top Rate		Corporate Rate
Current Rates	10%	15%	25%	28%	33%	35%	35%
Eliminate all Tax Expenditures	8%		14%		23%		26%

Lowering rates and ending special-interest spending in the tax code is what President Reagan did in 1986. Doing so again would be a win-win for taxpayers.

Low rates also relate back to fairness. The ideal tax rate is the rate at which government collects enough revenue to perform its essential functions and not a dime more. Another critically important principle when considering the ideal tax rate is something called "Hauser's Law," which shows that over the last six decades tax revenue as a percent of GDP has been about 19 percent, regardless of fluctuations in tax rates.[44] In other words, government has an impossible time collecting more than 19 or 19.5 percent of revenue even if it hikes tax rates considerably.

Simplicity

Simplifying the code by eliminating deductions, while lowering rates and reducing the number of tax brackets, would cut tax compliance costs dramatically. Remember, we spend $363 billion a year on tax compliance, which does nothing to create wealth and grow the economy.

Tax simplicity would redirect money away from the tax compliance industry and toward more productive activities and investments, which would create jobs and stimulate economic growth. Most important, tax simplicity would reward the risk takers, entrepreneurs, job creators, and consumers instead of politicians, lobbyists, and non–risk takers.

WHERE IS THE COURAGE TO REFORM THE CODE?

Even though both sides acknowledge the inefficiency and dysfunction of today's code, few politicians are willing to offer specific solutions and detail specific tax earmarks that should be eliminated or scaled back so we can lower rates. The American people can't afford to accept these nonanswers any longer.

One way to reform the code is to follow the Willie Sutton principle—go where the money is. This is difficult because much of the money in the tax code is within popular deductions like the mortgage deduction and charitable deductions. Few politicians have the guts to question the wisdom of some of these deductions even though they can harm consumers more than help them in the long run. For instance, if you think Washington has done a good job of managing the housing market after the subprime mortgage crisis, then you should like the mortgage interest deduction because the deduction is all about politicians manipulating the housing market through the code. The mortgage deduction gives consumers the illusion of saving money—and politicians the benefit of providing "affordable" housing—but what it really does is inflate the cost of housing. In reality, the deduction causes consumers to take out larger loans, which functions as an earmark—or subsidy—for mortgage brokers and real estate agents. The deduction is social engineering, not sound free-market economics.

It's true that provisions like the mortgage interest deduction can't be thrown out overnight because doing so would cause painful disruptions, but they can be scaled back and phased out in order to give the market a chance to correct itself and help future generations avoid our mistakes. In *Back in Black* I propose eliminating the deduction for second homes and equity lines of credit, combined with lowering the cap for the primary deduction to homes worth $500,000. This reform would save more than $187 billion over the next ten years. *Back in Black* includes dozens of other recommendations to eliminate tax expenditures large and small.

The point of my recommendations is to generate the kind of adult, grown-up conversation we have to have and responsible Americans want, if we are going to diffuse the debt bomb. Until we're willing to look at these high-dollar and costly tax earmarks, we will never have tax reform, grow our economy, and bring our debt down to a manageable level.

I'm convinced that if taxpayers are serious about getting our debt under control, we have to ask Washington to get out of the business of picking winners and losers through the tax code. As a nation, we can't have it both ways. We can't demand limited government and less debt while demanding the very spending that grows government and our debt.

Congress has tackled fundamental tax reform before and can do so again. In 1986, President Reagan passed a comprehensive tax reform plan that closed loopholes, lowered rates, simplified the code, and triggered our longest economic expansion since World War II. Reagan called the tax reform act "the best anti-poverty bill, the best pro-family measure and the best job-creation program ever to come out of the Congress of the United States." And as Martin Feldstein noted, federal revenues soared when this pro-growth reform was enacted.[45]

Congress has done bold tax reform in the past. It can and must do so again if we are going to survive in the twenty-first century.

THE SOLUTIONS:
THE PRINCIPLES OF THE TAX REFORMATION

1. The problem is overspending, not under-taxation.
2. There are not enough rich people to tax to get us out of debt.
3. The tax code's complexity rewards the well connected and wealthy.
4. Tax earmarks are spending programs to be eliminated, not tax cuts to be protected.
5. Tax earmarks are more consistent with socialism than with conservativism—they allow politicians to redistribute wealth through the code.
6. Tax earmarks keep rates artificially high—they are a tax increase on anyone who doesn't receive the benefit and can't hire a lobbyist or special-interest group to defend a perk.
7. Lower rates are preferable to higher rates and a complex code full of deductions, credits, loopholes, and earmarks.
8. Republicans who embrace tax earmarks desecrate the legacy of our founders and champions of limited government, such as Goldwater and Reagan.
9. Real tax reform that lowers rates and broadens the base would be an enormous economic stimulus and could create the momentum for a comprehensive deficit reduction agreement that would defuse the debt bomb.

12

Defense: Peace Through Strength Through Streamlining

This conjunction of an immense military establishment and a large arms industry is new in the American experience. The total influence—economic, political, even spiritual—is felt in every city, every statehouse, every office of the federal government. We recognize the imperative need for this development. Yet we must not fail to comprehend its grave implications. . . . In the councils of government, *we must guard against the acquisition of unwarranted influence, whether sought or unsought, by the military-industrial complex.* The potential for the disastrous rise of misplaced power exists and will persist. We must never let the weight of this combination endanger our liberties or democratic processes. . . . *Only an alert and knowledgeable citizenry can compel the proper meshing of the huge industrial and military machinery of defense with our peaceful methods and goals so that security and liberty may prosper together.*

—PRESIDENT DWIGHT D. EISENHOWER IN HIS FARE-
WELL ADDRESS TO THE NATION, JANUARY 17, 1961[1]

Few presidents have ever offered a more prophetic vision of government than Eisenhower in his famous speech about the military industrial complex. In the fifty-plus years since Eisenhower delivered his stark warning, his worst fears have been realized. We have the greatest military in the world and exceptional personnel. Yet, career politicians in Washington have rigged the system to defend themselves and, in the process, have undermined our national defense.

Of all the sacred cows that need to be tipped in Washington, defense spending is the biggest and most stubborn. It is tough to control for many reasons. First, it is one of the few legitimate constitutional roles of the federal government. Also, peace through strength is not a mere slogan but a reality of life. Maintaining a strong national defense is vital for our national security. Our strength is our best deterrent. Without it, our economy, freedoms, and liberty are all placed at risk.

However, wasting defense dollars neither defends our nation nor honors the sacrifice, heroism, and professionalism of our troops. In fact, spending money we don't have on things we don't need in such a large area of the budget as defense makes our greatest national security threat—our unsustainable national debt—more difficult to address.

Knowing what to keep and what to cut in the defense budget is our first responsibility as elected officials. Thinking critically about the defense budget is your responsibility as well. Eisenhower was exactly right when he said, "Only an alert and knowledgeable citizenry can compel the proper meshing of the huge industrial and military machinery of defense with our peaceful methods and goals so that security and liberty may prosper together."

How Defense Waste Threatens Our National Security

The military industrial complex tends to waste money in two primary ways—through bad contracting practices and old-fashioned parochialism.

Defense contracts often seem like they are designed to waste massive sums of money. For instance, many contracts are what are called "cost plus" contracts. In other words, DOD signs a contract with a company to deliver a system and then pays the company for any cost overruns. This creates a perverse incentive for initial contracts to be deliberately underbid and underestimated. After the contract is signed, contractors make money on cost overruns. A good example is the F-35 "Joint Strike Fighter," which has experienced cost overruns of 50 percent, bringing the total cost of the program to $388 billion.[2]

DOD contracting also suffers from what I call the "bells and whistles" problem. Because there are rarely adults with business experience in the room when contracting decisions are made, both companies and bureaucrats tend to add unnecessary requirements that can make otherwise effective systems prohibitively costly and subject to further delays. The desire to continually add new features has killed otherwise effective programs. The perfect becomes the enemy of the effective, affordable, and deployable. This phenomenon, which is also called "requirement creep" by defense experts, has cost taxpayers at least $30 billion in recent years and has led to cancellation of projects like the Comanche helicopter ($5.9 billion in lost costs) and Future Combat Systems—a collection of tanks, armored vehicles, and drones ($19 billion in lost costs).[3]

In other cases, good systems that could have benefited our troops in the field were delayed in order to add improvements. For instance, David Cote, CEO of Honeywell, explained to me how a backpack helicopter his company developed, which helps troops search for roadside bombs and do other reconnaissance, was delayed in order to add improvements when its immediate deployment may have been more beneficial.

Contracting lacks common sense in other ways. I'll never forget discussing the cost of producing the F-35 in my office with the CEO of Lockheed Martin, Robert Stevens. I asked Stevens what would happen if instead of producing the planes piecemeal across the country, we produced them in bulk.

"You could save 10 percent," Stevens responded.

When taxpayers are being asked to spend $388 billion on nearly twenty-five hundred F-35s, 10 percent is a lot of money. Congress wasn't even asking this question because it just wasn't how business was done. The fact that paying 10, 20, or 40 percent more than is necessary on a major weapons system just wasn't a problem brings us to the second major problem in defense spending I touched on earlier—parochialism.

Today, the military industrial complex has embedded itself in every congressional district and state across the country. Because career politicians tend to put their own parochial and political interests ahead of the country, efforts to streamline defense are met with fierce opposition.

The military industrial complex's war against change and efficiency came into clear focus last year when I met with Elon Musk, the CEO of a private space launch company, SpaceX, to discuss his desire to compete for Department of Defense space launch contracts. Musk, one of the top innovators and entrepreneurs in the world today, founded PayPal and served as its chairman and CEO before selling the company. Musk then used much of his own money to start SpaceX, the first company in the history of space flight to build a rocket that went into space and returned a capsule safely back to earth without government funding. For its efforts, SpaceX had already secured a contract with NASA to provide thirteen space launch missions to help resupply the International Space Station.

As we sat in my office, Musk discussed his goals for space flight. He said SpaceX was already able to deliver payloads into space at a third the cost of government and that he simply wanted to be given the opportunity to compete for contracts. He wanted to show that the savings they achieved at NASA could be replicated at DOD, where costs were spiraling out of control and where there is a de facto monopoly on space launches.

The military industrial complex and its agents in Congress had other ideas. The "United Launch Alliance" (ULA)—a joint venture with Boeing and Lockheed Martin—were working with the Air Force to lock out all competitors for contracts with the Department of Defense for the next five to seven years. The ULA had done good work, but they were not terribly efficient. The venture was supposed to decrease costs over the long term after an initial up-front investment by the government. That has not happened. Launch prices have doubled with the ULA and the Air Force could not give my office any specific savings that would be produced by locking out competitors.

Another problem with the status quo is the engines that launch our spy satellites are made in Russia. So, in other words, DOD was more interested in providing stimulus for Russia than in allowing competition. Incidentally, the GAO said, "The EELV (Evolved Expendable Launch Vehicle) program is dependent on Russian RD-180 engines for its Atlas line of launch vehicles, which according to the Launch Enterprise Transformation Study, is a significant concern for policymakers."[4] Yet, at the same time, Congress has somehow found a way to mandate that anchor chains for ships are made in the USA.[5] This was the perverse logic of the military industrial complex at work. It was fine for the engines that launched our spy satellites to be made in Russia as long as our anchor chains were made here in America.

My meeting with Musk was a reminder of the need to reform contracting to ensure that true innovators have a chance to compete. In the real world, economic stimulus means not giving people like Elon Musk a hard time. Pioneers like Musk and fellow space flight entrepreneur Jeff Bezos, the creator of Amazon.com, have the capability of creating entire industries and designing brand-new engines of economic growth.

Politicians and bureaucrats, on the other hand, will almost never do what is right and efficient when they can do what is safe and comfortable, especially if it involves helping a parochial interest or anchor chain maker back home.

Chris Edwards with the CATO Institute has described the parochialism problem very well. He writes:

> Defense contractors exploit this parochial self-interest of legislators, and they skillfully spread out research and production work across many states and districts to maximize congressional support. The $70 billion F/A-22 fighter program provides an example. *The Washington Post* noted in 2005 that the F/A-22 "is an economic engine, with 1,000 suppliers— and many jobs—in 42 states guaranteeing solid support in Congress." In 2009, Defense Secretary Robert Gates wanted to cancel further orders of the aircraft, but hundreds of lawmakers and state governors lobbied President Obama to keep the production lines going to preserve the 95,000 related jobs.[6]

This practice of spreading contracts out is well-known and taken for granted, even though it makes no economic or military sense. The F-22 was killed, but members of Congress tried to force the Pentagon to order a "second engine" for the F-35 the Pentagon did not want—so more states, and politicians, could benefit from DOD's largesse.[7] That effort was killed as well.

Many similar efforts, however, are not killed. Congress has a rich history of ordering ships and planes our generals did not ask for and do not need.[8] Sometimes the practice of earmarking defense funds has been shockingly blatant and harmful to our troops. For instance, in 2005 Representative David Wu, a Democrat from Oregon, forced the Marine Corps to purchase polyester T-shirts made by a company in his district called InSport after executives from the company donated thousands of dollars to his campaign. The problem with Wu's earmark is that polyester T-shirts were known to be extremely dangerous for troops serving in combat.

As David Heath and Hal Bernton reported in the *Seattle Times*:

> Polyester clothing melts in intense heat, adhering to the skin. "This essentially creates a second skin and can lead to horrific, disfiguring burns," said Capt. Lynn E. Welling, the 1st Marine Logistics Group head surgeon, who conducted research in Iraq in early 2006.
>
> Months after Wu's visit, a Marine wearing a polyester T-shirt was riding in an armored vehicle in Iraq when a bomb hidden on the road exploded. Even though the Marine wore a protective vest, the shirt melted in the explosion, contributing to severe burns over 70 percent of his body. Doctors had to extract the shirt's remains from the Marine's torso.[9]

The story gets worse. Instead of apologizing for his outrageous and reckless abuse of taxpayers and our troops, Wu slipped another $1 million earmark in the next defense bill to force the Marine Corps to purchase more T-shirts from the company in his district.

Wu's behavior is hardly an isolated incident. In 2007, for instance, career politicians put 2,700 earmarks in the defense bill, worth $11.8 billion. Both Republicans and Democrats have played games with the defense budget in a process my friend and fellow earmark critic Jeff Flake calls "circular fundraising."[10] Defense contractors large and small write politicians fund-raising checks, and politicians send defense contractors earmarked funds.

Another aspect of parochialism I've touched on is how the defense budget is also used as a jobs program across the country. There is nothing wrong with defense spending creating jobs, but spending money for projects that have no defense value is immoral.

In one such case I targeted for elimination a $7.5 million earmark for a company called 21st Century Systems Inc. (21 CSI) that had come under fire from the Omaha *World-Herald* for essentially being a holding company for earmarks. The vast majority of 21 CSI's funding came from federal grants that were mostly earmarks. As was the case with many such shell companies, 21 CSI had nine offices scattered strategically across the country in states represented by powerful members of the Senate Appropriations Committee. The Omaha *World-Herald* reported, "Only one piece of [21 CSI] software has been used—to help guard a single Marine camp in Iraq—and it was no longer in use."[11]

What made the 21 CSI case extraordinary was their response to my amendment striking one of their earmarks. The owner of 21 CSI threatened me with legal action for conducting oversight and questioning the wisdom of their earmarks. My amendment was a threat to their entire livelihood.

Defense porkers who didn't like my questioning their projects often insinuated I wasn't willing to look at spending in Oklahoma. That wasn't true. I not only refused to ask for earmarks for Oklahoma—for defense or any other area—but I also eliminated earmarks in my own state. For instance, when I heard about a $2 million earmark for an Urban Warfare Analysis Center (UWAC) in Shawnee, Oklahoma, boasting of hosting a "library" on this important subject, I decided to investigate.[12] It turns out the "library" was a four-foot bookshelf that contained perhaps twenty to twenty-five books. After a few phone calls among the delegation, the project was dead.

WHAT TO CUT FROM DEFENSE

In *Back in Black*, I call for $1 trillion in savings from defense over the next ten years. Here's why those savings are necessary.

Politicians love to ask for more defense spending, yet the fact is,

America's defenses have been decaying for decades despite increasing budgets. Over the last ten years, Congress increased annual appropriations to the Department of Defense by about 30 percent. In constant dollars, the annual base budget (excluding war spending) increased from $408 billion to $534 billion.[13]

Defenders of the status quo argue that defense spending as a percent of the economy is at its lowest level since World War II. That's true but misleading. The current nonwar budget is larger than our total defense budget during the defense buildup in the 1980s, when we faced the threat of a sophisticated global nuclear superpower with an overwhelming number of conventional forces in Europe. Today's nonwar defense budget also is larger than the total defense budget during the Vietnam War, when we had over 500,000 troops fighting overseas.[14] What the defense budget is lacking is not money but common sense.

Again, we have to ask: Has this significant increase in spending made us stronger or safer? The U.S. Navy has fewer combat ships than in any year since 1946; the U.S. Air Force has fewer combat aircraft; and the Army had the lowest levels of active-duty troops post World War II until around three years ago, when it added a small number of troops to its end strength.

We are spending more to get less. As the defense budget increased over time, our combat forces decreased. Former secretary Robert Gates noted in a speech in May 2010 that current submarines and amphibious ships are three times as expensive as their equivalents during the 1980s, and we have fewer of them.[15]

The growing cost of military hardware is certainly a key driver of our debt. The Government Accountability Office (GAO) releases an annual report of cost overruns of major weapon systems. Between 2001 and 2008, the GAO found nearly $300 billion in cost overruns and schedule delays for major defense acquisition programs.[16]

Rising personnel and benefit costs are another factor. Continuous military operations require adequate funding to recruit and retain military personnel. Ninety percent of all military personnel do not serve in a combat role, yet Congress chose to structure its pay and benefit increases across the military equally. Studies show that targeted bonuses for recruiting and enlisting are more effective ways to recruit and retain personnel. Even after nonpartisan experts recommended Congress change the way they compensate our military, Congress decided not to enact major reforms in this area.[17]

Aside from contracting reform, Congress can improve our readiness and national security in the following ways, which are outlined in more detail in *Back in Black*:

End the Subsidy for DOD-Administered Grocery Stores—$1.2 Billion[18]

The Defense Commissary Agency operates a worldwide chain of 254 grocery stores—called *commissaries*—on military bases around the world for military members, their families, and retirees. In 2009, it totaled nearly $6 billion in sales.[19] If the Defense Commissary Agency were a corporation, it would easily be one of the ten largest grocery store chains in the United States.[20] Instead, it is heavily subsidized by taxpayers to the tune of $1.2 billion a year.

Close DOD-Run Elementary Schools—$2 Billion

The Department of Defense operates 64 schools on 16 military installations in the United States, called the Domestic Dependent Elementary and Secondary Schools (DDESS), that cost an astonishing $51,000 per student, nearly three times as much as the worst public school system in the country—Washington, D.C.[21]

Today 26,000 students are taught by 2,300 teachers who are employees of the Department of Defense. Despite generous funding—$468 million in 2010—a recent report by the Center for Public Integrity noted, "Conditions are so bad [at military-run schools] that some educators at base schools envy the civilian public schools off base, which admittedly have their own challenges." Also, "Some of the new schools in town make our schools look like a prison," says David C. Primer, who uses a trailer as a classroom to teach students German at the vaunted Marine headquarters in Quantico, Virginia, just thirty miles south of the nation's capital, in one of the country's most affluent suburbs.[22]

When I tried to offer an amendment closing these schools, the National Education Association opposed my effort. Majority Leader Reid also did not want members to vote on the issue. I told the *Fiscal Times* the amendment was "not going anywhere because of the dysfunctionality of Congress, which is more worried about 'my base in my state' than giving kids a great education and saving the country money."[23]

Reduce Spending at the Congressionally Directed Medical Research Program on Nonmilitary-Specific Diseases—$2.7 Billion

Many Americans believe DOD is focused on only defense. Think again. Medical research is one of many areas in which DOD spends money that has nothing to do with fighting and winning wars. This proposal would reduce spending at the Congressionally Directed Medical Research Program (CDMRP) on nonmilitary-specific diseases. The CDMRP exists to "find and fund the best research to eradicate diseases and support the war fighter for the benefit of the American public."[24] It began in 1992 as a congressional earmark for breast cancer research. Over the last two decades, Congress funded CDMRP with nearly $6.5 billion for research into a variety of nonmilitary diseases with $500 million for 2010. Some projects directly relate to military concerns, such as a $463 million research effort into psychological health and traumatic brain injury. However, some other projects, such as $2.6

billion for breast cancer, $47.8 million for lung cancer, $113 million for prostate cancer, and $4.4 million for food allergies, have a vague connection to the military.

Not surprisingly, research on these diseases is specifically directed by the powerful defense committees in Congress during consideration of the annual appropriations bills.[25]

Reform Military Health Care—$115 Billion

The last area of the budget Washington politicians want to reform is veterans' health care. No one wants to be accused of being anti-veteran. And in spite of their desire to avoid hard choices and win reelection, members of Congress genuinely do want to do everything possible to provide the best possible care to our veterans and military retirees. Unfortunately, as members pursue this noble goal they sometimes treat veterans unfairly and make promises they can't keep.

One of the most controversial aspects of my proposal was to change what military retirees pay and receive from the government through a program called TRICARE, which serves more than nine million Americans who have served or are serving in the military as well as their family members.[26] Changing just a few aspects of TRICARE that provide extremely low-cost health insurance to military retirees (those who served twenty years) would save more than $100 billion over ten years.

One of the challenges in reforming military retiree health care is a lack of understanding regarding who these benefits are for, and why. TRICARE can refer to health care provided to active-duty troops, reservists, and National Guard that have been activated, as well as military retirees who have served twenty years and are no longer on active duty in the military. Spouses and dependents of active-duty troops also receive benefits. There are different benefits as well for military retirees upon retirement and a separate benefit plan for those who become eligible for Medicare. My budget proposals regarding TRICARE *only apply to military retirees and their families after retirement*—not to active-duty troops or their spouses and children.

Currently, military retirees who serve for twenty years are eligible for extremely low-cost health care coverage for life. This benefit is also extended to spouses and dependents (under the age of 26). However, the TRICARE benefit for military retirees is not awarded based on any sort of disability or injury suffered from military service or deployments to combat zones. TRICARE makes no distinction for military retirees that served in combat versus those that did not. There are retirees in the current system from the Cold War era who did not serve in a combat zone, while veterans who did multiple back-to-back deployments to Iraq and Afghanistan and leave the military after ten years or even fifteen years receive no TRICARE retiree health benefits.

To be clear, any veteran or retiree who suffers a disability or injury from combat or while on active military duty is entitled to free health care through the Department of Veterans Affairs.* However, TRICARE's purpose is to provide a health care benefit to military retirees whose need for health care is not connected to their military service. Therefore, my proposals to reform TRICARE for military retirees would not result in additional expenses for those retirees who were injured or disabled from combat service or any other injury sustained through their time in the military. In fact, the commonsense TRICARE reforms I have proposed would affect less than one in five veterans and their families.

TRICARE has become so costly because it has not been indexed to

---

* Veterans also receive a mileage reimbursement of 41 cents per mile for any travel to and from a VA health clinic or hospital for a visit involving an injury or disability connected to the veteran's military service. Veterans can elect to receive this benefit in cash at the time of the appointment.

keep up with the rising costs of health care, and no one in Congress has had the guts to acknowledge that costs are spiraling out of control. While the subsidy for military retirees has grown enormously, politicians have been terrified of putting on the brakes. The following chart from the Kaiser Family Foundation shows how employer and employee contributions to health plans have increased since 1999. What few Americans realize is that while the average family was paying $1,543 in 1999, the average military retiree family was paying only $460. In 2011, ten years later, military retirees were *still* paying only $460[27] while the average family is paying $4,129. In essence, their benefits have tripled. Indexing military retiree contributions to health plans the same way Medicare is indexed would save taxpayers more than $100 billion. Military retiree contributions would double, but military retirees would still be receiving extremely generous benefits.

Average Annual Worker and Employer Contributions to Premiums and Total Premiums for Family Coverage, 1999–2011

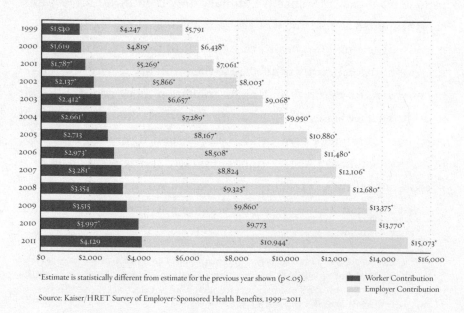

*Estimate is statistically different from estimate for the previous year shown (p<.05).

■ Worker Contribution
  Employer Contribution

Source: Kaiser/HRET Survey of Employer-Sponsored Health Benefits, 1999–2011

As I traveled the state, it was clear my proposal touched a nerve. In several town hall meetings, angry military retirees questioned why I would be going after their health care. I typically responded that while we were grateful for their service, they were not, in fact, promised extremely low-cost health care for life. In one particularly heated exchange, I asked a veteran, "Did you serve to only have to pay $230 a year for health care, or did you serve to protect our freedoms?"

This particular individual walked out, but the audience applauded. I explained that until we put everything on the table, asked the hard questions, and asked everyone to sacrifice, our nation would continue to be at risk.

I was also criticized by several letters to the editor in the *Daily Oklahoman* and other papers across the state that essentially asked, how dare you question veterans' benefits? Still, many Oklahomans were glad I was asking the hard questions, such as Jack C. Brown, who sent this comment to the *Daily Oklahoman*.

Several recent contributors to Your Views criticized Sen. Tom Coburn for his spending cut proposals. Whether you agree or disagree with specific proposals, you should applaud the fact we have a senator who's willing to provide a plan with details. Most government officials are cowards. They aren't willing to get into specifics for fear of alienating some constituency. "We must reduce spending" means nothing if you're not willing to provide specific suggestions and dollar amounts. So instead of criticizing Coburn, let's applaud a man who's trying to do something most won't even attempt. Proposals are not laws but rather starting points to a conversation we must have—reducing spending.[28]

Health care for veterans and military retirees is the very topic we have to debate if we are going to secure liberty for future generations.

Unfortunately, the emotionalism and misplaced sentimentality of these debates often obscure the facts. For instance, when I offered an amendment requiring that Agent Orange claims be awarded only to those who prove a causal link between their illnesses and the toxin, my amendment was rebuffed by a vote of 69 to 30. For years we had been throwing money at disabilities that were not caused by exposure to Agent Orange, but no one in Congress was willing to ask the hard questions based on science.

The amendment would have saved taxpayers $42.2 billion over the next ten years. I argued that if we pay for disabilities that aren't associated with service, we'll have less money for a veteran with a disability that is associated with service.

My list of proposed savings was far from perfect, but it was specific, which was very unusual for Washington. Several senators asked for more background.

In one meeting about which defense cuts to propose to the so-called supercommittee of 2011, Senator John McCain (R-AZ) asked a staffer, "Why can't we find the cuts Tom has? I want to do what Tom has done."

McCain then asked committee staff for a list of cuts. The committee responded, "The Pentagon should have a list of cuts for us by Friday."

"Why . . . do we have to wait on the Pentagon?" McCain asked calmly but firmly. "We should be giving them a list of cuts. Give them Tom's cuts!"

I will never know as much about military strategy as John McCain, nor will I ever have the experiences he has had. However, I do know something about management. The problem in Washington is the entire city and the military industrial complex are mobilized against people like John McCain who want to make hard choices.

With a budget worth hundreds of billions of dollars, the Pentagon should not force a senator like John McCain to "wait until Friday" to get a list of suggested cuts. Thankfully, waiting on the Pentagon wasn't good enough for McCain.

What was maddening was that even if the Pentagon had its list of cuts ready, the entire supercommittee process and its potential defense cuts would never happen. The process was wired to fail while giving politicians the appearance of doing something big and difficult on the budget.[29]

As a lobbyist for Americans for Tax Reform wrote to conservatives concerned about defense cuts, "The sequester [measure cutting defense spending] is written as a reduction in 050 (security) budget authority, where it's $500 over 10. This amounts to about $140 billion in 2013, hardly a huge pill to swallow, ESPECIALLY since the bill doesn't include limits on supplemental spending. Who's to say the 050 cut doesn't just show up in additional supplemental spending? Something to ponder for conservatives who are concerned about 'deep' defense cuts."

In other words, "conservatives" need not worry because regardless of how deep the defense cuts may look, they will never materialize. That's great news if you work for the military industrial complex, but bad news if you care about freedom. So it is okay with ATR to borrow billions for supplemental defense spending outside of the budget, but don't dare get rid of tax earmarks and more borrowing against our children. This type of thinking is what makes spending cuts and tax reform so difficult.

Still, it is true that an across-the-board sequestration of defense spending is a bad idea—it is like mowing the weeds along with the flower beds. Good projects will be cut along with bad projects. The smart thing to do is conduct oversight and cut what isn't working. The dollar goal of sequestration, though, was not the problem, just the method. Again, even with sequestration, defense spending would increase 16 percent over the next ten years compared to 23 percent without sequestration.[30]

Streamlining defense will strengthen, not weaken, our national security. History shows that all great powers eventually get the foreign policy they can afford, not what they want. As Will Durant warned, "A great civilization is not conquered from without until it has destroyed itself within."[31]

THE SOLUTIONS

We should be careful not to "gut" defense spending, but keeping defense spending off the table in budget talks is nonsense. Not all defense spending strengthens our national defense. In fact, billions in defense spending adds to our debt and compromises our national security.

The military industrial complex is more powerful today than ever. Both political parties treat the defense budget like a jobs program and an earmark slush fund.

Taxpayers should demand that defense spending receive the same degree of scrutiny as every other area of the budget.

13

The Debt Crisis Is a Moral Crisis

ONE OF MY POLITICAL HEROES IS WILLIAM WILBERFORCE, THE nineteenth-century British parliamentarian who led an unlikely and unpopular revolution against the slave trade in the British Empire. In 1787, Wilberforce famously wrote in his journal, "God has placed before me two great objects: the abolition of slavery and the reformation of manners in England."[1]

Amazingly, Wilberforce succeeded at both. On his deathbed he received word that the British Empire had abolished slavery, and his initiatives to reform the manners and morals of England marked the beginning of the Victorian era.

Today, we celebrate Wilberforce's success in abolishing slavery, which was the focus of a Hollywood film, *Amazing Grace*; but his accomplishment of helping to reform the culture of his time was equally impressive.

Wilberforce's example is worth looking at today for several reasons.

First, I would argue that preventing the collapse of our republic certainly qualifies as a "great object," which may be the great object that, as legislators, we have the greatest ability to address with our limited powers. Second, Wilberforce showed that so-called fiscal and social issues are deeply intertwined. The success of his two great objects depended on each other. This is an important lesson for today's conservatives, who tend to divide themselves into fiscal and social issue camps.

The reality is, the debt bomb was built by a culture, and it will be defused by a culture. As a nation, we have to make a decision to live within our means and embrace a government we can afford, not one we want.

LESSONS LEARNED FROM THE RELIGIOUS RIGHT

For many years, religious conservatives assumed that changing laws was the key aspect of cultural renewal. Obviously, changing laws is important. And it is true the law can be teacher. As Martin Luther King Jr. said, "It may be true that the law cannot make a man love me, but it can stop him from lynching me, and I think that's pretty important."[2]

Laws are pretty important, but they aren't the most important thing. As Wilberforce understood, politics and legislation are ultimately downstream from culture. Government is a reflection of the heart of the people. In Wilberforce's time, a culture that tolerated slavery would likely keep slavery legal. In order to change the slavery laws, you first had to change the culture. The same is true of our unsustainable and self-destructive fiscal policy.

The abortion debate proves this point. For instance, pro-life activists sometimes assume that overturning *Roe v. Wade* would be the decisive moment that would reduce the number of abortions. That isn't necessarily true. As Bill Wichterman, President Bush's liaison to faith-based groups, who is deeply pro-life, argues, the number of abortions did not increase substantially after the 1973 *Roe v. Wade* decision. What did cause the number of abortions to decline, however, was the *failure* of a legislative initiative to outlaw partial-birth abortion.[3] The debate was a great example of what I call the "winning by losing" principle. It educated the American people about life issues in a unique and compelling way that changed behavior and saved lives.

Viewing the debt crisis as a moral crisis does not require anyone to abandon his or her unique callings and gifts to be a voice for the unborn or to defend the sanctity of marriage and the family. In fact, if families— and especially fathers—took more responsibility, much of the debt crisis would go away. Sociologists have shown time and time again that stable families are one of the best defenses against poverty.

Fortunately, most thoughtful people of faith across America have thought through these issues, which is why the debt is a top concern among the public. Religious conservatives have learned the hard way that the power of government is severely limited in what it can do to transform a nation. Unfortunately, the religious left is now bowing to the same false god of government from the opposite side of the altar.

Lessons Not Yet Learned by the Religious Left

When the House of Representatives, under Paul Ryan's leadership, passed a historic budget in April 2011, many liberal clergy went apocalyptic.

"Speaker Boehner's budget eviscerates vital programs that protect the poor, the elderly, the homeless and at-risk pregnant women and children. This is not pro-life," said Stephen Schneck, director of the Institute for Policy Research & Catholic Studies at the Catholic University of America.[4]

Meanwhile, evangelical liberals like Jim Wallis were glibly asking, "How Christian is the Tea Party?" and "What Would Jesus Cut?"[5]

These exchanges expose what I call the left's *counterfeit compassion*. We hear a lot of talk about caring for the poor but very little evidence that the policies they espouse are working. In fact, the evidence shows government is harming the poor more than helping.

Imagine, for instance, if a conservative proposed a Medicaid reform that would result in 40 percent of doctors not seeing Medicaid patients, and 65 percent of specialists denying care to Medicaid patients. And then imagine if this same reform would cause Medicare patients to be rejected at a rate higher than that of private insurance. Finally, imagine if this reform idea would cause the bankruptcy of Medicare and the likely denial of benefits in five years. A conservative who would suggest such a thing would be castigated as uncaring. Yet these outcomes are already happening in the present, which begs the questions of those on the left: Where have you been? Where have you been while these programs have been disintegrating before our eyes?

The main lesson at the intersection of faith and politics is this: government can do justice, but not charity. Government simply was not designed to do charity. When a free citizen does charity, two people benefit—the person doing the charity and the person receiving the charity. When government does the charity, it creates dependency and denies the individual the benefit of providing charity.

CHANGE REQUIRES MORAL COURAGE

As I've shown throughout this book, the problem in Washington is not a lack of good intentions but the presence of double-minded careerism. Careerism is the sin of self-preservation. Real leaders, on the other hand, are obedient to a calling even unto death. Of course, for most politicians, death is not literal. Death may mean career death—losing an election—or loss of prestige or reputation.

Another great model of obedience was German theologian Dietrich Bonhoeffer, who risked his life to oppose Hitler and was eventually executed because of his connection to the plot to assassinate the Führer.[6] Even at the gallows, Bonhoeffer never doubted the justice of his cause. That is the kind of courage and clarity of conviction we need in Washington today.

THE MORAL RESPONSIBILITIES OF WE THE PEOPLE

In the book *The Tragedy of American Compassion*, Marvin Olasky asks readers to consider the criteria charities in America followed more than one hundred years ago when providing assistance.[7]

1. To give relief only after personal investigation of each case.
2. To give necessary articles and only what is immediately necessary.
3. To give what is least susceptible to abuse.
4. To give only in small quantities in proportion to immediate need; and less than might be procured by labor, except in cases of sickness.
5. To give assistance at the right moment; not to prolong it beyond duration of the necessity which calls for it.
6. To require of each beneficiary abstinence from intoxicating liquors.
7. To discontinue relieving all who manifest a purpose to depend on alms rather than their own exertions for support.

If the American people practiced these principles in their own families, communities, and neighborhoods, and required government to do the same, we would solve our debt crisis overnight.

In our free society, limited government only works when we re-establish the right relationship between government and the people. As government decreases, personal responsibility increases. Personal responsibility means you are personally taking responsibility not just for yourself but for others. Personal responsibility is not a license for self-interested materialism but a call to take responsibility for the common good without waiting on government or someone else to act.

And taking responsibility will require critical choices.

Conclusion

The Choices That Must Be Made

Few men are willing to brave the disapproval of their
fellows, the censure of their colleagues, the wrath
of society. Moral courage is a rarer commodity than
bravery in battle or great intelligence. Yet it is the one
essential, vital, quality for those who seek to change
a world which yields most painfully to change.

—ROBERT KENNEDY[1]

WASHINGTON TODAY IS A CITY THAT FIERCELY RESISTS CHANGE.
The forces of careerism—and cowardice—have so far prevented our
leaders from making the courageous choices these times require.
Washington may convince itself we can put off these choices a little longer. We could see an uptick in the economy or watch other nations
flounder and find comfort in our relative strength. Yet, the choices I've
laid out in this book are inescapable.

If America were one of my patients, I would tell her she had a 100 percent chance of experiencing a major cardiac event—a potentially fatal heart attack or stroke—if she failed to take immediate steps to get healthy. As a physician, when a patient's life is in imminent danger—as our economy is today—you first have to pursue the vital interventions to keep the patient alive.

THE LIFE-AND-DEATH ISSUES:
ENTITLEMENTS, TAXES, SPENDING

The vital interventions I've outlined—revamping our safety net, reforming our tax code, and reducing our lower-priority spending in all areas of government—will save the patient. But to get there, both citizens and legislators will be required to have an adult conversation and put the survival of the nation ahead of short-term politics. The good news is, all of these problems can be solved with choices that are not as hard as people in Washington may suggest.

With respect to the safety net, we have to abandon the language of entitlements once and for all. Yet, we do not need to abandon our desire to help those who truly cannot help themselves. In order to repair our safety net, we have to accept the economic fact that there is no longer any such thing as *my* or *your* Social Security or Medicare. The money for *my* benefits or *your* benefits does not exist. It will exist only if we persuade other nations and private investors to loan us the money to repay the funds politicians stole from the trust funds. Many other countries are facing the same dilemma. Today, we are living through the global collapse of the welfare state. We can either reform these programs, or we can watch the welfare state go bankrupt and bring our economy along with it.

We can avoid a catastrophe if we embrace straightforward structural reforms, such as relating benefits to income and increasing the retirement age for Social Security and Medicare recipients. If we take the additional step of allowing market forces to work in the health care economy, we'll see costs stabilize and quality increase.

With respect to tax reform, we have to reject the partisan argument that says the Bush tax cuts are the cause of our debt problem and acknowledge the fact that unsustainable entitlement spending on programs created eighty years ago is the real culprit. Also, we have to realize that trying to defuse the debt bomb by raising tax rates in a weak economy would kill a recovery and make our debt problem worse.

Those of us on the right have to realize the days of using tax purity pledges as a license to borrow and spend beyond our means are over. We also have to end the practice of hiding our earmarks in the tax code. We should not be afraid of putting revenue on the table, because that is the best way to prevent massive tax increases, financial repression, and an economic meltdown. As Friedman argued, inflation is a hidden tax and taxation without representation. An agreement that combines real entitlement reform with tax reform would be, in fact, a huge victory for limited-government constitutional conservatives.

Tax reform is the invitation and pathway to a solution. As Senate Democrat and Majority Whip Dick Durbin said in November 2011, "The fact that some Republicans have stepped forward to talk about revenue, I think, is an invitation for Democrats to step forward and talk about entitlement reform as well as spending cuts. Therein lies the core of an agreement."[2]

How to Secure Freedom, and Achieve a Real Recovery

This book has focused on the life-and-death issues described above, but, as a nation, we have to come to grips with the fact that these interventions alone will not be enough over the long haul. We have to save the patient and then embrace various lifestyle changes, so to speak, that will enable a recovery to take root and become sustainable.

One key lifestyle adjustment would be adopting an energy policy based on our national interest and sound economics rather than environmental fanaticism and left-wing special-interest fetishes. Our nation has the capability of becoming virtually energy independent while creating millions of jobs if we would embrace the reality that for the next twenty years at least, we will have a fossil fuel–based economy rather than an economy based on unproven "green" technologies. We also have to ask ourselves, which is the greater threat? Our debt bomb, which has brought down other nations throughout history, or the unproven threat of human-induced global warming? I would suggest we should organize our economy around proven threats.

We should, of course, be good stewards of the environment, but we should not let go of the principle that free economies also tend to be clean economies. We can remember that when the Berlin Wall fell, the buildings in communist East Berlin were covered in soot while, by contrast, those in West Berlin looked pristine. We can Google a picture of North and South Korea from space and see that North is as black as coal, while South is shimmering with light. Ending mindless regulations and restrictions will let the market work and create millions of jobs, stimulate real economic growth, and raise the revenue we need to get out of our economic hole.

North Dakota is a case study in what can happen with a sound energy policy. In North Dakota, unemployment went down to around 3 percent last year, compared to 9.2 nationwide.[3] The reason? New technologies that allow us to access the 4 billion barrels of oil in the Bakken field led to strong economic growth. A reasonable energy policy could create hundreds of thousands of jobs every year and hundreds of billions of dollars in additional revenue.

Unfortunately, our energy policy is not reasonable. It is schizophrenic.

Case in point: Early in 2012, President Obama rejected the approval of a major pipeline—the Keystone XL pipeline—from Alberta to the Gulf Coast. Alberta is expected to become the world's second-largest oil producer within a decade. The project would have created about 118,000 new jobs and reduced our dependence on Middle East oil. Yet, instead of seeing the pipeline as a blessing, Obama saw it as a political burden. So the Canadians may decide to build their pipeline west instead, toward China and the Pacific market.

Mary O'Grady highlighted the idiocy of the Obama administration position in the *Wall Street Journal*:

The province [Alberta] is on track to become the world's second-largest oil producer, after Saudi Arabia, within 10 years. Meanwhile Mr. Obama clings to his subsidies for solar panels and his religious faith in green jobs.

Haven't we heard, like forever it seems, that we need to wean ourselves from too much reliance on Middle East oil? Yes, we have. In fact, the Energy Department was created specifically to reduce America's dependence on oil from the Middle East. So is our Government celebrating Canada's new oil production, eagerly awaiting more oil right here in North America to replace foreign oil from the sheiks of Saudi Arabia? Wouldn't buying less oil from the sheiks mean they would have less money with which to plot terrorist attacks against us? Yes, yes, and yes. But no, no and no says Obama.

Much of America's vast untapped energy potential lies dormant because Mr. Obama's regulatory watchdogs have spent the past three years throwing sand in the gears of the permitting process for exploration and exploitation on federal lands.[4]

PRACTICAL STEPS FOR CONCERNED CITIZENS

As I've shown, the real resistance to change in Washington does not come from a deep ideological commitment to Marxism or socialism. Instead, the real problem is fear, combined with a lack of leadership, a shortage of courage, and leaders whose greatest desire is to win reelection. The way to break this logjam is to change who is serving in Washington.

Never underestimate the power of your leverage and influence over politicians. Again, most politicians live in a state of constant fear and will respond to what they perceive to be agitation in their states and districts.

Consider using these commonsense accountability tactics:

- *Write letters to your elected official.* If you get a form letter back that didn't answer your question, write again. I personally read every letter that comes into my office, and I approve every letter that goes out of my office. Very few elected officials do that, even though it is the most important part of our jobs. I don't personally write every letter at the keyboard, but every response is dictated by me and reflects my views, not those of a staff member or a lobbyist. Letters are very influential, especially handwritten ones. *One letter from a concerned citizen makes a difference.*
- *Create your own blog.* Every elected official receives news clips and articles that mention his or her name. Blogs sometimes, not always, appear in clips but are almost always noticed by staff. The Internet has given every citizen the power to be a journalist and commentator. Use that power to your advantage.
- *Attend town hall meetings and ask tough, direct, and thoughtful questions.* It is not unusual for a town hall exchange to make

local, state, and even national news. Politicians gauge what constituents are really feeling based on town hall meetings. Attend them whenever possible, and make your views heard.

- *Impose term limits.* There is no better way to break the culture of careerism than by arranging early retirements.

Term limits could be accomplished in two ways. One, through a constitutional amendment or, two, by simply firing career politicians at the polls who refuse to solve the nation's problems.

Personally, I'm a fan of the Jack Welch principle in reverse for Congress. Welch, the successful former CEO of General Electric, used what was called the 10 percent rule to maintain efficiency and productivity at his company. Every year the bottom 10 percent of the company would be replaced with new employees.[5] A better approach for Congress would be to fire 90 percent of members every election and only keep the 10 percent who were productive. This would defuse the debt bomb in one election cycle.

Another approach is to mount primary challenges for every incumbent every cycle. Members need to be reminded that serving in office is a privilege, not a lifetime appointment. Regular primary challenges will keep politicians honest. And if members do not agree to voluntarily limit their terms, don't elect them.

Finally, it's vital to elect and recruit people who have real-world, rather than just political, experience. As a nation, we have to look beyond the traditional political farm systems of state legislatures and elect people of character who have practical experience. Small business owners, machine workers, teachers, policemen, nurses, and military personnel would all be good candidates. In fact, a random sampling of 535 Americans would generate a solution to our debt crisis much quicker than the current group of entrenched career politicians.

The wonderful thing about new members is they have not yet learned what is not possible in Washington. Steve Jobs was right to complain that President Obama spent far too much time complaining about what could not be done.[6] Almost all career politicians are part of the axis of excuses. New members, on the other hand, operate on the basis of common sense rather than elite-Washington conventional wisdom. For most politicians, Washington "experience" really means unlearning what they knew when they were first elected.

Congress today is a stagnant pond that needs to be drained and refilled with a steady stream of new public servants. Only you can make that happen.

ADVICE TO ELECTED OFFICIALS

It is very easy to talk about cutting spending and reforming government, but doing it is very hard. When I came to the Senate I made a decision early on to focus on issues and solutions I believed would be "80 percent issues" and would seem like common sense to the average American. My goal was not to embarrass Democrats or gloss over Republican hypocrisy. Instead, I wanted to build a constituency for real change among Americans from all stripes and then show those smart Americans how out of touch Washington was, and is, with reality. For instance, I knew that even though 80 percent of Washington wanted to defend earmarks, 80 percent or more of Americans disagreed. The Bridge to Nowhere vote is the best example. I lost 82–15 among my colleagues but won at least 82–15 among the public. And, eventually, the public defeated the careerists.

I believe the same logic applies to my hold battles and efforts to forge unlikely coalitions around big solutions. Most Americans don't care how Washington lobbyists and special-interest groups define purity because they rightly assume the people developing those standards are operating out of self-interest and are disconnected from the real world.

No one in America wants the debt bomb to explode. Americans are far more interested in politicians reaching a solution than in their maintaining partisan positions or false standards of purity. While I don't apologize for trying to convert my colleagues to my conservative positions, I also don't apologize for trying to form coalitions with unlikely allies. Again, I'd much rather work with Democrats in our government than communists in the Chinese government who will one day force our hand if we don't do this work on our own.

But perhaps the best advice is to simply make the effort to fix this problem and not wait for a perfect political moment that will never arrive. In today's economy there is no excuse for not trying. Sometimes individual amendments can seem like taking a blowtorch to a glacier. Over time, however, a few strategic holes can undermine massive blocks of ice.

This is exactly what happened in the earmark debate. We "won" very few amendments, but we undermined the entire earmark culture and caused it to collapse.

I have a dry-erase board up in our legislative war room that reads:

What Does Not Cut Spending
- Commissions
- Caps
- Process reform
- Speeches
- Press releases (talkers, tweets, lunches, listserves, etc.)

What Does Cut Spending
- Rescissions
- Cuts
- Program eliminations

Here's a practical tip: *Relentlessly expose wasteful spending, then target it for elimination.* This seems obvious, but it is rarely done in Washington. There is no shortcut to doing the hard work of oversight and legislating. Process reforms can be helpful, but too often members hide behind proposals to balance the budget, for instance, without outlining how they would do so and what they would cut. Taxpayers should be very skeptical of politicians who lack specifics, especially if they have voted for the very borrowing and spending that have made balanced budgets so difficult to achieve.

All that I've outlined in terms of oversight is in the "Oversight and Investigations" section of my website at www.coburn.senate.gov and in appendix C.

Another tip: *Don't be a contestant in the partisan purity pageant.* There is nothing easier in politics than figuring out what people want to hear and then repeating it over and over again. That isn't good enough anymore. It will always be easier to join the talk show circuit than the oversight circuit. Today, far too many "conservatives" are populists without portfolios. Firing up the base is fine, but we have a crisis to solve today. We need real solutions.

Finally: *Expect to be criticized.* Regardless of what you do, you will be accused of being either extreme or a sellout or, most likely, both. Ignore the chatter and do your job, which is solving problems, not getting reelected.

A Challenge to the Media

Please spend more time covering real issues and less time covering the horse race. This applies to both liberal and conservative media. Change happens between elections. And change only happens when problems and solutions are explained and dissected. The media on the left and right find it much easier to cover the fight than the actual solutions. I've done everything I can do to identify possible solutions and highlight examples of government waste. No one has offered more amendments to cut spending, authored more original oversight reports, or held more bills than I have. If my solutions are not interesting enough, then find someone else's solutions to discuss so we can solve the nation's problems. The battle is before us right now. It's time to pay attention and cover news that matters.

ENCOURAGEMENT TO THE TEA PARTY AND OTHER GRASSROOTS MOVEMENTS

The rise of the Tea Party is the best thing to happen in American politics since 1994. Unlike in 1994, the Tea Party now has the capacity to force Congress to stay on course and not go native.

Real structural change is both a top-down and bottom-up phenomenon. That is precisely what is happening now in American politics with the Tea Party. The left wants to dismiss the Tea Party as a flash in-the-pan Astroturf phenomenon that was created by powerful politicians and big-money right-wing donors. That is wishful thinking.

The reality, which should be deeply encouraging to America, is the Tea Party is not an institution but a spontaneous movement of We the People that was already mobilizing before the elites knew what was happening. Elites can spend as much money as they want on activism, but it will accomplish nothing if there is not already a movement to mobilize.

To keep the movement on track, I'll close with these thoughts:

- *Don't institutionalize the movement and worry too much about branding.* Keep the tea party a lowercase movement, not an uppercase movement. The label is irrelevant and can change. The point is to keep the rumble organized and motivated until we solve our debt crisis. Don't forget that every positive development that has happened since 2005 has happened because concerned citizens were demanding change. You deserve the credit.

- *Be very suspicious of politicians who want to wrap themselves in the Tea Party banner.* As I've told national Tea Party leaders, I decline most invitations to speak at rallies because politicians tend to use the movement to boost their conservative credentials and assist their reelection campaigns.

- *Demand results, not rhetoric.* If "Tea Party" candidates refuse to offer specific solutions and fight for those solutions, replace them with candidates who will step up to the plate.

- *Ignore the critics.* The conventional wisdom about the Tea Party is that it is a movement of the unwashed masses who want to indiscriminately cut government. Most Tea Party activists I've met know a lot more about the real world than the typical Washington politician and are fighting for smart cuts and a thoughtful and compassionate vision of government that is a profound threat to the careerist status quo. Ignore the critics, and keep driving the national conversation toward a renewal of our founders' vision of limited government.

WE CAN'T WAIT ON A SOLUTION

The big question facing America now, and in the foreseeable future, is not who is going to win the next election but whether we are going to defuse a debt bomb that has put our very survival at risk. The battle is upon us now. Neither side can afford to be idle until a perfect political moment—or moment of total victory—that will never arrive.

The pessimists say America's best days are behind us and our decline is inevitable. I don't believe that's the case, not necessarily because of what I see in Washington, but because of what I see across America.

One of the privileges of being a United States Senator is reading letters from people across the country and especially from my home state of Oklahoma. Few have inspired me more than a letter I received from a retired veteran from my state.

Dear Senator Coburn:

I'm a retired military member and veteran, deployed four times during my career—having spent years of my life in some very dangerous places, away from home, and in tough conditions. I am very familiar with shared sacrifice. In all those days away, my sole purpose was to be prepared and ensure my soldiers were ready to deploy and return alive. In our current situation, it's easy to feel like we're (as a country) going into battle unprepared against an economic, financial enemy of political gridlock and no compromise; with two political parties vying for the next election.

I'm well aware that many proposals currently out there would potentially affect me.

However, I'm willing to work hard now and be part of a solution which solidifies our country's future versus robbing my kids and grandkids from the same opportunities our great country offers . . .

Please inform your colleagues—there are more people like me awaiting leadership and good decision making than there are left and right side uncompromising voters. These times call for briefings to the American people, not speeches. These times call for members of Congress to stand together . . . and to show how sacrifice now can lead to renewed prosperity later.

Sincerely,
Robin Boudiette, Jr.
Lawton, OK

Letters like this remind me why it is not too late for America to cheat history and avoid the fate of other great nations who lived beyond their means for far too long. From the New England liberal who sent me the framed image of the word "No" to this retired veteran from Lawton, America is still full of decent, brave, and sensible people who want a solution to the challenges we face. We are still what our founders envisioned—a republic of virtue.

Still, we face tremendous challenges. In his first inaugural address, George Washington said, "There is no truth more thoroughly established than that there exists in the economy and course of nature an indissoluble union between virtue and happiness."[7]

The pain so many Americans have experienced in this economy—especially in the housing collapse—can, in part, be traced to a breakdown in virtue. Banks took advantage of poorly written laws and regulations and acted out of greed. Politicians failed to do politically costly oversight of their donors and acted out of self-preservation. And sadly, individual Americans got swept up in schemes that seemed too good to be true. Everyone's worst instincts prevailed. It was a perfect storm of bad impulses and perverse incentives. Millions suffered, sometimes from their mistakes, but often from the mistakes of others.

The solution to what is a much greater economic threat—our debt bomb—will require us to reembrace virtue. The virtue we need in Washington more than any other right now is courage. I'm confident we can find a way to defuse our debt bomb because America, as a nation, and as individuals, is courageous. We've proven it time and time again.

The problems discussed in this book are not hard to solve. The solutions are not rocket science; many are commonsense answers that have been floating around Washington for years. What has been lacking is the courage to act on those solutions.

I certainly don't claim to have all of the solutions, but I do trust individual Americans to find them and support them. I hope I've done my part to suggest some ideas and make them a little less confusing.

From my vantage point, having spent hundreds of hours with people who have a sacred responsibility to solve this problem—from the president to congressional leaders—I believe a consensus for a solution already exists in the country and in Washington. In spite of all of the political theater and posturing Americans see in our nation's capital, both sides are largely in agreement about the magnitude of the fiscal challenges we face and are not as far apart as it seems in terms of a solution. The question, though, does come down to one of political will and courage. Will we be career politicians, or will we be statesmen? The fact is, a real solution will never fit into an election-year strategy. As long as the political strategists and branding experts prevail, our national security will be at risk. The good news is, there is a growing cadre of members of Congress in Washington who, like Mr. Boudiette, are ready to go into battle and to lay down their political lives for their country. With a little leadership and courage, we can get there sooner than you think.

The challenge before us is as great as any we have faced, but our nation has faced great challenges before and emerged stronger and more prosperous. Together, as a nation, we can make the choices that must be made, and preserve the brightest beacon of freedom the world has even known.

Acknowledgments

A VERY SPECIAL THANKS . . .

To our families for their love, support, and encouragement—especially Carolyn, Callie, Katie, and Sarah; and Kimberly, Nora, Jack, and Gabriel.

To Michael Schwartz—for showing us what it means to fight the good fight, finish the race, and keep the faith. Well done, good and faithful servant.

To my staff for their dedication, loyalty, hard work, and initiative—Cheryl Adams, Keith Ashdown, Katie Bailey, Matt Ball, Chris Barkley, Bryan Berky, Drew Berky, Becky Bernhardt, Joelle Cannon, John Carson, John Chapuis, Suzanne Chapuis, Jenny Clem, Andrew Dockham, Tyler Faught, Elizabeth Floyd, Aaron Fobes, Roland Foster, Jonathan Gray, Sarah Beth Groshart, Patrick Guinn, Janice Hagan, Jeremy Hayes, Donna Henley, Dan Hourigan, Michael Junk, Caleb Krautter, Clay Lightfoot, Jerry Morris, Sekemia Mwonyoni, Tripp Parks, Connie Pearson, Laura Pence, Justin

Rood, Michael Schwartz, Paige Scott, Leigh Sethman, Courtney Shadegg, Emily Shipley, Craig J. Smith, Kyle Springer, Gabe Sudduth, Elizabeth Taylor, Brian Treat, Josh Trent, Laura Villarreal, and Joni Williams.

To the original Porkbusters—Glenn Reynolds and Rob Neppell.

To the experts who have given their time to educate me and other members of Congress, and who influenced this work—Kyle Bass, Veronique de Rugy, Neal McCluskey, Carmen Reinhart, Kenneth Rogoff, and many others.

To the team at Thomas Nelson for seeing the urgency of this threat and helping us raise these issues for the American people—Kristi Henson, Janene MacIvor, Joel Miller, Kristen Parrish, and Walter Petrie.

And to my colleagues in Congress and friends at the other end of Pennsylvania Avenue—thank you for listening to my doomsday speeches. I love and respect each of you even when we passionately disagree, and even when I support the challenger. We are all on America's team. Let's lay down our political lives and cheat history together.

Appendix A

Savings Breakdown from *Back in Black*

Discretionary and Other Mandatory	Deficit Reduction
General Government Reforms	$974.08 billion
Congress	$4.28 billion
Executive Branch	$5.40 billion
Judiciary Branch	$7.78 billion
Department of Agriculture	$346.40 billion
Department of Commerce	$26.84 billion
Department of Defense	$1.006 trillion
Department of Education	$409.10 billion
Department of Energy	$101.77 billion
Department of Health and Human Services	$106.70 billion
Department of Homeland Security	$23.29 billion
Department of Housing and Urban Development	$88.73 billion
Department of the Interior	$26.44 billion
Department of Justice	$34.54 billion

Department of Labor	$268.04 billion
Department of State and Foreign Aid	$192.12 billion
Department of Transportation	$192.22 billion
Department of Treasury and GSEs	$39.72 billion
Department of Veteran Affairs	$13.57 billion
U.S. Army Corps of Engineers	$5.28 billion
Environmental Protection Agency	$33.67 billion
NASA	$51.15 billion
National Science Foundation	$14.20 billion
Small Business Administration	$3.22 billion
Other Independent Agencies	$48.89 billion
SSI and SSDI	$17.17 billion

Entitlements

Medicare and Medicaid	$2.64 trillion
Social Security	75+ Years Solvent

Revenue

Reform Tax Expenditures	$962.02 billion
Other Government Revenue	$30.34 billion
Interest	$1,360 trillion
Total	$9,032 trillion

Actions Speak Louder than Words—Key Votes

MEMBERS ON BOTH SIDES OF THE AISLE LIKE TO PRESENT themselves as fiscally responsible, but their votes tell a different story. Since 2005, I have offered 705 amendments to cut spending and reduce the size of government. Below are a few votes that illustrate the Senate's refusal to set commonsense priorities and cut wasteful spending. The entire list can be found in the "Porkbusters" section of my website, www. coburn.senate.gov.

October 6, 2005: Senate tables amendment (*tabling* means the Senate refuses to take a straight up or down vote on the substance of the amendment) to curtail waste under the DOD web-based travel system. [65–32]

October 20, 2005: Senate votes to protect funding for Bridge to Nowhere in Alaska. [15–82]

March 28, 2007: Senate rejects amendment to provide farm assistance in fiscally responsible manner. [23–74]

May 15, 2007: Senate rejects amendment to prioritize federal spending to ensure the needs of Louisiana residents who lost their homes as a result of Hurricane Katrina and Rita are met before spending money to design or construct a nonessential visitors center. [11–79]

May 15, 2007: Senate rejects amendment to prioritize federal spending to ensure the residents of the city of Sacramento are protected from the threat of floods before spending money to add sand to beaches in San Diego. [12–77]

September 11, 2007: Senate tables amendment to prohibit the use of funds for bicycle paths so that the funds can be used to improve bridge and road safety. [80–18]

September 11, 2007: Senate tables amendment to prohibit funds from being used for earmarks until all structurally deficient and functionally obsolete bridges have been repaired. [82–14]

September 12, 2007: Senate tables amendment to prohibit the use of funds for the construction of a baseball facility in Billings, Montana, and to reduce the amounts made available for the Economic Development Initiative and the Community Development Fund. [63–32]

September 12, 2007: Senate rejects amendment to require that the housing needs of all Louisiana residents displaced by Hurricanes Katrina and Rita are met before spending money to design or construct a Wetland Center in Lake Charles, Louisiana. [32–63]

October 23, 2007: Senate rejects amendment to require Congress to provide health care for all children in the United States before funding special-interest pork projects. [26–68]

October 30, 2007: Senate rejects amendment to ensure Amtrak no longer consistently loses money on food and beverage services. Potential savings: $244.5 million. [24–67]

March 19, 2009: Senate rejects amendment eliminating low-priority spending for a birthday party for St. Augustine, Florida; botanical gardens in Hawaii and Florida; a salmon restoration project in California; a study of Alexander Hamilton's boyhood estate in the Virgin Islands; and historic shipwreck exploration. [27–70]

March 19, 2009: Senate rejects amendment requiring an annual report detailing total size and cost of federal property. [39–58]

March 19, 2009: Senate tables amendment to prohibit funding for earmarks for wasteful and parochial pork projects. [70–27]

August 4, 2009: Senate rejects amendment that would have eliminated $3 billion in federal funding for the specialty cheese industry in Wisconsin and Vermont. [**voice vote**]

September 16, 2009: Senate rejects amendment to allow states to opt out of a provision requiring them to purchase transportation enhancements, such as gigantic coffeepots and transportation museums, instead of allowing them to fix deficient bridges in their states. [39–59]

October 6, 2009: Senate rejects amendment to restore $166 million for the armed forces to prepare for and conduct combat operations by eliminating earmarks. [25–73]

January 26, 2010: Senate rejects amendment that would have cut $245 million from Congress's budget for itself. [46–48]

March 24, 2010: Senate rejects amendment to eliminate fraudulent payments and prohibit Viagra coverage for child molesters and rapists and for drugs intended to induce abortion. [57–42]

April 14, 2010: Senate rejects amendment to pay for the full cost of extending additional unemployment insurance and other supplemental spending by reducing waste, inefficiency, and unnecessary spending within the federal government. [53–45]

June 29, 2011: Senate rejects amendment to prevent the creation of duplicative and overlapping federal programs. [63–34]

September 15, 2011: Senate rejects amendment to save at least $7 billion by consolidating duplicative and overlapping programs. [54–45]

October 21, 2011: Senate rejects amendment to end payments to landlords who are endangering the lives of children and needy families. [59–40]

Appendix C

Oversight Reports

IN THIS BOOK I TALK A GREAT DEAL ABOUT OVERSIGHT AND WHY it matters. In the real world, oversight is essentially maintenance—the often unpleasant but critically important tasks like taking out the trash, shoveling the driveway, and even disciplining children that, if ignored, lead to considerable pain and discomfort. Our government is so wasteful because members prefer to spend new money rather doing the maintenance—oversight—on existing programs. If your member of Congress is spending more time creating new programs than doing maintenance on existing programs, there is a good chance he or she is part of the problem in Washington. All my oversight reports are in the "Oversight and Investigations" section of my website at www.coburn.senate.gov.

June 2007: *CDC Off Center* examines how the Centers for Disease Control and Prevention has lost sight of its core mission. The American people expect CDC to spend its $10 billion budget treating and preventing disease and dealing with public safety threats, including the threat of bioterrorism. Instead, CDC has spent hundreds of millions of tax dollars on failed prevention efforts, international junkets, and lavish facilities, while failing to demonstrate it is controlling disease.

May 2008: *For the Farmers for Fun: USDA Spends over $90 Million in Conference Costs* examines federal agencies' lavish spending on conferences at the Department of Agriculture (USDA). USDA recently reported to Congress that it spent $19.4 million on conferences in 2006—almost tripling the amount it spent in 2000. There are approximately 112,000 employees at USDA, and in 2006, the agency sent 20,959 employees to 6,719 conferences and training events across the nation and around the world.

August 2008: *The XVII International AIDS Conference* is a review of federal agency spending on an international conference that is costing taxpayers almost half a million dollars—dollars that could have helped prevent HIV/AIDS and treat those living with the disease.

August 2008: *Missing in Action: AWOL in the Federal Government* looks at the time federal employees are absent from their jobs without permission. Between 2001 and 2007, the number of work hours lost to AWOL employees rose steadily. In total, there were nearly 20 million AWOL hours in just seven years across 18 departments and agencies.

October 2008: *Justice Denied: Waste & Management at the DOJ* exposes extensive waste and mismanagement at the Department of Justice, costing taxpayers more than $10 billion.

December 2008: *2008: Worst Waste of the Year* highlights more than $1 billion in taxpayer funding that Washington bureaucrats and politicians wasted on more than 60 examples of waste: everything from an inflatable alligator to training for casino workers to an unsuccessful search for Alaskan ice worms and extraterrestrial life forms.

May 2009: *Washed Out to Sea—How Congress Prioritizes Beach Pork over National Needs* details just how beachfront communities, D.C. lobbyists, and members of Congress have teamed up to "save" beaches with federally funded sand— an effort that always results in additional requests for sand projects in the future.

June 2009: *100 Stimulus Projects: A Second Opinion* discloses one hundred of the worst examples of waste in the American Recovery and Reinvestment Act, or stimulus bill. The projects in the report—worth $5.5 billion—range from Maine to California, and even include two from the state of Oklahoma.

July 2009: *Out of Gas: Congress Raids the Highway Trust Fund for Pet Projects While Bridges and Roads Crumble* examines the $78 billion from the Highway Trust Fund not being spent on bridges or roads, but instead being spent on projects such as bike paths, pedestrian walkways, "scenic beautification," and roadkill prevention tunnels.

December 2009: *Stimulus Checkup: A Closer Look at 100 Projects Funded by the American Recovery and Reinvestment Act* highlights 100 wasteful projects in the first $200 billion spent in the $787 billion stimulus bill passed in February 2009.

July 2010: *Bad Medicine: A Checkup on the New Federal Health Law* highlights some of the problems with the law and its consequences. Published 100 days after the law was passed, the report reveals new information and goes through a litany of problems with this flawed legislation.

July 2010: *Party at the D.O.J.* describes how the Department of Justice is wasting millions of taxpayer dollars on recreational activities that are undermining DOJ's core mission to enforce the law, prevent crime, and administer justice.

August 2010: *Summertime Blues* highlights questionable stimulus projects that are wasteful, mismanaged, and generally unsuccessful in creating jobs.

September 2010: *Pork 101: How Education Earmarks School Taxpayers* shows how Congress's parochial education projects are harming students, delaying reform, and undermining our future.

October 2010: *Grim Diagnosis: A Checkup on the Federal Health Law* details how many of the consequences of the new law are worse than anticipated.

October 2010: *Federal Programs to Die For: American Tax Dollars Sent Six Feet Under* exposes more than $1 billion that has been sent to the deceased in the past decade. Washington paid for dead people's prescriptions and wheelchairs, subsidized their farms, helped pay their rent, and even chipped in for their heating and air-conditioning bills.

November 2010: *Wastebook 2010* highlights some of the most egregious examples of government waste in 2010.

February 2011: *Help Wanted: How Federal Job Training Programs Are Failing Workers* highlights examples of waste, fraud, and mismanagement in federal job training programs.

April 2011: *The National Science Foundation: Under the Microscope* is a report on the National Science Foundation, identifying billions lost to waste, mismanagement, and duplication.

July 2011: *Oklahoma Waste Report* exposes wasteful government spending in Oklahoma. The "Oklahoma Waste Report" questions the merit of over 30 federal programs throughout the state costing taxpayers at least $170 million.

July 2011: *Back in Black* outlines how the federal government can reduce the deficit by $9 trillion over the next 10 years and balance the federal budget.

November 2011: *Subsidies for the Rich and Famous* illustrates how under the current tax code, the federal government is giving billions of dollars to individuals with an annual gross income (AGI) of at least $1 million, subsidizing their lavish lifestyles with the taxes of the less fortunate.

November 2011: *Shooting the Messenger: Congress Targets the Taxpayers' Watchdog* shows that while Congress is steadily losing its ability to conduct effective oversight, it has simultaneously been cutting off resources of its own investigative agency, the Government Accountability Office (GAO).

December 2011: *Wastebook 2011* highlights some of the most wasteful and low-priority spending in 2011, providing over $6.5 billion in examples of some of the most egregious ways taxpayer dollars were spent in the past year.

Notes

Introduction

1. Definition of debt bomb: A debt bomb occurs when a major financial institution, such as a multinational bank, defaults on its obligations that causes disruption not only in the financial system of the institution's home country, but also in the global financial system as a whole. A debt bomb can occur also if consumer spending is based heavily on debt. For example, if a nation incurred huge credit card debt, individual debt holders could default en masse and create trouble for creditors. This book argues the same can occur on a national level. Read more: http://www.investopedia.com/terms/d/debtbomb.asp#ixzz1m3As0F7j, accessed February11, 2012.

2. John Adams to John Taylor, April 15, 1814, in *The Works of John Adams, Second President of the United States: with a Life of the Author, Notes and Illustrations, by his Grandson Charles Francis Adams* (Boston: Little, Brown and Co., 1856). 10 volumes.

3. Thomas Jefferson to Edward Carrington, Paris, May 27, 1788, in *The Papers of Thomas Jefferson*, ed. Julian P. Boyd, Charles T. Cullen, John Catanzariti, Barbara B. Oberg, et al (Princeton: Princeton University Press, 1950-), 13:208–9. The misspelling is of *yield* is Jefferson's original spelling.

4. Thomas Jefferson to Albert Gallatin, October 1809, "To Albert Gallatin," EDITION: Washington ed. v, 477, EDITION: Ford ed., ix, 264, PLACE: Monticello, DATE: Oct. 1809, http://etext.virginia.edu/etcbin/ot2www-foley?specfile=/texts/english/jefferson/foley/public/JefCycl.o2w&act=surround&offset=4047444&tag=3348.+GALLATIN+(Albert),+Cabinet+dissensions.+--+--+[continued].+&query=in+an+eminent+degree&id=JCE3348.

5. Jeanne Sahadi, "Tax cuts push debt to new milestone," *CNN Money*, June 8, 2011, accessed February 7, 2012, http://money.cnn.com/2011/06/08/news/economy/tax_cuts_national_debt/index.htm.

6. Office of Management and Budget, *Historical Tables*, accessed February 7, 2012, http://www.whitehouse.gov/omb/budget/Historicals.

7. Ibid.

8. "GOP Congressional Committee says U.S. borrows $4 billion a day for spending," PolitiFact Rhode Island, accessed February 7, 2012, http://www.politifact.com/rhode-island/statements/2011/may/04/national-republican-congressional-committee/gop-congressional-committee-says-us-borrows-4-bill/.

9. Oklahoma Policy Institute, "FY '12 Budget Highlights," *Factsheet*, accessed February 7, 2012, http://okpolicy.org/files/FY%2712Hi-Lites.pdf.

10. Congressional Budget Office, *Monthly Budget Review: November 2011*, accessed February 7, 2012, http://www.cbo.gov/doc.cfm?index=12541.

11. Central Intelligence Agency, *The World Factbook 2011*, accessed February 7, 2012, https://www.cia.gov/library/publications/the-world-factbook/index.html.

12. Carmen M. Reinhart and Kenneth S. Rogoff, *This Time Is Different: Eight Centuries of Financial Folly*, 1st ed. (Princeton University Press, 2009), p. 25.

13. Ronald Reagan (farewell address, White House, Washington, DC, January 11, 1989), accessed February 7, 2012, http://reagan2020.us/speeches/Farewell.asp.

14. Lucy Madison, "Congressional approval at all-time low of 9%, according to new CBS News/New York Times poll," CBS News, October 25, 2011, accessed February 7, 2012, http://www.cbsnews.com/8301-503544_162-20125482-503544/congressional-approval-at-all-time-low-of-9-according-to-new-cbs-news-new-york-times-poll/.

15. Tom Coburn, *Back in Black: A Deficit Reduction Plan* (July 2011), accessed February 7, 2012, http://www.coburn.senate.gov/public/?p=deficit-reduction.

16. C. S. Lewis, *The Weight of Glory*, rev. ed. (1949; repr., New York: HarperCollins, 2001), 162.

Chapter 1

1. Laura Bassett, "Adm. Mike Mullen: 'National Debt Is Our Biggest Security Threat,'" *Huffington Post*, June 24, 2010, accessed February 7, 2012, http://www.huffingtonpost.com/2010/06/24/adm-mike-mullen-national_n_624096.html.

2. Note to reader: In 2011, a key Republican leader admitted privately he would not pursue entitlement reform in 2012 if Republicans took the Senate.

3. Mary Pilon and Matt Phillips, "Pimco's Gross Has 'Lost Sleep' Over Bad Bets," *Wall Street Journal*, August 30, 2011, accessed February 7, 2012, http://online.wsj.com/article/SB10001424053111903352704576539093167112076.html.

4. Editorial, "40 Under 40: 15. Michael Hasenstab," *CNN Money*, last updated October 25, 2011, accessed February 7, 2012, http://money.cnn.com/galleries/2011/news/companies/1110/gallery.40_under_40.fortune/15.html.

5. Niall Ferguson, "Sun Could Set Suddenly on Superpower as Debt Bites," *Real Clear World*, July 28, 2010, accessed February 7, 2012, http://www.realclearworld.com/articles/2010/07/28/sun_could_set_suddenly_on_superpower_as_debt_bites_99088.html.

6. Opinion Editorial, "Too Much Debt Means the Economy Can't Grow: Reinhart and Rogoff," *Bloomberg View*, July 13, 2011, accessed February 7, 2012, http://www.bloomberg.com/news/2011-07-14/

too-much-debt-means-economy-can-t-grow-commentary-by-reinhart-and-rogoff.html.

7. Christina Romer and Jared Bernstein, "The Job Impact of the American Recovery and Reinvestment Plan," (January 9, 2009), accessed February 7, 2012, http://otrans.3cdn.net/ee40602f9a7d8172b8_ozm6bt5oi.pdf.

8. Stephen Foley, "US house price fall 'beats Great Depression slide," *Independent* (UK), June 1, 2011, accessed February 7, 2012, http://www.independent.co.uk/news/business/news/us-house-price-fall-beats-great-depression-slide-2291491.html.

9. Dan Balz, "Obama's debt commission warns of fiscal 'cancer,'" *Washington Post*, July 12, 2010, accessed February 7, 2012, http://www.washingtonpost.com/wp-dyn/content/article/2010/07/11/AR2010071101956.html.

10. Rob Bluey, "Federal Government's Debt, Unfunded Obligations Grew Rapidly Last Year," *The Foundry*, June 7, 2011, accessed February 7, 2012, http://blog.heritage.org/2011/06/07/governments-unfunded-obligations-now-total-534000-per-household/.

11. Michael D. Tanner, "Bankrupt: Entitlements and the Federal Budget," *CATO Institute Policy Analysis* 673, March 28, 2011, accessed February 7, 2012, http://www.cato.org/pub_display.php?pub_id=12880.

12. Jon Ward, "Bernanke headlines a day of grim warnings about the nation's fiscal standing," *Daily Caller*, February 4, 2011, accessed February 7, 2012, http://dailycaller.com/2011/02/04/bernanke-headlines-day-grim-warnings-nations-fiscal-standing/#ixzz1D1f6XUus, emphasis added.

13. Ibid.

14. Paul Ryan, "A Roadmap for America's Future," accessed February 7, 2012, http://www.roadmap.republicans.budget.house.gov/.

15. Bureau of Public Debt, *Monthly Statement of the Public Debt of the United States: January 31, 2011*, accessed February 7, 2012, http://www.treasurydirect.gov/govt/reports/pd/mspd/2011/opds012011.pdf.

16. "S&P Cuts US Ratings Outlook to Negative from Stable," *Moneynews*, April 18, 2011, accessed February 7, 2012, http://www.moneynews.com/FinanceNews/S-PRevisesUSOutlooktoNegativeFromStable/2011/04/18/id/393191.

17. "Italy Govt Bonds 10 Year Gross Yield," *Bloomberg*, accessed February 7, 2012, http://www.bloomberg.com/quote/GBTPGR10:IND.

18. "Greece Govt Bond 10 Year Acting as Benchmark," *Bloomberg*, accessed February 7, 2012, http://www.bloomberg.com/quote/GGGB10YR:IND.

19. Gerald F. Seib, "As Budget Battle Rages On, a Quiet Cancer Grows, *Wall Street Journal: Capital Journal*, March 11, 2011, accessed February 7, 2012, http://online.wsj.com/article/SB10001424052748703883504576186163767307644.html.

20. Chris Arnold, "Debt's Impact Could Be Worse If Interest Rates Rise," July 22, 2011, accessed February 7, 2012, http://www.npr.org/2011/07/22/138590769/debts-impact-could-be-worse-if-interest-rates-rise.

21. Allysia Finley, *Wall Street Journal Political Diary*, December 14, 2011.

22. Reinhart and Rogoff, *This Time Is Different*, 66.

23. Ibid., 174.

24. Ibid., 175.

25. Milton Friedman, *Monetary Correction: a proposal for escalator clauses to reduce the costs of ending inflation* (London: Institute of Economic Affairs, 1978), 27.

26. Cullen Roche, "The Mythical Collapse in American Living Standards," *Pragmatic Capitalism*, October 20, 2011, figure 2, accessed February 7, 2012, pragcap.com/the-mythical-collapse-in-american-living-standards.

27. Tara Andringa, "Senate Investigations Subcommittee Releases Levin-Coburn Report on the Financial Crisis," Homeland Security and Governmental Affairs Permanent Subcommittee on Investigations, April 13, 2011, accessed February 7, 2012, http://hsgac.senate.gov/public/index.cfm?FuseAction=Press.MajorityNews&ContentRecord_id=51bf2c79-5056-8059-76a0-6674916e133d.

28. Rick Hampson, "Poll: Washington to blame more than Wall Street for economy," *USA Today*, October 18, 2011, accessed February 7, 2012, http://www.usatoday.com/news/nation/2011-10-17-poll-wall-street-protests.htm.

29. Heather Scoffield, "There will be blood," *Globe and Mail*, February 23, 2009, last updated April 19, 2009, accessed February 7, 2012, http://www.theglobeandmail.com/report-on-business/there-will-be-blood/article973785/singlepage/#articlecontent.

30. Turner Catledge, "Roosevelt Seeks 10% Economy Cuts – Moves to Slash Spending by All Departments Except Outlay for National Defense," *The New York Times*, June 4, 1940.

31. Amy Belasco, "The Cost of Iraq, Afghanistan, and Other Global War on Terror Operations Since 9/11," Congressional Research Service, March 29, 2011, http://www.fas.org/sgp/crs/natsec/RL33110.pdf, accessed February 10, 2012.

32. "Fighting Fraud and Abuse, Funding Reform," *Healthcare Matters*, Thomson Reuters, accessed February 7, 2012, http://info.thomsonhealthcare.com/?elqPURLPage=475.

33. Congressional Budget Office, *CBO's 2011 Long-Term Budget Outlook: June 2011*, accessed February 7, 2012, http://www.cbo.gov/doc.cfm?index=12212.

34. Ibid.

35. "Jin Liquin: Europe induces 'sloth, indolence,'" *Al Jazeera*, November 9, 2011, accessed February 7, 2012, http://www.aljazeera.com/programmes/talktojazeera/2011/11/2011114434664695.html.

36. Bruce Bartlett, "How Excessive Government Killed Ancient Rome," CATO Journal 14, no. 2 (Fall 1994), accessed February 7, 2012, http://www.cato.org/pubs/journal/cjv14n2-7.html.

37. Reinhart and Rogoff, *This Time Is Different*, xxv.

Chapter 2

1. John Adams to Thomas Jefferson, February 2, 1816, *The Writings of Thomas Jefferson*, editor H.A. Washington, New York : H.W. Derby, 1861, http://www.yamaguchy.com/library/jefferson/1816.html

2. Coburn, *Back in Black*.

3. Senator Tom Coburn, *Subsidies of the Rich and Famous* report, November 2011, http://www.coburn.senate.gov/public//index.cfm?a=Files.Serve&File_id=544ae3e7-195b-40ad-aa84-334fdd6a5e1f accessed February 11, 2012

4. Lewis, *Weight of Glory*, 154.

5. Kevin Spak, "Abramoff: Reforms Won't Stop 'Bribery' in Congress," *Newser*, November 3, 2011, accessed February 7, 2012, http://www.newser.com/story/132523/abramoff-reforms-wont-stop-bribery-in-congress.html.

6. United States Senate, "Oath of Office," accessed February 7, 2012, http://www.senate.gov/artandhistory/history/common/briefing/Oath_Office.htm.

7. Chuck Neubauer and Tom Hamburger, "Will the pork stop here?" *Los Angeles Times*, November 13, 2006, accessed February 7, 2012, http://www.latimes.com/news/nationworld/la-na-earmarks13nov13,0,5238569.story

8. Julio Ochoa, "A Mack daddy of a controversy; Congressman linked to developer east of I-75," *Naples News*, June 14, 2007, last updated June 15, 2007, accessed February 7, 2012, http://www.naplesnews.com/news/2007/jun/14/analyst_macks_ties_aronoff_raise_more_questions_ab/.

9. Julio Ochoa, "Report shows someone edited federal transportation bill," *Naples News*, August 8, 2007, updated August 9, 2007, accessed February 7, 2012, http://www.naplesnews.com/news/2007/aug/08/lee_county_metriopolitan_planning_organization_rel/?breaking_news.

10. George Will, "The Earmark Culture Thrives in Washington," Townhall.com, February 10, 2008, accessed February 7, 2012, http://townhall.com/columnists/georgewill/2008/02/10/the_earmark_culture_thrives_in_washington.

11. Reid Wilson, "Name and Shame? Obama May Go Public with Lawmakers' Funding Requests," *National Journal*, November 5, 2011, updated November 7, 2011, accessed February 7, 2012, http://www.nationaljournal.com/whitehouse/name-and-shame-obama-may-go-public-with-lawmakers-funding-requests-20111105.

12. Coburn, *Back in Black*.

13. Erick Erickson, "The Tax Compromise Must Now Die," *Redstate*, December 10, 2011, accessed February 7, 2012, http://www.redstate.com/erick/2010/12/10/the-tax-compromise-must-now-die/.

14. Senator Pete Domenici (R-NM) during debate on the Consolidated Natural Resources Act of 2008, S. 2739, Cong. Rec. S2865, (daily ed. Apr. 10, 2008), http://www.gpo.gov/fdsys/pkg/CREC-2008-04-10/pdf/CREC-2008-04-10-pt1 PgS2861.pdf#page=5.

15. Senator Tom Coburn (R-OK) during debate on the Consolidated Natural Resources Act of 2008, S. 2739, Cong. Rec. S2877, (daily ed. Apr. 10, 2008).

16. Paul Kiel, "K Street Project (All Rights Reserved)," *TMP Muckraker*, April 14, 2006, accessed February 7, 2012, http://tpmmuckraker.talkingpointsmemo.com/archives/000379.php.

17. Mark Hemingway, "Rubio: 'We Don't Need New Taxes. We Need New Taxpayers'" *Weekly Standard*, July 7, 2011, accessed February 7, 2012, http://www.weeklystandard.com/blogs/rubio-makes-strong-speech-senate-jobs-and-taxes_576380.html.

18. Tony Blankley, "Governing While Drunk on Partisanship, *Washington Times*, April 18, 2011, accessed February 7, 2012, http://www.washingtontimes.com/news/2011/apr/18/governing-while-drunk-on-partisanship/.

19. David Brooks, "The Mother of All No-Brainers," *New York Times*, July 4, 2011, accessed February 7, 2012, http://www.nytimes.com/2011/07/05/opinion/05brooks.html?src=me&ref=general.

20. Ibid.

21. Doug Mataconis, "Incumbent Re-Election Rates in the 2010 Mid-Terms," *Outside the Beltway*, November 9, 2010, accessed February 7, 2012, http://www.outsidethebeltway.com/incumbent-re-election-rates-in-the-2010-mid-terms/.

22. U.S. House of Representatives, "Historial Highlights: General George Washington resigning his commission in Annapolis, Maryland, December 23, 1783" Office of the Clerk, accessed February 7, 2012, http://artandhistory.house. gov/highlights.aspx?action=view&intID=451.
23. "The Address of General George Washington To The People of The United States of America," *American Daily Advertiser*, September 17, 1796.

Chapter 3

1. Thomas Jefferson, "The Kentucky Resolutions of 1798," accessed February 7, 2012, http://www.constitution.org/cons/kent1798.htm.
2. Thomas Jefferson (first inaugural address, Senate Chamber, Capitol building, Washington, DC, March 4, 1801).
3. James Madison, Speech at the Virginia Convention to ratify the Federal Constitution, 6 June, 1788, http://www.constitution.org/rc/rat_va_05.htm.
4. Wickard v. Filburn, 317 U.S. 111 (1942).
5. Senate Committee on the Judiciary: *S. Hrg. 111-1044, The Nomination of Elena Kagan To Be an Associate Justice of the Supreme Court of the United States*, 111th Cong. (2010), accessed February 7, 2012, http://www.gpoaccess.gov/congress/ senate/judiciary/sh111-1044/browse.html.
6. Ibid.
7. James Oliphant, "Kagan slips on fruits and vegetables in Senate panel questioning," *Los Angeles Times*, July 1, 2010, accessed February 7, 2012, http:// articles.latimes.com/2010/jul/01/nation/la-na-kagan-hearings-20100701.
8. Michael Barone, "Obama skirts rule of law to reward pals, punish foes," *Washington Examiner*, May 24, 2011, accessed February 7, 2012, http://washingtonexaminer.com/politics/2011/05/ obama-skirts-rule-law-reward-pals-punish-foes#ixzz1YeD3tACb.
9. Alexandra Alper, "House panel to scrutinize Cordray appointment," Reuters, January 23, 2012, accessed February 7, 2012, http://www.reuters. com/article/2012/01/23/us-cordray-idUSTRE80M1ZV20120123. The four appointments are Richard Cordray to lead the Consumer Financial Protection Bureau (CFPB) and three members to serve on the National Labor Relations Board (NLRB). Appointees include: democratic union lawyer Richard Griffin, democratic Labor Department official Sharon Block, and republican NLRB lawyer Terence Flynn.
10. Peter Wehner, "Why the Constitution—and What It Means— Matters," *Commentary*, January 6, 2011, accessed February 7, 2012, http://www.commentarymagazine.com/2011/01/06/ why-the-constitution-%E2%80%94-and-what-it-means-%E2%80%94-matters/.
11. George F. Will, "More Questions for nominee Elena Kagan," *Washington Post*, June 28, 2010, accessed February 7, 2012, http://www.washingtonpost.com/ wp-dyn/content/article/2010/06/27/AR2010062703256.html?hpid=opinionsbox1.
12. West Virginia State Board of Education v. Barnette, 319 U.S. 624 (1943).
13. Barack Obama (news conference, November 25, 2008), accessed February 7, 2012, available at http://www.clipsandcomment.com/2008/11/25/ transcript-barack-obama-news-conference-the-economy-november-25-2008/.

14. Social Security Administration Office of Budget, *FY2011 President's Budget, Key Tables* (February 1, 2010), tables 4–5, accessed February 7, 2012, http://www.ssa.gov/budget/FY11%20Key%20Tables.pdf.

15. Umar Moulta-Ali, Congressional Research Service, Primer on Disability Benefits: Social Security Disability Insurance (SSDI) and Supplemental Security Income (SSI) , 7-9557 (August 8, 2011) (RL32279).

16. Coburn, *Back in Black*, 540.

17. Population of the United States, US Census Bureau, 313 when accessed February 9, 2012, http://www.census.gov/main/www/popclock.html.

18. Damian Paletta and Dionne Searcey, "Two Lawyers Strike Gold in U.S. Disability System," *Wall Street Journal*, December 22, 2011, accessed February 7, 2012, http://online.wsj.com/article/SB10001424052970203518404577096632862007046.html?mod=WSJ_WSJ_US_News_5.

19. Amy Graff, "National Geographic features adult babies," *San Francisco Chronicle*, accessed February 7, 2012, http://blog.sfgate.com/sfmoms/2011/05/03/national-geographic-features-adult-babies/.

20. Bill Costello, "The Schools Scandal," *American Thinker*, September 6, 2010, accessed February 7, 2012, http://www.americanthinker.com/2010/09/the_schools_scandal.html.

21. National Center for Education Statistics, *Digest of Education Statistics* (Washington: Institute of Education Sciences, 2007), table 61, accessed February 7, 2012, http://nces.ed.gov/programs/digest/d07/tables/dt07_061.asp.

22. Ian Millhiser, "Coburn Channels Failed Tenther Candidates Who Claim Department of Education Is Unconstitutional," *ThinkProgress* (blog), December 7, 2010, accessed February 7, 2012, http://thinkprogress.org/politics/2010/12/07/133728/coburn-education-dpmt/.

23. Ibid.

24. Ibid., emphasis added.

25. Neal McCluskey, "On Federal Education, Think Progress Should Think Harder," *Cato@Liberty*, December 8, 2010, accessed February 7, 2012, http://www.cato-at-liberty.org/on-federal-education-think-progress-should-think-harder/.

26. James Madison to James Robertson, Montpellier, 20 April 1831, in *Letters and Other Writings of James Madison*, vol. 4, 1829–1836 (Philadelphia: J. B. Lippincott and Co., 1865), 171–172.

27. McCluskey, "On Federal Education."

28. David Boaz, "Education and the Constitution," *Cato@Liberty*, May 1, 2006, accessed February 7, 2012, http://www.cato-at-liberty.org/education-and-the-constitution/.

Chapter 4

1. "Candidates Clash Over Voting Records in Close Oklahoma Senate Race," *Online NewsHour*, PBS, September 24, 2004, accessed February 7, 2012, http://www.pbs.org/newshour/updates/ok_09-24-04.html.

2. Tom A. Coburn, *Breach of Trust: How Washington Turns Outsiders into Insiders* (Nashville, WND Books, 2003), xix.

3. John Stossel, Glenn Ruppel, and Ann Varney, "The Real Price of Pork Barrel Spending," *ABC News*, September 9, 2005.

4. Senator Tom Coburn (R-OK) during debate on the Transportation, Treasury, the Judiciary, Housing and Urban Development and Related Agencies Appropriations Act, 2006, H.R. 3058, Cong. Rec. S11606-11607 (daily ed. Oct. 20, 2005).

5. Senator Ted Stevens (R-AK) during debate on the Transportation, Treasury, the Judiciary, Housing and Urban Development and Related Agencies Appropriations Act, 2006, H.R. 3058, Cong. Rec. S11628-S11630 (daily ed. Oct. 20, 2005).

6. Senator Lisa Murkowski (R-AK) during debate on the Transportation, Treasury, the Judiciary, Housing and Urban Development and Related Agencies Appropriations Act, 2006, H.R. 3058, Cong. Rec. S11630-11631 (daily ed. Oct. 20, 2005).

7. Senator Ted Stevens (R-AK) during debate on the Transportation, Treasury, the Judiciary, Housing and Urban Development and Related Agencies Appropriations Act, 2006, H.R. 3058, Cong. Rec. S11633 (daily ed. Oct. 20, 2005).

8. Senator Kit Bond (R-MO) during debate on the Transportation, Treasury, the Judiciary, Housing and Urban Development and Related Agencies Appropriations Act, 2006, H.R. 3058, Cong. Rec. S11611 (daily ed. Oct. 20, 2005).

9. Senator Patty Murray (D-WA) during debate on the Transportation, Treasury, the Judiciary, Housing and Urban Development and Related Agencies Appropriations Act, 2006, H.R. 3058, Cong. Rec. S11611-11612 (daily ed. Oct. 20, 2005).

10. "The U.S. Congress Votes Database," *Washington Post*, October 20, 2005, accessed February 7, 2012, http://projects.washingtonpost.com/congress/109/senate/1/votes/262/.

11. Tom Coburn, "Dr. Coburn's Efforts to Reduce Wasteful Washington Spending and Reform the Federal Budget Process," Tom Coburn, M.D., August 25, 2011, accessed February 7, 2012, http://www.coburn.senate.gov/public/?p=PorkBusters.

12. Editorial, "Harvard study shows earmarks cost jobs," *Examiner*, June 2010, accessed February 7, 2012, http://washingtonexaminer.com/opinion/editorials/harvard-study-shows-earmarks-cost-jobs.

13. Senator Mitch McConnell (R-KY) speaking in support of an Earmark Moratorium, Cong. Rec. S7872-7873 (daily ed. Nov. 15, 2010).

Chapter 5

1. Thomas Jefferson letter to John Talyor, 1816, TITLE: *To John Taylor*. EDITION: Washington ed. vi, 608. EDITION: Ford ed., x, 31. PLACE: Monticello DATE: 1816, http://etext.virginia.edu/etcbin/ot2www-foley?specfile=/texts/english/jefferson/foley/public/JefCycl.o2w&act=surround&offset=4025799&tag=3328.+FUNDING,+Posterity+and.+--+&query=swindling+futurity&id=JCE3328

2. Rick Klein, Jonathan Karl, and Huma Khan, "Democratic Senator Evan Bayh Retiring: 'I Do Not Love Congress,'" *ABC News*, February 15, 2010, accessed February 7, 2012, http://abcnews.go.com/Politics/indiana-democratic-senator-evan-bay-announces-retirement/story?id=9841970#.TsXJ1lZtl8E.

3. Ruth Marcus, "Both parties lose as Bayh leaves," *Washington Post*, February 17, 2010, accessed February 7, 2012, http://www.washingtonpost.com/wp-dyn/content/article/2010/02/16/AR2010021603553.html.

4. Evan Bayh, "Why I'm Leaving the Senate," *New York Times*, February 20, 2010, accessed February 7, 2012, http://www.nytimes.com/2010/02/21/opinion/21bayh. html?pagewanted=all.

5. Marcus, "Both parties lose."

6. Howard Fineman, "Six Reasons Evan Bayh Is Retiring," *Daily Beast*, February 15, 2010, accessed February 7, 2012, http://www.thedailybeast.com/ newsweek/2010/02/15/six-reasons-evan-bayh-is-retiring.html.

7. *Broken Government*, CNN, accessed February 7, 2012, http://www.cnn.com/ CNN/Programs/broken.government/.

8. Jim DeMint, "Constitution of No," *National Review*, June 8, 2010, accessed February 7, 2012, http://www.nationalreview.com/articles/229909/ constitution-no/jim-demint.

9. "Holding Spending," Tom Coburn, M.D., accessed February 7, 2012, http:// coburn.senate.gov/public/?p=HoldingSpending.

10. Igor Volsky, "Coburn On Emmett Till Bill: 'They're Playing Games,'" *ThinkProgress* (blog), July 24, 2008, accessed February 7, 2012, http:// thinkprogress.org/economy/2008/07/24/172280/coubrn-till/.

11. Fran Visco, "Coburn to Breast Cancer Community: Drop Dead," *HuffPost Healthy Living*, October 1, 2006, accessed February 7, 2012, http://www. huffingtonpost.com/fran-visco/coburn-to-breast-cancer-c_b_30709.html.

12. Ibid.

13. Senator Harry Reid (D-NV) during debate on the "Coburn Omnibus" Advancing America's Priorities Act, S. 3297, Cong. Rec. S7552 (daily ed. Jul. 28, 2008). *"Emmitt"* is misspelled in the Congressional Record and corrected in text as *"Emmett."*

14. "Frist knocks Edwards over stem cell comment," CNN, October 12, 2004, accessed February 7, 2012, http://articles.cnn.com/2004-10-12/politics/edwards. stem.cell_1_cell-research-cell-policy-adult-cells?_s=PM:ALLPOLITICS.

15. Sherrilyn A. Ifill, "FBI Shuts Down Civil Rights Era Investigations: Agency will let old murder cases stay cold," *The Root*, March 10, 2010, accessed February 7, 2012, http://www.theroot.com/views/fbi-shuts-down-civil-rights-era-investigations.

16. Letter to Vice President Joseph Biden from Ronald Weich, Assistant Attorney General, enclosing a report to Congress about the Department of Justice's activities regarding civil rights era homicides, as required by the Emmett Till Unsolved Civil Rights Crimes Act of 2007, September 23, 2011. Full Report: Attorney General Eric Holder, *The Attorney General's Third Annual Report to Congress pursuant to the Emmett Till Unsolved Civil Rights Crime Act of 2007*, (Dep't of Justice Sept. 23, 2011), available at http://nuweb9.neu.edu/civilrights/ wp-content/uploads/Attorney-Generals-3rd-Annual-Report-to-Congress.pdf.

17. *New York Post* editorial, "Museum madness," February 1, 2012, http://www. nypost.com/p/news/opinion/editorials/museum_madness_w0W0d8CoS1S6v54B vFLe8K#ixzz1m6nCIvhI accessed February 11, 2012.

18. *"Meet the Press* transcript for January 15, 2012," NBC, accessed February 7, 2012, http://www.msnbc.msn.com/id/46004652/ns/meet_the_press-transcripts/t/ meet-press-transcript-jan/.

19. United States Senate, "Roll Call Votes 112th Congress: 1st Session (2011)," accessed February 7, 2012, http://www.senate.gov/legislative/LIS/roll_call_lists/vote_menu_112_1.htm.

20. United States Senate, "Roll Call Votes 110th Congress: 1st Session (2007)," accessed February 7, 2012, http://www.senate.gov/legislative/LIS/roll_call_lists/vote_menu_110_1.htm.

Chapter 6

1. Barack Obama (inaugural address, Washington, DC, January 20, 2009), accessed February 7, 2012, http://www.whitehouse.gov/blog/inaugural-address.

2. Milton Friedman and Rose Friedman, *Free to Choose: A Personal Statement* (1979; repr., Orlando: Mariner Books, 1990), 116.

3. Ibid., 116–17.

4. For more on this debate see "'Fear the Boom and Bust,' a Hayek vs. Keynes Rap Anthem," YouTube video, 7:33, posted by "EconStories," October 28, 2011, accessed February 7, 2012, http://www.youtube.com/watch?v=d0nERTFo-Sk.

5. John Maynard Keynes, *The General Theory of Employment, Interest and Money* (New York: Classic Books America, 2009), 331.

6. Amity Schlaes, "Cheering for Obama Stimulus Buys Into 1930s Myth," February 18, 2009, accessed February 7, 2012, http://www.bloomberg.com/apps/news?pid=newsarchive&sid=aPQDtpOebjKI; Michael Barone, "Real Lesson of the Great Depression," *Washington Times*, accessed February 7, 2012, http://www.washingtontimes.com/news/2009/feb/17/real-lesson-of-the-great-depression/.

7. "Draft: Working Group Stimulus Plan," updated February 2, 2009, accessed February 7, 2012, http://www.cbsnews.com/htdocs/pdf/RealStimulus.pdf?tag=contentMain;contentBody

8. Robert J. Barro, "Government Spending Is No Free Lunch," *Wall Street Journal*, January 22, 2009, accessed February 7, 2012, http://www.econ.nyu.edu/user/violante/NYU%20Teaching/AMF/barro_multipliers.pdf.

9. Reuters, "FutureGen clean-coal project gets $1 billion from U.S." August 6, 2010, http://news.cnet.com/8301-11128_3-20012870-54.html.

10. "Dr. [Tom] Coburn Statement Opposing Passage of Stimulus Bill" (press release), *Tom Coburn, M.D., US Senator of Oklahoma*, February 10, 2009, accessed February 7, 2012, http://coburn.senate.gov/public/index.cfm/pressreleases?ContentRecord_id=61bdaa5d-802a-23ad-483d-803ae7e74eb2&ContentType_id=d741b7a7-7863-4223-9904-8cb9378aa03a&Group_id=7a55cb96-4639-4dac-8c0c-99a4a227bd3a.

11. "Table 1. Five-Year Relative Survival Rates for Cancer of Different Sites, US and European Cancer Registries," accessed February 7, 2012, http://4.bp.blogspot.com/_otfwl2zc6Qc/SoG4Vv5-y-I/AAAAAAAAK3A/afilDKt_4ks/s1600-h/cancer.bmp.

12. Tom Coburn, *100 Stimulus Projects: A Second Opinion* (June 2009), accessed February 7, 2012, http://coburn.senate.gov/public/index.cfm?a=Files.Serve&File_id=59af3ebd-7bf9-4933-8279-8091b533464f; Tom Coburn and John McCain, Stimulus Checkup: A closer look at 100 projects funded by the American Recovery and Reinvestment Act (December 2009), accessed February

7, 2012, http://coburn.senate.gov/public/index.cfm?a=Files.Serve&File_
id=a28a4590-10ac-4dc1-bd97-df57b39ed872; Coburn and McCain, Summertime
Blues: 100 stimulus projects that give taxpayers blues (August 2010), accessed
February 7, 2012, http://coburn.senate.gov/public//index.cfm?a=Files.
Serve&File_id=a7e82141-1a9e-4eec-b160-6a8e62427efb.

13. Amy Lester, "New Boynton Sidewalk Makes List of Top Wasteful Stimulus
Projects," *News on 6* (Oklahoma), August 3, 2010, updated August 5, 2010,
accessed February 7, 2012, http://www.newson6.com/story/12917360/new-
boynton-sidewalk-makes-list-of-top-wasteful-stimulus-projects?redirected=true.

14. Jonah Goldberg, "The Shrine of FDR: Why the Left worships there," *National
Review Online*, January 26, 2009, accessed February 7, 2012, http://www.
nationalreview.com/articles/226860/shrine-fdr/jonah-goldberg.

15. Douglas W. Elmendorf to Judd Gregg, 4 February 2009, Congressional Budget
Office, accessed February 7, 2012, http://cbo.gov/ftpdocs/96xx/doc9619/Gregg.pdf.

16. Ibid, page 8

17. Bureau of Labor Statistics, Labor Force Statistics from the Current Population
Survey, http://data.bls.gov/timeseries/LNS14000000, accessed February 11, 2012.

18. Barack Obama (remarks at the Signing of the American Recovery and
Reinvestment Act, Denver Museum of Nature and Science, Denver, Colorado,
February 17, 2009), accessed February 7, 2012, http://www.whitehouse.gov/
the_press_office/Remarks-by-the-President-and-Vice-President-at-Signing-of-
the-American-Recovery-an/.

19. Veronique de Rugy, "Why Should We Trust Their Stimulus
Predictions? *National Review*, September 9, 2011, accessed
February 7, 2012, http://www.nationalreview.com/corner/276801/
why-should-we-trust-their-stimulus-predictions-veronique-de-rugy.

20. Christina Romer and Jared Berstein, "The Job Impact of the American Recovery
and Reinvestment Plan," January 9, 2009, page 4, http://otrans.3cdn.net/
ee40602f9a7d8172b8_ozm6bt5oi.pdf

21. Bureau of Labor Statistics, Labor Force Statistics from the Current Population
Survey, http://data.bls.gov/timeseries/LNS14000000, accessed February 11, 2012.

22. Congressional Budget Office, "Estimated Impact of the American Recovery
and Reinvestment Act on Employment and Economic Output from July 2011
Through September 2011," November 2011, page 8, http://www.cbo.gov/
ftpdocs/125xx/doc12564/11-22-ARRA.pdf accessed February 11, 2012.

23. Congressional Budget Office, "Estimated Impact of the American Recovery and
Reinvestment Act on Employment and Economic Output from October 2009
Through December 2009," February 2010, http://www.cbo.gov/ftpdocs/110xx/
doc11044/02-23-ARRA.pdf accessed February 11, 2012.

24. Friedrich August Hayek, *The Fatal Conceit: The Errors of Socialism* (1988), 76.

25. Friedrich August Hayek, *The Road to Serfdom*, (George Routledge and Sons,
1944), 65, http://books.google.com/books?id=eTve6XEUbYIC&q=most+of+the
m+do+not+want+at+all#v=snippet&q=journey&f=false.

26. A. Barton Hinkle, "Obama's Crony Capitalism –What the Solyndra debacle
reveals about Obama's economic strategy," Reason.com, September 9, 2011,
http://reason.com/archives/2011/09/09/obamas-crony-capitalism

27. Rich Lowry, "Innovation is the Thing," *National Review Online*, December 3, 2010, http://www.nationalreview.com/articles/254393/innovation-thing-rich-lowry, accessed February 11, 2012.

28. Joel Pollak, "AEI's Arthur Brooks: Make the Moral Case for Freedom," BigGovernment.com, January 11, 2012, http://biggovernment.com/jpollak/2012/01/11/aeis-arthur-brooks-make-the-moral-case-for-freedom/ accessed February 11, 2012.

Chapter 7

1. "The Moment of Truth," Report of the National Commission on Fiscal Responsibility and Reform, December 2010, accessed February 7, 2012, http://www.fiscalcommission.gov/sites/fiscalcommission.gov/files/documents/TheMomentofTruth12_1_2010.pdf.

2. "Dr. Coburn in debt commission 12.1.2010," YouTube video, 8:42, posted by "SenatorCoburn," December 1, 2010, accessed February 7, 2012, http://www.youtube.com/watch?v=KxkLoZqfvpM.

3. "Senators Coburn, Crapo Announce Support for Debt Commission Plan" (press release), *Tom Coburn, M.D., US Senator from Oklahoma*, December 2, 2010, accessed February 7, 2012, http://www.coburn.senate.gov/public/index.cfm/pressreleases?ContentRecord_id=94a738d2-5fff-4bf7-8b66-c675a91ca031&ContentType_id=d741b7a7-7863-4223-9904-8cb9378aa03a&Group_id=7a55cb96-4639-4dac-8c0c-99a4a227bd3a&MonthDisplay=12&YearDisplay=2010.

4. Stephen Moore, "Tax Reform's Moment?—Where else is the growth going to come from?" *Wall Street Journal*, August 5, 2011. Note: Moore here is later citing a Gang of Six breakthrough on tax reform, which was modeled after Simpson-Bowles, http://online.wsj.com/article/SB10001424053111903366504576486082360723602.html, accessed February 12, 2012.

5. Michael Warren, "CBO: We Can't Score Obama's Budget Plan Because It's Just a Speech," *Weekly Standard*, June 23, 2011, accessed February 7, 2012, http://www.weeklystandard.com/blogs/cbo-director-we-dont-estimate-speeches_575464.html.

6. Jon Ward, "Coburn willing to block debt limit increase to force spending cuts," *Daily Caller*, November 3, 2010, accessed February 7, 2012, http://dailycaller.com/2010/11/03/coburn-willing-to-block-debt-limit-increase-to-force-spending-cuts/#ixzz1lWfSxjhL.

7. "President Obama Briefs the Press on Progress in Deficit Talks," The White House, July 19, 2011, http://www.youtube.com/watch?v=k-bBzSvp3rY.

8. Tom Coburn, "Why I voted against the debt deal," *Washington Post*, Opinions, August 2, 2012, accessed February 7, 2012, http://www.washingtonpost.com/opinions/why-i-voted-against-the-debt-deal/2011/08/02/gIQArHlopI_story.html.

9. "S&P downgrades US credit rating: Coburn says the announcement is long overdue," *Daily Progress* (Claremore, OK), August 6, 2011, accessed February 7, 2012, http://claremoreprogress.com/business/x541066197/S-P-downgrades-US-credit-rating.

10. Veronique de Rugy, "Update: Federal Spending Without & With Sequester Cuts FY2012-2021," Mercatus Center, George Mason University, November 18, 2011, accessed February 7, 2012, http://mercatus.org/publication/update-federal-spending-without-sequester-cuts-fy2012-2021.

11. "Sen. Tom Coburn: We Have Taken a Stupid Pill," *NewsOK*, 3:56, posted by "Chris Casteel," November 29, 2011, accessed February 7, 2012, http://blog.newsok.com/politics/2011/11/29/sen-tom-coburn-we-have-taken-a-stupid-pill/.

12. Dan Mitchell, "Sequestration Is a Small Step in Right Direction, not Something to Be Feared," *International Liberty* (blog), November 1, 2011, accessed February 7, 2012, http://danieljmitchell.wordpress.com/2011/11/01/sequestration-is-a-small-step-in-right-direction-not-something-to-be-feared/.

Chapter 8

1. Will Roger's Weekly Articles: The Hoover Years, 1931-1933, Oklahoma State University Press, Feb 1, 1982, p 133.

2. Congressional Budget Office, *Budget and Economic Outlook: Fiscal Years 2011 to 2021*, January 2011, accessed February 7, 2012, http://www.cbo.gov/doc.cfm?index=12039.

3. Z. Byron Wolf, "GAO: Duplication, Waste Costs Taxpayers Billions Each Year, Coburn Says Report Makes Congress Look Like 'Jackasses,'" *The Note* (blog), ABC News, March 1, 2011, accessed February 7, 2012, http://abcnews.go.com/blogs/politics/2011/03/gao-duplication-waste-costs-taxpayers-billions-each-year-coburn-says-report-makes-congress-look-like/.

4. Scott Wong, "Coburn: Report will make us 'look like jackasses,'" *On Congress*, Politico, February 28, 2011, accessed February 7, 2012, http://www.politico.com/blogs/glennthrush/0211/Coburn_report_will_make_us_look_like_jackasses_html.

5. United States Government Accountability Office, Report to Congressional Addressees, *Opportunities to Reduce Potential Duplication in Government Programs, Save Tax Dollars, and Enhance Revenue*, GAO-11-318SP (March 1, 2011), accessed February 7, 2012, http://www.gao.gov/new.items/d11318sp.pdf.

6. "Duplication in Federal Programs," accessed February 7, 2012, http://coburn.senate.gov/public//index.cfm?a=Files.Serve&File_id=72c84d4e-bac2-4d6c-8aea-8b6de7a2a00f.

7. Gregory Korte, "Job training sprawl costs U.S. $18B per year," *USA Today*, February 9, 2011, accessed February 7, 2012, http://www.usatoday.com/news/washington/2011-02-09-1Ajobtraining09_ST_N.htm.

8. Friedman and Friedman, *Free to Choose*, 116–17; "The Four Different Ways to Spend Money by Milton Friedman," *Financial Samurai* (blog), posted by "Sam," accessed February 7, 2012, http://www.financialsamurai.com/2010/07/30/the-four-different-ways-to-spend-money-by-milton-friedman/.

9. Dennis Jacobe, "U.S. Unemployment Ticks Up in Mid-November," *Gallup Economy*, November 17, 2011, accessed February 7, 2012, http://www.gallup.com/poll/150794/Unemployment-Ticks-Mid-November.aspx.

10. GAO-11-318SP, 126.

11. United States Government Accountability Office, Report to Congressional Requesters, *Multiple Employment and Training Programs: Providing Information on Colocating Services and Consolidating Administrative Structures Could Promote Efficiencies*, GAO-11-92 (June 2011), accessed February 7, 2012, http://www.gao.gov/new.items/d1192.pdf.

12. As listed in "Dr. Coburn Releases Oversight Report on Job Training Programs," February 8, 2011, accessed February 7, 2012, http://coburn.senate.gov/public/index.cfm/pressreleases?ContentRecord_id=cf7fa487-7be6-4d72-b701-a36e7ea541fe. To view my full report, Help Wanted: How Federal Job Training Programs Are Failing Workers, visit http://coburn.senate.gov/public//index.cfm?a=Files.Serve&File_id=9f1e1249-a5cd-42aa-9f84-269463c51a7d (accessed February 7, 2012).

13. GAO-11-318SP, 144.

14. Ibid.

15. Tom Coburn and John McCain, *Out of Gas: Congress Raids the Highway trust Fund for Pet Projects While Bridges and Roads Crumble* (July 2009), accessed February 7, 2012, http://coburn.senate.gov/public/index.cfm?a=Files.Serve&File_id=80b3458b-b6e2-470a-be24-bb82b93d10c2.

16. "Science, Technology, Engineering, and Mathematics Education—Strategic Planning Needed to Better Manage Overlapping Programs across Multiple Agencies," Government Accountability Office, January 20, 2012, http://gao.gov/products/GAO-12-108

17. Executive Committee, *President's Private Sector Survey on Cost Control* (January 15, 1984), accessed February 7, 2012, http://www.uhuh.com/taxstuff/gracecom.htm.

18. Senator Harry Reid (D-NV), during debate on the Full-Year Continuing Appropriations Act of 2011, H.R. 1,Cong. Rec. S1249 (daily ed. Mar. 4, 2011).

19. Senator Jeanne Shaheen (D-NH), during debate on the Full-Year Continuing Appropriations Act of 2011, H.R. 1, Cong. Rec. S1189 (daily ed. Mar. 3, 2011).

20. Senator Mark Kirk (R-IL), remarks on government spending, Cong. Rec. S1086 (daily ed. Mar. 2, 2011).

21. Ross Reily, "Update: McCain versus Mississippi catfish," *Mississippi Business Journal: Editor's Notebook*, March 9, 2011, accessed February 7, 2012, http://msbusiness.com/editorsnotebook/2011/03/09/mccain-sticks-it-to-catfish-farmers/.

22. "Pelosi Floor Speech on Short-Term Continuing Resolution" (press release), *Congresswoman Nancy Pelosi*, March 15, 2011, accessed February 7, 2012, http://pelosi.house.gov/news/press-releases/2011/03/pelosi-floor-speech-on-short-term-continuing-resolution.shtml.

23. Senator Pat Roberts (R-KS), remarks on energy regulations, Cong. Rec. S1314 (daily ed. Mar. 7, 2011).

24. Senator Tom Coburn website, "Duplication Nation" under "Legislation and Issues" and "Key Issues," http://www.coburn.senate.gov/public/index.cfm/duplication-nation accessed February 11, 2012.

25. "Shooting the Messenger: Congress Targets the Taxpayers' Watchdog, A Report by Tom A. Coburn, M.D., U.S. Senator, Oklahoma" (November 2011), accessed February 7, 2012, http://coburn.senate.gov/public//index.cfm?a=Files.Serve&File_id=c6bdbe64-ad37-4571-9c6a-8d97a3154253.

26. GAO-11-318SP, 2.
27. Office of Management and Budget, Historical Tables, 143; all adjusted for inflation.
28. Senator Tom Coburn, "Wastebook 2011," December 2011, http://www.coburn. senate.gov/public//index.cfm?a=Files.Serve&File_id=2b11ca9d-1315-4a7c-b58b-e06686e3aece accessed February 11, 2012.
29. Timothy P. Carney, "GOP and Dems get taxpayer subsidies for conventions," *Examiner*, June 2011, accessed February 7, 2012, http://washingtonexaminer.com/ politics/2011/06/gop-and-dems-get-taxpayer-subsidies-conventions.

Chapter 9

1. "Coburn-Lieberman press conference on Medicare debt reduction plan (pt. 1), "YouTube video, 11:41, June 28, 2011, uploaded by "SenatorCoburn," accessed February 7, 2012, http://www.youtube.com/watch?v=alFr2Jouj2s.
2. House Budget Committee Chairman Paul Ryan, "The Choice of Two Futures" (March 2011), accessed February 7, 2012, http://budget.house.gov/UploadedFiles/ marchlisteningsessions.pdf.
3. Ibid
4. "Medicare," Kaiser Family Foundation, accessed February 7, 2012, http://www. kff.org/medicare/index.cfm.
5. "Medicaid/CHIP," Kaiser Family Foundation, accessed February 7, 2012, http:// www.kff.org/medicaid/index.cfm.
6. Ibid.
7. "Moment of Truth."
8. C. Eugene Steuerle and Stephanie Rennane, "Social Security and Medicare Taxes and Benefits Over a Lifetime," Urban Institute, updated June 2011, accessed February 7, 2012, http://www.urban.org/UploadedPDF/social-security-medicare-benefits-over-lifetime.pdf.
9. Congressional Budget Office, *The Budget and Economic Outlook, Fiscal Years 2010–2020,* January 2010, accessed February 7, 2012, http://www.cbo.gov/ ftpdocs/108xx/doc10871/01-26-Outlook.pdf.
10. "2011 Annual Report of the Boards of Trustees of the Federal Hospital Insurance and Federal Supplementary Medical Insurance Trust Funds," Centers for Medicare and Medicaid Services, 25, accessed February 7, 2012, https://www. cms.gov/ReportsTrustFunds/downloads/tr2011.pdf.
11. Ibid., 52.
12. Government Accountability Office, *Fiscal Pressures Could Have Implications for Future Delivery of Intergovernmental Programs,* July 2010, accessed February 7, 2012, http://www.gao.gov/new.items/d10899.pdf.
13. Thomas Jefferson to J. W. Eppes, June 1813, in Washington ed. vi, 136; Ford Ed., ix, 389, *To John W. Eppes,* http://etext.virginia.edu/etcbin/ot2www-foley?specfile=/texts/english/jefferson/foley/public/JefCycl.o2w.
14. Thomas Jefferson to Albert Gallatin, 1820, in Ford ed., x, 176, *To Albert Gallatin,* from UVA digital library.
15. "Hiking Taxes to Pay for Entitlement Would Require Doubling Tax Rates," 2011 Budget Chart Book, Heritage Foundation, accessed February 7, 2012, http://www. heritage.org/budgetchartbook/entitlements-double-tax-rates.

16. Ezra Klein, "You can't save Medicare by raising taxes," *Washington Post*, May 18, 2011, accessed February 7, 2012, http://www.washingtonpost.com/blogs/ezra-klein/post/you-cant-save-medicare-by-raising-taxes/2011/05/09/AFU9BT6G_blog.html.

17. Ryan, "Roadmap for America's Future."

18. Douglas W. Elmendorf to Paul D. Ryan, 17 November 2010, Congressional Budget Office, accessed February 7, 2012, http://www.cbo.gov/ftpdocs/119xx/doc11966/11-17-Rivlin-Ryan_Preliminary_Analysis.pdf.

19. House Committee on the Budget Chairman Paul Ryan of Wisconsin, "The Path to Prosperity: Restoring America's Promise," Fiscal Year 2012 Budget Resolution, accessed February 7, 2012, http://budget.house.gov/UploadedFiles/PathToProsperityFY2012.pdf.

20. "Bipartisan Health Options," U.S. Senator Ron Wyden, accessed February 7, 2012, http://wyden.senate.gov/issues/issue/?id=ab82bb35-a617-4d66-b6e2-c9f9b4758c59.

21. "Restoring America's Future," Debt Reduction Task Force, Bipartisan Policy Center, November 2010, accessed February 7, 2012, http://www.bipartisanpolicy.org/sites/default/files/BPC%20FINAL%20REPORT%20FOR%20PRINTER%2002%2028%2011.pdf.

22. Joe Lieberman, "Washington Post Op-Ed: How Medicare can be saved," *Washington Post*, June 10, 2011, accessed February 7, 2012, http://lieberman.senate.gov/index.cfm/news-events/speeches-op-eds/2011/6/washington-post-oped-how-medicare-can-be-saved.

23. "Lieberman, Coburn Reveal Bipartisan Proposal to Save Medicare, Reduce Debt," *Tom Coburn, M.D., US Senator from Oklahoma*, June 28, 2011, accessed February 7, 2012, http://www.coburn.senate.gov/public/index.cfm/pressreleases?ContentRecord_id=ae711529-741a-4f52-89eb-4e6ef1c861a7.

24. "Life Expectancy: United States," Data360, accessed February 7, 2012, http://www.data360.org/dsg.aspx?Data_Set_Group_Id=195; Congressional Budget Office, *Budget Options, vol. 1, Health Care*, December 2008, 37, accessed February 7, 2012, http://www.cbo.gov/ftpdocs/99xx/doc9925/12-18-HealthOptions.pdf.

25. Social Security Administration, "Retirement Benefits," SSA Publication no. 05-10035, ICN 457500, (September 2011) accessed February 7, 2012, http://www.ssa.gov/pubs/10035.html.

26. "Coburn-Lieberman press conference on Medicare debt reduction plan (pt. 1)," YouTube video, 11:41, June 28, 2011, uploaded by "SenatorCoburn," accessed February 7, 2012, http://www.youtube.com/watch?v=alFr2Jouj2s.

27. Robert Kelley, "Where can $700 billion in waste be cut annually from the U.S. Healthcare System?" Thomson Reuters, October 2009, accessed February 7, 2012, http://www.factsforhealthcare.com/whitepaper/HealthcareWaste.pdf; "The price of excess: Identifying waste in healthcare spending," PricewaterhouseCoopers LLP, April 2008, accessed February 7, 2012, http://www.pwc.com/us/en/healthcare/publications/the-price-of-excess.jhtml.

28. Government Accountability Office, *High-Risk Series: An Update*, February 2011, accessed February 7, 2012, http://www.gao.gov/new.items/d11278.pdf.

29. Ibid.

30. Information provided by Centers for Medicare and Medicaid Services to Office of Senator Tom Coburn, M.D.
31. Congressional Budget Office, "Combined OASDI Trust Funds, January 2011 Baseline," accessed February 7, 2012, http://www.cbo.gov/budget/factsheets/2011/5-oasdi.pdf.
32. Jacob Lew, "Opposing view: Social Security isn't the problem," *USA Today*, editorial, February 21, 2011, accessed February 7, 2012, http://www.usatoday.com/news/opinion/editorials/2011-02-22-editorial22_ST1_N.htm.
33. Executive Office of the President of the United States, *Analytical Perspectives: Budget of the United States Government*, Fiscal Year 2000, accessed February 7, 2012, http://www.gpoaccess.gov/usbudget/fy00/pdf/spec.pdf; emphasis added.
34. William G. Gale, John B. Shoven, Mark Warshawsky, eds., Private Pensions and Public Policies (Washington: Brookings Institute, 2004), 246.
35. Ibid.
36. Samuel C. Thompson Jr., *The Missing Ingredient in the Budget Debate: Phasing Out Social Security and Medicare for High Income Retirees*, Pennsylvania State University Legal Studies Research Paper no. 11-2011, available at http://ssrn.com/abstract=1852749, quoted at http://www.scribd.com/doc/73147962/Coburn-Taxes, (both accessed February 7, 2012).
37. Tevi Troy, "The Fog of Mediscare," *Commentary*, September 2011, accessed February 7, 2012, http://www.commentarymagazine.com/article/the-fog-of-mediscare/.
38. Glenn Thrush, "Obama: SSN checks in jeopardy," *Politico*, July 13, 2011, accessed February 7, 2012, http://www.politico.com/politico44/perm/0711/senior_scare_85a220d7-f653-4d32-ae8c-2d5218d273ff.html.
39. Peter J. Peterson, "Will America Grow Up Before It Grows Old?" *Atlantic Monthly*, May 1996, accessed February 7, 2012, http://www.theatlantic.com/past/docs/issues/96may/aging/aging.htm.
40. Ibid.

Chapter 10

1. P. J. O'Rourke, "The Liberty Manifesto," CATO Institute, May 6, 1993, accessed February 7, 2012, http://www.cato.org/pub_display.php?pub_id=6857.
2. Tyler Cowen, "Poor U.S. Scores in Health Care Don't Measure Nobels and Innovation," *New York Times*, October 5, 2006, accessed February 7, 2012, http://www.nytimes.com/2006/10/05/business/05scene.html?ei=5090&en=5889b48 19eaf787a&ex=1317700800&adxnnl=1&partner=rssuserland&emc=rss&adxnnlx=1322719679-+0u1mtvoV6nxFZ4vK8lO8w.
3. Congressional Budget Office, *CBO's 2011 Long-Term Budget Outlook*, 35, accessed February 7, 2012, http://www.cbo.gov/ftpdocs/122xx/doc12212/06-21-Long-Term_Budget_Outlook.pdf.
4. Kelley, "$700 Billion in Waste."
5. "Wages and Benefits: A Long-Term View," Kaiser Family Foundation, November 2009, accessed February 7, 2012, http://www.kff.org/insurance/snapshot/chcm012808oth.cfm.

6. "New CRS Report Shows Government Already Controls Heath Care in the U.S." (press release), *Tom Coburn, M.D., US Senator from Oklahoma*, December 4, 2009, accessed February 7, 2012, http://goo.gl/rBF6J.

7. "Medicaid Expansion in Health Law to Cost States $118 Billion Through 2023" (press release), March 1, 2011, accessed February 7, 2012, http://finance.senate.gov/newsroom/ranking/release/?id=8e7cb991-2d90-42b8-8f20-bc3370462e99.

8. "Physician Study: Quantifying the Cost of Defensive Medicine," Jackson Healthcare, October 2009, accessed February 7, 2012, http://www.jacksonhealthcare.com/healthcare-research/healthcare-costs-defensive-medicine-study.aspx.

9. "AAMC Releases New Physician Shortage Estimates Post-Reform" (press release), American Association of Medical Colleges, September 30, 2010, accessed February 7, 2012, https://www.aamc.org/newsroom/newsreleases/2010/150570/100930.html.

10. "Physician perspectives about health care reform and the future of the medical profession," Deloitte Center for Health Solutions, December 2011, accessed February 7, 2012, http://www.deloitte.com/assets/Dcom-UnitedStates/Local%20Assets/Documents/us_lshc_PhysicianPerspectives_121211.pdf, 31.

11. Ibid., 37.

12. Tom Coburn and John Barrasso, *Bad Medicine: A Check-Up on the New Federal Health Law* (July 2010), 2, accessed February 7, 2012, http://coburn.senate.gov/public/index.cfm?a=Files.Serve&File_id=722faf8b-a5be-40fd-a52b-9a98826c1592.

13. Phil Bredesen, *Fresh Medicine: How to Fix Reform and Build a Sustainable Health Care System*, (New York: Atlantic Monthly Press, 2010), 31.

14. "Many U.S. employers to drop health benefits: McKinsey," Reuters, June 7, 2011, accessed February 7, 2012, http://www.reuters.com/article/2011/06/07/us-health-benefits-idUSTRE7564VR20110607.

15. "PPACA One Year Later: Small Business Owners Expect Costs to Rise" (press release), NFIB, July 25, 2011, accessed February 7, 2012, http://www.nfib.com/press-media/press-media-item?cmsid=57614.

16. Ibid.

17. "Employers Committed to Offering Health Care Benefits Today; Concerned About Viability of Insurance Exchanges," Towers Watson, August 24, 2011, accessed February 7, 2012, http://www.towerswatson.com/united-states/press/5328.

18. "Employer Health Benefits 2011 Annual Survey," Kaiser Family Foundation, accessed February 7, 2012, http://ehbs.kff.org/.

19. Tom Coburn, "The Health Bill is Scary," *Wall Street Journal*, December 16, 2009, accessed February 7, 2012, http://online.wsj.com/article/SB10001424052748703514404574588842779569168.html.

20. Patient Protection and Affordable Care Act, §3021 (2009).

21. Senators Tom Coburn and John Barrasso, "Medicare & You 2012," accessed February 7, 2012, http://coburn.senate.gov/public/index.cfm?a=Files.Serve&File_id=8f52a1d3-bce5-453c-b359-24b86e1a95dc.

22. Sarah Bosely, "Up to 15,000 older cancer patients die prematurely each year, study says," *Guardian* (UK), June 25, 2009.

23. Social Security Act, 42 U.S.C. 1395 §1801, accessed February 7, 2012, http://www. ssa.gov/OP_Home/ssact/title18/1801.htm.

24. Byron York, "How Obamacare hits industry and threatens jobs," *Washington Examiner*, March 23, 2010, accessed February 7, 2012, http://washingtonexaminer. com/politics/how-obamacare-hits-industry-and-threatens-jobs.

25. Ibid.

26. "U.S. Medical Innovation at Risk: Fewer New Companies and Therapies Receiving Funding, Says Report" (press release), National Venture Capital Association, October 6, 2011, accessed February 7, 2012, http://www.nvca.org/ index.php?option=com_docman&task=doc_download&gid=796&Itemid=93.

27. Walter Williams, "FDA has become our killer agency," *Journal* (Martinsburg, WV), February 15, 2011, accessed February 7, 2012, http://journal-news.net/page/ content.detail/id/556179/FDA-has-become-our-killer-agency.html?nav=5195.

28. Ibid.

29. Richard M. Burr and Tom Coburn, "Caution kills: FDA's go-slow approval approach shortens lives," *Washington Times*, February 15, 2011, accessed February 7, 2012, http://www.washingtontimes.com/news/2011/feb/15/caution-kills/print/.

30. "The Estimated Effect of the Affordable Care Act on Medicare and Medicaid Outlays and Total National Health Care Expenditures," Testimony before the House Committee on the Budget, January 26, 2011, by Richard S. Foster, F.S.A. Chief Actuary Centers for Medicare & Medicaid Services, accessed February 7, 2012, http://budget.house.gov/UploadedFiles/fostertestimony1262011.pdf.

31. "Medicaid Expansion in the New Health Law: Costs to the States," Joint Congressional Report by Senate Finance Committee, accessed February 7, 2012, http://energycommerce.house.gov/media/file/PDFs/030111MedicaidReport.pdf.

32. "The Fiscal Survey of States," Spring 2011, National Governors Association and the National Association of State Budget Officers, accessed February 7, 2012, http://www.nga.org/files/live/sites/NGA/files/pdf/FSS1106.PDF.

33. Senators Coburn and Barrasso, "Grim Diagnosis: A check-up on the federal health law" (October 2010), 11, emphasis added, accessed February 7, 2012, http://www.coburn.senate.gov/public//index.cfm?a=Files. Serve&File_id=0d0b33ae-292e-42ba-ba94-43ff234961a2.

34. John Shatto and Kent Clemens, "Projected Medicare Expenditures under an Illustrative Scenario with Alternative Payment Updates to Medicare Providers," Office of the Actuary, Centers for Medicare and Medicaid Services, August 5, 2010, accessed February 7, 2012, http://www.cms.gov/ActuarialStudies/Downloa ds/2010TRAlternativeScenario.pdf.

35. "52% Still Favor Repeal of National Health Care Law," Rasmussen Reports, January 23, 2012, accessed February 7, 2012, http://www.rasmussenreports.com/ public_content/politics/current_events/healthcare/health_care_law.

36. Patients' Choice Act, summary, accessed February 7, 2012, http://www.coburn.senate.gov/public/index.cfm?a=Files. Serve&File_id=d2f94455-368c-45b5-8d56-fc195a833884.

37. John Sheils and Randall Haught, "The Cost of Tax-Exempt Health Benefits In 2004," *Health Affairs* (2004), accessed February 7, 2012, http://content. healthaffairs.org/cgi/reprint/hlthaff.w4.106v1.pdf.

38. "Employer Health Benefits 2011 Annual Survey," (Chicago: Kaiser Family Foundation and Health Research and Educational Trust, 2011), accessed February 7, 2012, http://ehbs.kff.org/pdf/2011/8225.pdf.
39. Bob Lyke, "The Tax Exclusion for Employer-Provided Health Insurance: Policy Issues Regarding the Repeal Debate," *CRS Report for Congress* (November 21, 2008), 3, accessed February 7, 2012, http://www.allhealth.org/BriefingMaterials/RL34767-1359.pdf.
40. U.S. Senate Republican Policy Committee, "Health Care Costs and Their Impact on Middle-Class Wages," *RPC Bulletin*, October 1, 2008, accessed February 7, 2012, http://rpc.senate.gov/public/_files/BulletinImpactofHealthCostsonMiddleClass100108.pdf.
41. Scott Gottlieb, "What Medicaid Tells Us About Government Health Care," Wall Street Journal, January 8, 2009, accessed February 7, 2012, http://online.wsj.com/article/SB123137487987962873.html.
42. "Communities Putting Prevention to Work," Centers for Disease Control and Prevention, modified November 20, 2008, accessed February 7, 2012, http://www.cdc.gov/communitiesputtingpreventiontowork/.
43. Victoria, Colliver, "Preventive Health Program May Prevent Cost Increases," *San Francisco Chronicle*, February 11, 2007, accessed February 7, 2012, http://www.sfgate.com/cgi-bin/article.cgi?file=/c/a/2007/02/11/BUG02O20R81.DTL&type=printable.
44. R. J. Ozminkowski, D. Ling, et al., "Long-Term Impact of Johnson & Johnson's Health & Wellness Program on Health Care Utilization and Expenditures," *Journal of Occupational and Environmental Medicine* 44(1): 21–29, 2002, accessed February 7, 2012, http://http://www.ncbi.nlm.nih.gov/pubmed/11802462.
45. Florida, South Carolina, Nebraska, Texas, Utah, et al, vs. United States Department of Health and Human Services, Secretary of the United States Department of Health and Human Services, United States Department of the Treasury Secretary of the United States Department of Treasury, United States Department of Labor, Secretary of the United States Department of Labor, Nos. 11-11021, 11-11067 (4th Cir. 2011), accessed February 7, 2012, http://www.courthousenews.com/2011/08/12/vinson.pdf.

Chapter 11

1. Barry M. Goldwater, *The Conscience of a Conservative* (New York: MJF Books, 1990), 47.
2. Scott A. Hodge, J. Scott Moody, and Wendy P. Warcholik, "The Rising Cost of Complying with the Federal Income Tax," Tax Foundation (January 2006), accessed February 7, 2012, http://www.taxfoundation.org/files/federalcompliancecosts-20061026.pdf.
3. Warren E. Buffett, "Stop Coddling the Super-Rich," *New York Times*, August 14, 2011, accessed February 7, 2012, http://www.nytimes.com/2011/08/15/opinion/stop-coddling-the-super-rich.html?_r=1.
4. David S. Logan, "Warren Buffett's Proposed Tax Hikes Would Provide Insignificant Revenue," *Tax Foundation Tax Policy Blog*, August 19, 2011, accessed February 7, 2012, http://www.taxfoundation.org/blog/show/27547.html.

5. Ibid.

6. Urban Institute and Brookings Institution, "Who Doesn't Pay Federal Taxes?" Tax Policy Center, accessed February 7, 2012, http://www.taxpolicycenter.org/taxtopics/federal-taxes-households.cfm.

7. Margaret Thatcher, interview by Llew Gardner, *Thames TV This Week*, February 5, 1976, accessed February 7, 2012, http://www.margaretthatcher.org/speeches/displaydocument.asp?docid=102953.

8. Tom A. Coburn, "Subsidies of the Rich and Famous" (November 2011), accessed February 7, 2012, http://coburn.senate.gov/public/index.cfm?a=Files.Serve&File_id=bb1c90bc-660c-477e-91e6-91c970fbee1f.

9. Tom Coburn, "End welfare for the wealthy," CNN, December 1, 2011, accessed February 7, 2012, http://www.cnn.com/2011/12/01/opinion/coburn-welfare-to-wealthy/index.html?iref=allsearch.

10. Tonya Somanader, "Super Committee Member Sen. Kerry: Grover Norquist is 'The 13th Member of this Committee,'" *ThinkProgress* (blog), November 21, 2011, accessed February 7, 2012, http://thinkprogress.org/economy/2011/11/21/373269/supercommittee-norquist-13th-member/.

11. "*Meet the Press* transcript for November 27, 2011," NBC, accessed February 7, 2012, http://www.msnbc.msn.com/id/45445090/ns/meet_the_press-transcripts/t/meet-press-transcript-november/.

12. "The Pledge: Grover Norquist's hold on the GOP," *60 Minutes*, CBS, November 20, 2011, accessed February 7, 2012, http://www.cbsnews.com/8301-18560_162-57327816/grover-norquist/?tag=currentVideoInfo;videoMetaInfo.

13. "Debt Talks Complicated by Definition of a Tax Increase," *Moneynews*, July 6, 2011, accessed February 7, 2012, http://www.moneynews.com/Economy/Debt-Talks-Complicated Definition/2011/07/06/id/402719.

14. Grover Norquist, testimony before the Simpson-Bowles commission, June 30, 2010, page 8. Note: Norquist calls for making *all expiring tax cuts permanent* but fails to call for tax simplification and the elimination of special interest tax earmarks and spending in the code, which he defines as "tax cuts."

15. Paul Singer, "Debate Over Tax Cuts, Earmarks Stirs Right," Roll Call, February 10, 2009, accessed February 7, 2012, http://www.rollcall.com/issues/54_86/-32196-1.html.

16. Editorial, "Coburn vs. Norquist: The Senator is right on ethanol and, in this case, on tax subsidies," *Wall Street Journal*, April 5, 2011, accessed February 7, 2012, http://online.wsj.com/article/SB10001424052748703712504576233053869526920.html.

17. Alexander Bolton, "Coburn spars with Norquist over tax breaks for ethanol," *The Hill*, March 29, 2011, accessed February 7, 2012, http://thehill.com/homenews/senate/152609-coburn-spars-with-norquist-over-tax-breaks-for-ethanol.

18. Michael Munger, "A pious Congress, shilling indulgences," *Herald-Sun* (Durham, NC), July 26, 2011, accessed February 7, 2012, http://www.heraldsun.com/view/full_story/14848446/article-A-pious-Congress--shilling-indulgences?instance=hs_guest_columnists#ixzz1Xz85a900.

19. "About," Americans for Tax Reform, accessed February 7, 2012, http://www.atr.org/americans-tax-reform-a2878.

20. Eric Wasson, "Coburn demands ATR shift policy as tiff with Norquist heats up," *The Hill*, March 29, 2011, accessed February 7, 2012, http://thehill.com/blogs/on-the-money/budget/152503-coburn-demands-atr-shift-policy-as-tiff-with-norquist-heats-up.

21. "Feinstein Calls for Repeal of Corn Ethanol Subsidy, Reduction of Ethanol Tariffs" (press release), *Dianne Feinstein, United States Senator for California*, March 9, 2011, accessed February 7, 2012, http://www.feinstein.senate.gov/public/index.cfm/press-releases?ID=9ced81dd-5056-8059-76ac-e29ebd7af65e.

22. "Dr. Coburn's Statement on Ethanol Vote," *Tom Coburn, M.D., US Senator from Oklahoma*, June 14, 2011, accessed February 7, 2012, http://coburn.senate.gov/public/index.cfm/pressreleases?ContentRecord_id=b8ae344d-b4ac-4a25-9621-b5138d7abb54&ContentType_id=d741b7a7-7863-4223-9904-8cb9378aa03a&Group_id=7a55cb96-4639-4dac-8c0c-99a4a227bd3a.

23. Jonah Goldberg, "Late to the Ethanol Party," *National Review*, June 17, 2011, accessed February 7, 2012, http://www.nationalreview.com/corner/269871/late-ethanol-party-jonah-goldberg.

24. Andrew Stiles, "The Norquist-Coburn Feud Reignites," *National Review*, June 16, 2011, accessed February 7, 2012, http://www.nationalreview.com/articles/269802/norquist-coburn-feud-reignites-andrew-stiles?page=2.

25. Ibid.

26. Ibid.

27. Ibid.

28. Ibid.

29. Editorial, "Coburn vs. Norquist."

30. "The fiscal purists go mad: A quarrel over ethanol lays bare Republican divisions on tax," *The Economist*, April 7, 2011, accessed February 7, 2012, http://www.economist.com/node/18529711.

31. Andrew Stiles, "Grover Rallies His Troops," *National Review*, June 24, 2011, accessed February 7, 2012, http://www.nationalreview.com/corner/270482/grover-rallies-his-troops-andrew-stiles.

32. Charles Krauthammer, "The Norquist myth," *STLtoday.com*, November 27, 2011, accessed February 7, 2012, http://www.stltoday.com/news/opinion/columns/charles-krauthammer/charles-krauthammer-the-norquist-myth/article_15c70357-d80f-5f9b-920f-56b5d691af4e.html.

33. Paul Ryan, "3 Steps to Pro-Growth Tax Reform: Fair. Competitive. Simple," September 14, 2011, accessed February 7, 2012, http://paulryan.house.gov/News/DocumentSingle.aspx?DocumentID=260105.

34. Donald B. Marron, "Spending in Disguise," *National Affairs*, Summer 2011, accessed February 7, 2012, http://www.urban.org/uploadedpdf/1001542-Spending-In-Disguise-Marron.pdf.

35. Thomas L. Hungerford, "Tax Expenditures and the Federal Budget," CRS RL34622, June 1, 2011, Page 2, accessed February 7, 2012, http://www.fas.org/sgp/crs/misc/RL34622.pdf.

36. Ibid.

37. Martin S. Feldstein, "Raise Taxes, but Not Tax Rates," *New York Times*, May 4, 2011, accessed February 7, 2012, http://www.nytimes.com/2011/05/05/opinion/05feldstein.html.

38. Citizens for Tax Justice, "Twelve Corporations Pay Effective Tax Rate of Negative 1.4% on $175 Billion in Profits; Reap $63.7 Billion in Tax Subsidies," June 1, 2011, accessed February 7, 2012, http://ctj.org/ctjreports/2011/06/twelve_corporations_pay_effective_tax_rate_of_negative_15_on_171_billion_in_profits_reap_624_billion.php.

39. Peter Blank, "Extraordinary Tax Deductions," *Kiplinger*, March 2010, accessed February 7, 2012, http://kiplinger.com/features/archives/extraordinary-tax-deductions.html.

40. Congressional Research Service, "Response to Office of Senator Coburn: 'Deductibility of Certain Expenses and Exemption for Certain Gambling Winnings,'" July 11, 2011.

41. Ibid.

42. "Moment of Truth," 28.

43. Ibid., 29.

44. W. Kurt Hauser, "There's No Escaping Hauser's Law," *Wall Street Journal*, November 26, 2010, accessed February 7, 2012, http://online.wsj.com/article/SB10001424052748703514904575602943209741952.html?KEYWORDS=hauser.

45. Martin Feldstein, "The Tax Reform Evidence from 1986," *Wall Street Journal*, October 24, 2011, accessed February 7, 2012, http://online.wsj.com/article/SB10001424052970204002304576629481571778262.html.

Chapter 12

1. Emphasis added.

2. "Still More F-35 Cost Growth to Come," Center for Defense Information, April 9, 2010, accessed February 7, 2012, http://www.cdi.org/program/document.cfm?DocumentID=4599&StartRow=1&ListRows.

3. "Army Strong: Equipped, Trained and Ready, Final Report of the 2010 Army Acquisition Review," Secretary of the Army (January 2011), 163, accessed February 7, 2012, http://usarmy.vo.llnwd.net/e2/c/downloads/213465.pdf.

4. United States Government Accountability Office, Report to Congressional Requesters, "Evolved Expendable Launch Vehicle," September 2011, GAO-11-641, accessed February 7, 2012, http://www.gao.gov/assets/520/511460.pdf.

5. Defense Department Appropriations Act, Pub. L. No. 112-10 (2011).

6. Chris Edwards, "Government Cost Overruns," CATO Institute, March 2009, accessed February 7, 2012, http://www.downsizinggovernment.org/government-cost-overruns.

7. Paul Bedard, "Killed by Tea Party GOP, Second F-35 Engine Revived," *U.S. News and World Report*, May 4, 2011, accessed February 7, 2012, http://www.usnews.com/news/blogs/washington-whispers/2011/05/04/killed-by-tea-party-gop-second-f-35-engine-revived.

8. "U.S. troop funds diverted to pet projects," *Washington Times*, October 15, 2009, accessed February 7, 2012, http://www.washingtontimes.com/news/2009/oct/15/troop-funds-diverted-to-pet-projects/?page=all.

9. David Heath and Hal Bernton, "$4.5 million for a boat that nobody wanted," *Seattle Times*, October 14, 2007, accessed February 7, 2012, http://seattletimes.nwsource.com/html/nationworld/2003948586_favorfactory14m.html.

10. Kay B. Day, "Flake on C-SPAN: Earmark process is 'circular fundraising,'" *US Report*, July 28, 2009, accessed February 7, 2012, http://www.theusreport.com/the-us-report/flake-on-c-span-earmark-process-is-circular-fundraising.html.

11. Robert D. Novak, "Shame of the Senate," July 2007, accessed February 7, 2012, http://www.creators.com/opinion/robert-novak/shame-of-the-senate.html.

12. Office of Management and Budget, Urban Warfare Analysis Center (UWAC), 2008, accessed February 7, 2012, http://earmarks.omb.gov/earmarks-public/2008-earmarks/earmark_344482.html.

13. *National Defense Budget Estimates for FY 2012*, Office of the Undersecretary of Defense (Comptroller), March 2011, accessed February 7, 2012, http://comptroller.defense.gov/defbudget/fy2012/FY12_Green_Book.pdf.

14. Ibid.

15. Robert Gates (remarks at Navy League Sea-Air Space Exposition, Gaylord Convention Center, National Harbor, Maryland, May 3, 2010), accessed February 7, 2012, http://www.defense.gov/speeches/speech.aspx?speechid=1460.

16. United States Government Accountability Office, Report to Congressional Committees, "Defense Acquisitions: Assessments of Selected Weapon Programs," March 2008, GAO 08-467SP, accessed February 7, 2012, http://www.gao.gov/new.items/d08467sp.pdf.

17. *Report of The Tenth Quadrennial Review of Military Compensation*, vol. 1, Cash Compensation, Department of Defense, February 2008, accessed February 7, 2012, http://www.whs.mil/library/doc/Tenth.pdf.

18. Unless otherwise noted, savings are over ten years.

19. Defense Commissary Agency, *Annual Report 2010*, accessed February 7, 2012, http://www.commissaries.com/press_room/documents/AnnualReport.pdf.

20. "Fortune 500 2011: Industry: Food and Drug Stores," *CNN Money*, May 23, 2011, accessed February 7, 2012, http://money.cnn.com/magazines/fortune/fortune500/2011/industries/148/index.html.

21. DOD, "Fiscal Year 2011 Budget Estimate, Department of Defense Dependents Education (DoDDE)," February 2010, accessed February 7, 2012, http://comptroller.defense.gov/defbudget/fy2011/budget_justification/pdfs/01_Operation_and_Maintenance/O_M_VOL_1_PARTS/DoDDE_FY11.pdf.

22. Kristen Lombardi, "Daddy, Why Is My School Falling Down?" *Daily Beast*, June 27, 2011, accessed February 7, 2012, http://www.newsweek.com/2011/06/26/military-children-s-schools-in-disrepair.html.

23. Eric Pianin, "Deep Defense Cuts Are Unlikely," *Fiscal Times*, December 6, 2011, accessed February 7, 2012, http://www.thefiscaltimes.com/Articles/2011/12/06/Deep-Defense-Cuts-Are-Unlikely.aspx#page1.

24. U.S. Army Medical Research and Materiel Command, *Congressionally Directed Medical Research Programs: Annual Report*, September 30, 2010, 1, accessed February 7, 2012, http://cdmrp.army.mil/pubs/annreports/2010annrep/2010annreport.pdf.

25. Don J. Jansen, *Military Medical Care: Questions and Answers*, CRS Report RL33537, 16, May 14, 2009, accessed February 7, 2012, http://www.fas.org/sgp/crs/misc/RL33537.pdf.

26. Evaluation of the TRICARE Program, Fiscal Year 2011 Report to Congress, p. 16, accessed February 7, 2012, http://www.tricare.mil/hpae/_docs/2011eval/TRICARE2011_02_28_11v8.pdf.

27. *USA Today* editorial, "Our view: Military's Tricare benefits are too sweet a deal," June 1, 2011, http://www.usatoday.com/news/opinion/editorials/2011-06-01-Militarys-Tricare-benefits-too-sweet-a-deal_n.htm accessed February 12, 2012.

28. "Applaud Sen. Coburn for cost-cutting efforts," *NewsOK*, September 14, 2011, accessed February 7, 2012, http://newsok.com/article/3603766.

29. Dan Mitchell, "Sequestration Is a Small Step in Right Direction, Not Something to Be Feared," *International Liberty* (blog), November 1, 2011, accessed February 7, 2012, http://danieljmitchell.wordpress.com/2011/11/01/sequestration-is-a-small-step-in-right-direction-not-something-to-be-feared/.

30. Veronique de Rugy, "Defense Spending Excluding War Funding," Mercatus Center, George Mason University, December 5, 2011, accessed February 7, 2012, http://mercatus.org/publication/defense-spending-excluding-war-funding.

31. Will Durant, *The Story of Civilization*, vol. 3 (XXX: Simon and Shuster, 1944) Caesar And Christ. Epilogue—Why Rome fell).

Chapter 13

1. John Pollock, *Wilberforce* (New York: St. Martin's Press, 1977), 69.

2. Martin Luther King, Jr. quoted in the *Wall Street Journal*, November 13, 1962.

3. Mark Rodgers and Bill Wichterman, Faith and Law lecture series, "Culture: Upstream From Politics—Why Christians are foolish to think they can change a nation through politics alone" June 10, 2011, http://faithandlaw.org/past-lectures/, accessed February 12, 2012.

4. Dan Nejfelt, Faith in Public Life, May 11, 2011, http://www.faithinpubliclife.org/blog/catholic_scholars_teach_boehne/.

5. See Jim Wallis, "How Christian Is Tea Party Libertarianism?" *Huff Post Religion*, May 27, 2010, accessed February 7, 2012, http://www.huffingtonpost.com/jim-wallis/how-christian-is-tea-part_b_592170.html; Jim Wallis, "What Would Jesus Cut?" Huff Post Religion, February 10, 2011, accessed February 7, 2012, http://www.huffingtonpost.com/jim-wallis/what-would-jesus-cut_b_821555.html.

6. Eric Metaxas, *Bonhoeffer: Pastor, Martyr, Prophet, Spy* (Nashville: Thomas Nelson, 2011).

7. Correspondence of Mary Richmond, June 3, 1899, in *The Heritage of American Social Work*, Ralph and Muriel Pumphrey, eds., (New York: Columbia University Press, 1961), 266.

Conclusion

1. Robert F. Kennedy, speech at University of Capetown, Capetown, South Africa, June 6, 1966, John F. Kennedy Presidential Library and Museum, http://www.jfklibrary.org/Research/Ready-Reference/RFK-Speeches/Day-of-Affirmation-Address-news-release-text-version.aspx.

2. Paul Scicchitano, "Coburn: Govt Subsidizing Millionaires," *NewsMax*, November 15, 2011, accessed February 7, 2012, http://www.newsmax.com/InsideCover/coburn-millionaires-tax-breaks/2011/11/15/id/418134.

3. Brian A. Shactman, "Unemployed? Go to North Dakota," *USA Today*, August 28, 2011, accessed February 12, 2012, http://www.usatoday.com/money/economy/story/2011-08-27/Unemployed-Go-to-North-Dakota/50136572/1.

4. Mary O'Grady, "Canada's Oil Sands Are a Job Gusher," *Wall Street Journal*, September 12, 2011, accessed February 7, 2012, http://online.wsj.com/article/SB10001424053111904836104576560933917369412.html.
5. "Create Candor in the Workplace, Says Jack Welch," Stanford Graduate School of Business, April 1, 2005, accessed February 12, 2012, http://www.gsb.stanford.edu/news/headlines/vftt_welch.shtml.
6. Corbett B. Daly, "Steve Jobs: Obama's focus on excuses 'infuriated' him," *CBS News*, October 21, 2011, accessed February 12, 2012, http://www.cbsnews.com/8301-503544_162-20123670-503544/steve-jobs-obamas-focus-on-excuses-infuriated-him/.
7. President George Washington, First Inaugural Address, April 30, 1789, accessed February 12, 2012, http://www.bartleby.com/124/pres13.html.

About the Author

Senator Tom Coburn is a former business owner and practicing physician. He was first elected to the U.S. House of Representatives in 1994. A true citizen legislator, he honored his self-imposed term limits pledge and left Congress in 2001. He returned to public service in 2005 after a successful campaign for the U.S. Senate. As he did in the House, he has limited his terms in the Senate and will be leaving after two terms, in 2016.

John Hart is an award-winning writer who has served as Dr. Coburn's communications director since 2005. He previously served as Dr. Coburn's press secretary from 1997 until 2000 and also collaborated with Dr. Coburn on *Breach of Trust*. John lives in Washington DC with his wife, Kimberly, and three children.

Index